THE PUBLIC INTEREST

NOMOS

V

NOMOS:

Yearbook of The American Society for Political and Legal Philosophy

PUBLISHED SIMULTANEOUSLY IN GREAT BRITAIN

BY PRENTICE-HALL INTERNATIONAL, LONDON

NOMOS
V

THE PUBLIC
INTEREST

Edited by CARL J. FRIEDRICH

ATHERTON PRESS   70 FIFTH AVENUE, NEW YORK   1962

NOMOS V: THE PUBLIC INTEREST
Carl J. Friedrich, editor

Copyright © 1962 by Prentice-Hall, Inc.
Atherton Press, New York, New York

Published simultaneously in Great Britain by
Prentice-Hall International, Inc.
28 Welbeck Street, London W. 1, England

Copyright under International, Pan American,
and Universal Copyright Conventions

Atherton Press, A Division of Prentice-Hall, Inc.
70 Fifth Avenue, New York 11, New York

Library of Congress Catalogue Card Number   *62-19400*

Printed in the United States of America   *62353*

Designed by Polly Cameron

PREFACE

In presenting NOMOS V to the members of the American Society for Political and Legal Philosophy as well as to the general reader, it behooves the editor to point out that its topic, *The Public Interest,* chosen by the membership for their meeting with the American Political Science Association in 1960, has received some special attention in recent years. The American Philosophical Association fostered a special research project on this subject which was put in charge of Wayne A. R. Leys and Charner Perry. In the last chapter of this volume, Leys presents a general appraisal of this enterprise's results; they are referred to in a number of other contributions. The viewpoints expressed in the various papers vary widely in outlook and methodology, ranging from a reasoned conviction that the public interest is a central concern of political and legal philosophy to the pointedly argued rejection of it as merely a façade for special interests and partisan position in the political battle. The range and content of the papers did not suggest any obvious or self-evident sequence, either in terms of the several fields' approaches or the positions taken. There is not to be discerned any distinctly philosophical, legal or political-scientific approach, though some of the authors lean more in one direction, some more in the other. Nor is there agreement as to the scope of the application of this concept; some would include external affairs and foreign relations, others would exclude them, still others are silent on the issue. Some would stress the governmental sphere, others would make the term more inclusive, and so forth. It has, therefore, seemed best to adhere somewhat to the structure of the meeting which was built around the papers of Lasswell, Musgrave, and Braybrooke, especially since a few papers are in essence brief comments on these papers, namely Friedman, Nakhnikian, Cohen, and Pennock. Some papers were, as in previous years, solicited by the editor from scholars who did not participate in the meeting at all, but were believed to have something to contribute. Others were elaborations of points made in the discussion and constituting significant aspects of the over-all range of issues involved in the problem of the public interest. Schubert's and Sorauf's papers were presented at the joint meeting with the American Political Science Association, and distributed in mimeograph form to members of that association. Since Schubert's paper contains considerable matter also presented in his book dealing with our subject, the permission of The Free Press of Glencoe to use this paper is gratefully acknowledged.

It remains to say a word of thanks to all who have cooperated in making this volume possible, more especially the Twentieth Century Fund for their continued support, and my editorial assistant Miss Roberta Hill for her never failing helpfulness. Brian Barry kindly read the entire manuscript and gave helpful criticism on a number of the papers.

CARL J. FRIEDRICH

Cambridge, Mass.
August, 1962

CONTENTS

ix

CONTRIBUTORS

STEPHEN K. BAILEY
Political Science, Syracuse University

BRIAN M. BARRY
Social Philosophy, University of Birmingham

EDGAR BODENHEIMER
Law, University of Utah

DAVID BRAYBROOKE
Philosophy, Yale University

C. W. CASSINELLI
Political Science, University of Washington

JULIUS COHEN
Law, Rutgers University

GERHARD COLM
Economics, National Planning Association, Washington

W. FRIEDMANN
Law, Columbia University

ERNEST S. GRIFFITH
Political Science, The American University

HAROLD D. LASSWELL
Political Science, Yale University Law School

WAYNE A. R. LEYS
Philosophy, Roosevelt University

WILLIAM S. MINOR
Philosophy, West Virginia University

JOHN D. MONTGOMERY
Political Science, Boston University

R. A. MUSGRAVE
Economics, Johns Hopkins University

GEORGE NAKHNIKIAN
Philosophy, Wayne State University

GERHART NIEMEYER
Political Science, University of Notre Dame

J. ROLAND PENNOCK
Political Science, Swarthmore College

GLENDON SCHUBERT
Political Science, Michigan State University

FRANK J. SORAUF
Political Science, University of Minnesota

THE PUBLIC INTEREST

NOMOS
V

1

PUBLIC INTEREST
AND PRIVATE UTILITY

GERHART NIEMEYER

R. A. Musgrave has reminded us of the classical economist's view of the public interest as the aggregate of individual
utilities. Consumer satisfaction, a synonym for private utility,
was the standard of efficiency of the economic system; such efficiency is the main public interest. While this is an economist's
view, I do not consider it unrepresentative of contemporary
political reality. Economic efficiency judged in terms of consumer
satisfaction has indeed become the accepted formula for the
public interest, so much so that the merit of newly emerging
political entities is assessed almost wholly in terms of rising
standards of living. Incoming administrations seek to identify
themselves above all with two goals: the economic satisfaction
of as many citizens as possible and superior national defense. Of
these two, the second depends on the first, since defense secures
only whatever the public interest maintains at home, which in
our case is an aggregate of individual utilities. Acknowledging
the aptness of Musgrave's term in our own situation, we should
all the same raise the question of the validity of such a concept
of the public interest. There are various conceivable relations
between public interest and private utility, and a comparison

1

between a number of them is likely to lead to the emergence of standards of criticism. I should like briefly to compare four concepts of the public interest in terms of their relation with private utility, represented, respectively, by (1) Plato and Aristotle, (2) Augustine and Aquinas, (3) Locke, Adam Smith, Mill, and (4) Marx and Lenin.

PLATO AND ARISTOTLE

While there is no explicit distinction between "public" and "private" in Plato and Aristotle, a distinction emerges from the analysis of what it is that generates community among men. This analysis turns on the recognition of a rational element in the soul, and of the divine character of this element. The rational part of the human soul responds to the *logos,* the all-pervading law in the multitude of phenomena. Heraclitus had already spoken of the *logos* as that which is common to human lives.[1] Participation in the *logos,* or *nous,* is the substance of public community; common awareness of the transcendent reason enables men to live together in order and friendship. The distinction between public and private hinges on the identification of another part of the soul, characterized by concupiscence and passion: the appetitive element. It is the energy of this part of the soul that serves for self-preservation, but the appetites in their self-centeredness are not capable of generating community and sustaining order. The appetites can only make their contribution to public order when under the higher rule of reason. When not so ruled, they tend to disorient and pervert human life.

Both Plato and Aristotle assigned to the appetites not merely the role of craving what is needed for self-preservation but also that of impelling production of the needed material goods. Both put the production of wealth under the care of what they considered "private" impulses, impulses oriented toward private utility rather than the common good. This position is remarkable in view of Plato's and Aristotle's insistence that it is economic interdependence from which arises the need for public

---

1 Diels 32, fr. 2.

order. Economic interdependence is, however, not the substance of, but only the occasion for, public order. The substance of order is found in the rational relation of natures with one another and with the transcendent structure of existence: justice is found in men's "general dealings with one another." [2] Starting from economic interdependence, Plato and Aristotle do not make commerce, the division of labor, or even unified management of production the substance of community but assign public status only to the general order of the *nous*. Material production is thereby relegated to the sphere of private individual concerns. Hence, the procurement of material goods for the sustenance of life is called "household-management" (*oikonomia*). It is an activity of the appetitive energies of the soul, and the materials it uses and procures are held in private control as private property.

Nor does Plato abandon this distinction between the public sphere of the *nous* and the private sphere of economics when postulating communal possessions for the guardians of the Republic. The brotherhood of the guardians is not an arrangement for the purpose of communal labor but for the philosophical rule of the community. Private property is not eliminated from the community as a whole but only from among the guardians, and this elimination has not an economic but a philosophical meaning: it is to free the guardians from all possible motives of private utility so that they can wholly give themselves to the public good. The community's wealth is still produced by men in whose souls the appetites prevail, private utility being their propelling motive. The guardian's public maintenance is then the method by which the fruits of private appetites are ordered to the common good.

Equally noteworthy is Aristotle's insistence on private property as the basis of economic production, even though Aristotle himself insisted that the resulting division between rich and poor must always create the besetting troubles in all political communities. Like Plato, he felt that material production properly belongs to the appetitive forces of the soul. Economic

---

2 Plato, *The Republic*, II, §372.

activities then are essentially motivated by private utility, while the public interest is oriented toward the awareness (*noesis*) of the rational order of justice (*dikē*). The public interest corresponding to Plato's and Aristotle's concept of order may be termed *dikaio-noesis*.

AUGUSTINE AND AQUINAS

For the Greeks, the ultimate fulfillment of man's destiny was conceivable only within the framework of the political order. The experience of the Incarnation and the Crucifixion of the Son of God led to a new view. Man's destiny was now perceived as the salvation of his individual soul. Accordingly, the religious Community of Saints rather than the political community of the polis was of ultimate significance. Salvation being from God, it could not be attained or even rationally pursued by public political agencies. As a result of Augustine's identification of the City of God as man's highest community, the meaning of the political community was strictly confined to peace, order, and a minimal justice.

The City of God is a community and the Kingdom of God an ultimate common good, but in relation to the political order every man's salvation still figured as his personal interest, a "private" concern—one does not dare call it a utility—which now is acknowledged side by side with the public political interest as an ordering force. Here is the root of the concept of limited government. Government was subjected to a twofold limitation. Functionally speaking, an entire realm of human life was staked off in which government must not intrude: the realm of the salvation of souls. Hierarchically speaking, government was limited by the higher authority of the overarching natural law to which human laws ought to defer. The individual interest—the salvation of each person's soul—was in itself the basis of order, although in its religious aspects it bypassed the government, as it were, and thus established a direct "non-public" relation between man and God. Thus the right ordering of individual lives was the criterion common to the sphere of public interest, the ecclesiastical sphere, and the private sphere.

The over-all purpose of salvation created order overlapping the three spheres: it invented moral rules for private economic activities, drove individual rulers to public acts of personal penitence, and produced such hybrid phenomena as the Inquisition with its mixture of concern for public order and concern for individual salvation.

Essential to the Augustinian-Thomistic concept of order then is the limitation of government to the functions of peace, minimal justice, and defense, and the simultaneous elevation of individual salvation to the rank of a publicly recognized though not publicly organized concern—the meaning of "public" here connoting "governmental." The corresponding public interest is still *dikaio-noetic* in Aristotle's sense, but no longer oriented toward conversion in Plato's sense. We have here the emergence of politics as a strictly practical occupation dealing with the problems of public order and judicial administration. But in the Christian order the public interest is characterized not merely by the limitation of government to peace, defense, and justice, but rather by the participation of this limited government in the transcendent origin and destination of human life. The Augustinian-Thomistic synthesis strongly emphasizes the structural transcendent dimensions of existence, with God as the Supreme Existent and the ultimate end of all action. In this structure the government, limited in function, participates in a twofold sense. It participates in the prime cause, the existential ground of all things, through the natural law that pervades its ordinances. It participates in the final cause, the ultimate end of all existence, through its deference to the realm of salvation. Peace is indeed the public interest, but not peace as such. It is peace, order, justice in the framework of participation, the participation in transcendent existence and destiny, which is the characteristic Christian formula for the public interest. If we were to think of a suitable term, we might call this public interest *pax participians*.

LOCKE, ADAM SMITH, MILL

Contrary to both Greek and Christian views of public order, Locke builds the political community not on what is

common to men but rather on men's individual needs and aspirations. Civil society, for him, exists for the sake of private
utility. He is consistent with Plato and Aristotle in seeing material acquisition as the substance of private utility. Property
being "the great and chief end of men uniting into common-
wealths," [3] the political order serves above all to promote for
men's acquisitive appetites a greater degree of satisfaction than
would be possible under conditions of anarchy. By common
consent, men have "found out and agreed on a way how a man
may, rightfully and without injury, possess more than he himself can make use of. . . ." [4] This way is to be secured and improved by suitable public arrangements. Locke does acknowl-
edge a natural law, but it is no longer the substance of the *dikē*
that is the common element among men. The content of Locke's
natural law is determined by pleasure and pain, so that natural
law for him is, in the last analysis, nothing but an aggregate
of private utilities. Only a generation after Locke, this implication was brought out into the open through the pleasure-pain
calculus of Helvétius and Bentham.

Locke's problem is to find what kind of public arrangement
will promote the assurance of individual satisfactions. This kind
of problem is subject to widely differing solutions, according to
what one chooses to assume regarding the direction and relative
strength of individual appetites and what one believes regarding the suitability of various public means to serve the satisfaction of these appetites. Locke's own answer was that man's
acquisitiveness would fare best in a regime characterized by what
is in German called *Rechtssicherheit*—i.e., the certainty and consistency of systematized laws which would secure a higher degree
of predictability for human affairs. Thus civil society, as seen
by Locke, centers not in Aristotle's justice but rather in a
calculable, manipulatable legality, or "rules of the game."

Adam Smith added to this notion the concept of the Invisible
Hand, the assumption of a self-regulating harmony between
individual appetitive activities and individual satisfactions.[5] It

---

3 Locke, *Second Treatise*, 124.
4 *Second Treatise*, 50.
5 Adam Smith, *Wealth of Nations*, Bk. IV, Ch. 2.

was a concept logically required by, though not yet included in, the Lockean scheme. Without the premise that somehow the strivings of individual appetites would fit together into a whole, one could not go on conceiving of a community based on private utility. Adam Smith's contribution, moreover, led to a new version of limited government. As in the Christian order, public authority was held subject to a twofold limitation. Functionally speaking, a realm of private initiative and aspiration was staked off, in which the government was not to intrude. Hierarchically speaking, government was limited by the overarching natural order of "society," the self-adjusting and self-equilibrating system of private activities, to which public laws ought to defer. Thus the individual acquisitive interest was in itself also a source of order. Its aim, consumer satisfaction, was the criterion common to the sphere of government and the sphere of the Invisible Hand, and it provided the substance of the standards of judgment: "good government," "efficient economy."

Unlike the Christian order, however, one cannot here speak of participation, for while the many can participate in what is common to all, the community cannot participate in the diversity of countless private appetites and aspirations. It can only allow them the widest possible play. Hence freedom from government is the key concept in the new order. Freedom is to the liberal scheme of things what participation is to the Christian order. In the name of freedom, Mill removed from the public sphere the *nous* which, according to the Ancients, is the common element par excellence. The doctrine of free speech relegated the rational activities of men's souls to the realm of the Invisible Hand, which put them out of bounds for public laws and public interest. What remained in the public realm was a power which, shorn of any intellectual substance, is nothing but power and which, quite consistently, is given by Mill the function to do everything required to defend itself "from injury or molestation." [6] But if freedom in the liberal order is the equivalent of participation in the Christian scheme, it is the setting rather

---

[6] Mill, *On Liberty,* Ch. IV.

than the function of government. Liberal government has the purpose to make such public arrangements as will enhance the satisfaction of private utilities. This function has been variously conceived, the concepts ranging from night-watchman, through umpire, to insurance agency, and from negative protection to positive promotion. An additional problem is the relation between the government and the system procured by the Invisible Hand. The reasons for these vacillations are inherent in the difficulties of crystallizing an intelligible public interest out of private utilities.

The government is supposed to defer to the "natural order" of self-adjusting private activities, as in the Christian order the government is supposed to defer to the natural law. Unlike the natural law, however, the "natural order" of economic private activities is not a merely noetic but an operating system liable (1) to break down, (2) to give rise to undesirable results, and (3) to fail to ensure individual satisfactions. In that case the government, in the very name of private utility, will enter the forbidden compound and take the Invisible Hand under its public management. When this happens, the above-mentioned hierarchical limitation of government is suspended and, with repeated suspensions, tends to vanish. Instead of limited government we have then a type of government that is no longer required to defer to an overarching order and guided only by its concept of expedience.

Another difficulty of the liberal order stems from the necessity of making more or less arbitrary assumptions about individual aims, assumptions which any government must make that wants to serve the private utilities of countless personally unknown individuals. At the same time, assumptions must be made about the most vexing obstacles in the way of greater individual satisfaction, and the means by which such obstacles can be removed. Locke thought of fixed and certain laws as the most suitable means; Mill, of a hands-off policy in matters of speech and thought. Others, by contrast, have looked for public means to secure full employment, or the redistribution of wealth. Public assumptions about private aspirations tend not only to statistical averages but often postulate the existence of aspirations in order

to meet them by public policies. Where satisfaction is thus offered, appetite soon appears, so that public assumptions of this
kind are self-fulfilling propositions.

There is thus an inescapable tendency to progress from negative protection to the public promotion of individual utility.
Public management moves to extend both to the conditions affecting individual satisfactions and to individual activities and
aspirations themselves. This tendency gradually eliminates the
above-mentioned functional limitation of government, so that
government, for the sake of consumer satisfaction, intrudes more
and deeper into the staked-off sphere of individual initiative and
aspiration. It is a tendency that inheres in the ambiguities of a
public order oriented toward private utility. The public interest
in this order is thus not sharply definable but tends to range
from *laissez faire* to public management of labor and resources,
the entire range coming under the heading of public management of private satisfactions. Musgrave rightly called attention
to the spectral nature of the liberal public interest when speaking of "certain 'welfare conditions' for resource allocation which
would be met by perfect competition and socialist planning
alike." If one could designate the entire range of these "welfare
conditions" by a concept of public interest, I should like to
propose the term *hēdononomia*—from *hēdonē* (pleasure, satisfaction) and *nomos* (rule, management).

The orientation of public interest toward private utility thus
tends to a kind of socialism, a tendency that has made itself felt
insistently, from the eighteenth century French *philosophes*
through the Mill of the last years to Franklin D. Roosevelt. One
can speak here of socialism in so far as a public concern for
private utility converts itself into an expanding public management of economic activities and resources. A socialism motivated
by private utility and consumer satisfaction should, however, be
distinguished from socialism of the Marxist variety. Even when
the public interest motivated by private utility assumes social-
istic directions, it is still likely to retain private property as the
basis of individual livelihood and freedom of contract as the
basis of employment. Retention of private property is not wholly
incompatible with government direction or regulation of large-

scale industries that have assumed the form of vast bureaucracies. If we have socialism in the West today, it is then one of the varieties of a liberal order that assigns to the public interest the task of satisfying private aspirations.

MARX AND LENIN

For Marx material production could not be, as it was for Plato and Aristotle, a private matter. For unlike Aristotle who said: "More than anything else, reason *is* man," Marx might have said: "More than anything else, labor *is* man." The rejection of the transcendence is for Marx the basis of communism. Having discounted the *logos*, Marx sees the substance of man's humanity in his relations with immanent nature. Man is essentially a being that, in the objects of his labor, produces his own life. If labor is based on private property, the exclusive character of that property separates man from man, resulting in estrangement and alienation. "The positive transcendence of *private property* . . . is, therefore, the positive transcendence of all estrangement—that is to say, the return of man . . . to his *human,* i.e., social mode of existence." [7] Labor, through which man's humanity must be actualized, must be communal rather than private. The social order is thus essentially the order of collective labor and its management. Marx accepts the traditional definition of politics as the sphere of the rational and general intellectual substance, but he denies the reality of such substance. Public truths are either illusory or ideological, rationalizations of economic power of man over man. That is why the order of politics will be replaced by the order of labor once the conditions of labor are fully socialized and labor has become a public interest. For the future society, the first society that will be fully human, Marx defines the public interest as that of labor management. In human history, however, this is a public interest that, according to Wittfogel, has also been characteristic of certain societies based on large-scale water works.[8] Whether the Marxist type of public interest resembles that of Oriental despotic societies or not, we have

---

[7] Marx, *Economic and Philosophic Manuscripts,* XXXIX, 3.
[8] Karl Wittfogel, *Oriental Despotism* (1957).

here obviously one of the conceivable types, to which I should like to attach the term *ergononomia*—from *ergon* (labor) and *nomos* (rule, management).

Marx aims at the conversion of what is now a private utility into the public interest. After this conversion, no private utility is left, not even consumer satisfaction. Men, of course, have different needs, and this difference is recognized by Marxism. But these needs and particularly their differences are not supposed in any way to motivate individual actions. Socialist man is supposed to be wholly absorbed by the motive of public labor. The full satisfaction of all his needs is confidently predicted, but this satisfaction is not to figure as the purpose of either private or public action. Nor is the *bios theōretikos,* the reflective life, to become a matter of private utility, as one might surmise from the one-time socialist slogan "religion is a private matter." Contemplation unrelated to the production of material objects challenges the entire dogma of the centrality of the labor process and is thus antisocial.

This concept of the public interest in a socialized order is the same for Marx and for Lenin. Lenin adds a concept to define the public interest in the period of transition from the "false" world of the present to the "real" world of the future. Throughout the entire period of transition, struggle is the "law of laws." Lenin's doctrine therefore deals above all with the organization of conflict instruments and conflict strategies. The period of transition is of indeterminable duration. Lenin speaks of "protracted struggle." His followers have indicated that the struggle is likely to last longer than a lifetime, possibly longer than a succession of lifetimes. From Lenin's elaboration of Marxism there has thus emerged a peculiar type of public interest, the type of interest that is connected with the idea of a combat party and a combat government. For the duration of the period of transition, the public interest represented by militant communism is conflict management, for which I should like to suggest the term *polemonomia*—from *polemos* (strife) and *nomos* (rule, management). Although this concept is designed for a period of indefinite duration, it is nevertheless for a transitional period and need not be listed among the permanent conceivable types.

INDIVIDUAL MAN AND PUBLIC AUTHORITY

The four main types of public interest that have been discussed can be grouped by two's with respect to the kind of relation which they admit between individual man and public authority. The Greek and the Christian order resemble each other in so far as the public authority in both represents a common orientation of the intellect and the spirit. The liberal and the Marxist order resemble each other in so far as the public authority in both administers material needs. It is true that the hedonistic orientation of the liberal order is not necessarily materialistic, but when public management of consumer satisfaction has so far progressed that most private economic activities depend for their success on public policies, then the public authority represents the guarantee of private livelihoods and welfare in its hands. In this capacity, it is second cousin to the public authority in the Marxist order which alone can dispense employment and consumer goods to individuals. We can thus distinguish a relation between individual man and public authority founded on material dependence from a relation founded on public truth or established dogma.

The latter relation depends on the public sharing of what Varro has called *theologia civilis*. The weight of authority will be felt, when it is asserted, more in words and thoughts, including the public uniformities of laws, cults, hierarchies, ceremonies, and beliefs. The other relation resembles that between employer and employee, and the weight of authority will—or can—be much less directly asserted. In a relation of material dependence, individuals can be manipulated through their material needs, the withholding of work, the denial of income, or the provision of incentives. The power of authority in a relation of material dependence is less harsh or direct, but also less resistible. For the relations of production are, as Marx himself emphasized, a "realm of physical necessity," which even in a socialist order "still remains a realm of necessity." [9] In a relation based on public truth, public authority is likely to press on individuals' minds in a way

---

[9] *Capital*, Vol. 3, Ch. XLVIII, 111.

that becomes more insufferable the less individuals are capable freely to share in the public beliefs. Such comparisons, however, raise entirely new questions which cannot be answered in the present context.

2

THE ETHICAL FOUNDATIONS
OF THE PUBLIC INTEREST

ERNEST S. GRIFFITH

The concept of "public interest" has been variously defined. Extreme Bentleyites even claim that the public interest is nonexistent. "If the realistic approach to the legislative process is accepted, one can then obtain absolute standards of judgment only by regarding as absolute the aims and views of one social group, or cluster of groups, among the contestants in the legislative struggle. . . . The only final decisions are made on the basis of power in one form or another." [1]

The concept of public interest may be broadly viewed, even to the extent of treating it as roughly synonymous with "general welfare." Such a definition holds it capable of permeating all action, both individual and institutional. On the other hand, it can be construed narrowly, as an attribute of certain acts confined to the governmental sector of human activity. In this case there is the further problem of whether the viewpoint is to be national or international and, if the latter, by what instrument it can be defined and effected. Here is the closed circle of the "national" interest of Kennan and others, who hold that the

---

[1] Bertram Gross, *The Legislative Struggle* (1953), p. 10.

14

acts of a nation-state cannot, and in fact should not, attempt to transcend the interests of those from whom the authority of its governing body is derived.

For our present purpose we shall for the most part confine our consideration to public interest as manifested in governmental activity, but with full recognition that in a pluralistic society this constitutes but a subheading, albeit an important one, under the broader heading of "general welfare."

Definitions devoid of ethical content are deceptively easy at this juncture. Positivist thinking has so deeply permeated our social science that the word "public" has frequently come to be applied to purely procedural considerations. Many lawyers and political scientists are prepared to endow any and all acts which conform to "legitimitized" procedure with the attribute or quality of public interest. When pressed for an operative definition of "legitimitized," such scholars fall back upon such concepts as "constitutional," and then seek to discover a common denominator among acts of despots (benevolent or otherwise), of sophisticated and long enduring democracies, and of polite fictions such as the "Republic of the Congo." The word "interest" will not survive such universal application, even though the word "public" may come through relatively unscathed by confining its identification to a process.

Economists of kindred approach do little if any better. "Free consumer choice" replaces "legitimacy" as the criterion of public interest, and governmental activity designed to promote such choice is therefore clearly intended to be "in the public interest." Antitrust legislation and regulations designed to promote honesty in advertising and branding will serve as examples. This concept of public interest does at least have the merit of focusing attention upon persons, theoretically *all* persons, and by that much we are nearer operationally to both "public" and "interest."

To the observant sociologist, the public interest in a given society at a given time is that which conforms to the mores of the society. Here is the basis for ethical relativism. According to the viewpoint of the particular society, given acts may be deemed in or not in the public interest. The trouble at this point in providing guide lines or enlightenment for individual conduct is that other societies with different mores will come up with different answers. A further difficulty is that within a given society—or nation—various groups will likewise have different mores or will cloak their particular interests with the sanctity of the mores, and even as an operational definition the sociologist's criterion is almost as likely to be obscurantist as useful. The problem is even worse in transitional cultures, where the mores do not have even the temporary stability of a "settled" society. However, the sociologist's approach does at least have the merit of identifying the "value" element, ethical in nature, in the search of the individual for value guidance—even though the value is relativistic and not absolute. This approach also calls attention to the enormous power of the traditional in limiting the scope and speed of efforts to attain any universally acceptable definition of an operable public interest.

These definitions are therefore either purely procedural (legalist) or based on atomistic personal preference (economist) or relativistic and ephemeral (sociologist). The legalistic approach, greatly favored by the positivists, has been singularly sterile and deceptive in international matters. As deVisscher has so cogently pointed out it "legitimatizes" the most arrogant and nationalistically centered conduct, provided only the forms are observed. To identify this conduct with the public interest is an inexcusable distortion of terms. The political scientist is somewhat more successful on the domestic front when he equates public interest with procedures designed to achieve majority rule. Here he is akin to the aforementioned orthodox economist, but with the same defects as well as strengths, in that considerations of value are bypassed or equated with voter choice—however self-centered. Perhaps we are conveniently glossing over a shift or distinction in the use of the word "public" from its application to all voters regardless of motivation and voters "publicly" motivated. There is involved also the attractive and subtle question of whether selfishly motivated electorates may at times deliberately choose altruistically motivated leaders. Considerations such as these are important, but take one too far afield.

Man's apparently inborn need for and belief in a categorical imperative has never been long content with description and relativism. He demands meaning as well as fact; significance as well as event. Here we are in the very center of the historical dialogues concerned with ethics and value. While this essay cannot become deeply involved with this central problem of all life, neither can it totally ignore it. Inexorably the concept of public interest leads one to search for criteria of general welfare, and the latter postulates values.

The humanist who lacks a hypothesis that includes deity seeks objective norms in the biological, psychological, and social "nature" of man—postulating the latter as the end, not the means, of the evolutionary and social process. Whether even a successful outcome of his search would include or carry with it the necessary sanctions to motivate conformity is dubious. The chances are each individual—particularly if he is in a position of power—will refuse to accept as applicable to him the social and altruistic values, if such in fact emerge from the search as transcendent.

The Communist claims not to be troubled with doubts. As of a given moment the "party line" gives him the ethical absolutes necessary to define the public interest according to Marx, Lenin, Stalin, Khrushchev—or whoever is the latest word in orthodoxy in the party hierarchy. The trouble is that these absolutes do not stay put, and as time passes their intellectual absurdity or internal contradictions or use for selfish power maintenance purposes may undermine the blind faith in the infallibility of party dogma. For the time being, however, communism must be classified with those philosophies which vest public interest with an ethical content, however irrational such content appears to the noncommunist world. Its touchstone is the triumph of the proletariat in a world revolution.

Among other contemporary absolutes with substantial support, there remain the norms of religion, revealed or otherwise. I propose to use Christianity as a case study in this connection, largely because it is the religion most familiar to the majority of my readers, and also because it is the only one I know at all well. It is therefore used throughout in no pre-emptive sense, but for illustrative purposes. Those who care to do so may undertake similar analyses of other faiths. The Christian hierarchy of conduct, for example, treats love of one's fellow man (derived from the love of God) as the absolute good in human relations. Although it is not necessary at this point to elaborate the doctrine, from it flows other subsidiary elements directed toward general welfare—respect for personality, the human ends of power, integrity in discussion, the functional view of activity (economic and otherwise), responsible behavior, the obligation to serve.

It will be noted at once that these elements are subjective or motivational in character. In other words, Christian ethics are a matter of intent rather than result. On the other hand, "general welfare" or "public interest" is object or goal, to be measured in terms of results.

This factor gives credence to the attempts of many analysts to find "public interest" in terms of such results and not of motives. The essential philosophic error of many of the extreme laissez-faire economists, though operatively it was nevertheless a part truth, was their belief that, if self-interest be the primary motivation in a competitive society, it would automatically produce this common good or general welfare. Jeremy Bentham basically reasoned in the same fashion in his utilitarian political thought, holding that a democracy in which individuals voted what they regarded as most making for their own happiness would spell the greatest happiness for the greatest number— which for convenience we may call his idea of the "public interest." Much the same thought occurs in contemporary "group utilitarianism" in that the common good or public interest is seen as the upshot of group struggle and compromise—or in the ascendancy of labor as the greatest of the "mass" groups. One still lacks criteria for identifying the public interest in an objective sense.

What then are the Christian criteria of general welfare and public interest? For these I believe we must re-examine the Christian absolutes mentioned above. In objective terms these mean the development of the kind of a society in which Christian values have the maximum opportunity to flourish and flourish *freely*. Coerced morality is not morality in Christian terms. On the other hand, one would be safe in saying that the creation of a wholesome environment for childhood and youth would clearly be in the public interest in Christian terms. This would involve adequate nourishment, opportunities for education and development of artistic and intellectual potentialities, protection against bodily harm and moral corruption, health and physical fitness, and character education, including such matters as cross-cultural understanding, acceptance of responsibility, opportunities for unpaid service. Beyond childhood and youth we run into a clear dilemma between individual responsibility and social justice as components of public interest, which will be discussed in more detail later. It is assumed, of course, that during youth (and even childhood) the educational process aforementioned will involve a growth in individual responsibility.

We may summarize at this point by saying that those who are motivated to seek the public interest would undertake action designed to maximize freedom *and* justice. The ethical element in motivation translates or expresses itself in an ethic of consequences in terms of public interest. The nexus between the two is *intelligence* in the sense of the capacity to discern the public interest correctly. In other words public interest is ultimately identified with the achievement of a society based upon or pervaded by *intelligent good will*. We can dispense neither with the motivation that inspires nor the intelligence with which the persons so motivated confront the persons and the society affected by their decisions and their behavior. It is intelligence that is the source of *effective* action in the public interest.

Such an analysis clearly raises a number of serious questions. For example, by what authority may it be claimed that these elements are "absolutes"? To establish the credentials of such authority is basic to acceptance of the Christian faith (or for that matter of any other absolute ethic, including Marxian). An author may say, "I believe this to be true," and state reasons therefor. The reasons can establish probabilities, at least to the author's satisfaction; but, for the present, certainty is denied them. Faith then becomes "a willingness to act on probabilities," which is enough for the purpose. This faith differs from ethical relativism, in that the claim is made as to the probability that this particular dogma is the correct one, rather than that all codes or faiths are more or less equally valid or invalid. The

laboratory test of trying out the Christian dogma would appear
to result in (1) maximizing a sense of happiness or inward harmony or personal fulfillment, as well as, or through (2) a minimiz-
ing of social conflicts and consequent frustrations, and in (3) the
socializing or functionalizing of the economic and other groups
which are central to our contemporary pluralistic society. This
is Christianity's pragmatic proof, reinforcing its claim to be "revealed." This is also akin to the usual result of the search (referred to above) of secular humanists for norms in the nature
of man, with, however, the tremendously powerful added sanction of conformity to divine will and purpose, whether or not
the promise of heaven or threat of hell is thrown in. It differs
from fascism in its universality, from communism in its means,
philosophical undergirding, and views as to the nature and end
of man.

The answers to these questions as to what these Christian absolutes are can therefore be at least approximated in motivational terms, which is enough for the purpose. With such a
norm, whether arrived at by Christianity, secular humanism, or
otherwise, ethical relativity is not only dangerous and, if you
will, "heretical," but quite unnecessary. With altruism and good
will we search for or seek to build the society or community in
which these qualities may express themselves to the fullest—adult,
mature, responsible, intelligent. This is the target in general
welfare, of which the "public interest" is adjectival in all joint
or collective or co-operative efforts. We recognize fully that tac-
tically the building of such a society must make room for differences in tradition and culture and religious faith, and stra-
tegically must pay tribute to the values inherent in the variety
of life implicit in such differences. At the same time, one per-
ceives at this point that one of the basic factors favorable to
the success of a democracy is a public imbued with the public
interest.

Motivationally the problem may be simply stated. It lies in
the apprehension of the Christian insight of growth from "law"
to "spirit." Whether one postulates the individual's life as a
struggle against "original sin" or toward "fulfillment," the prob-

lem from this angle is one of acceptance of the goal, and the will and grace to pursue it.

It is, however, far from simple in terms of intelligent choice in a given situation. Here one runs into the fact that in the aforesaid ethic of consequences the average decision is mixed. What helps one person or group may hurt another. Just as the late Isaiah Bowman well stated, "No one principle ever exhausts the meaning of a situation," so in a more mundane fashion a full illumination of the short- and long-range consequences of a given decision usually shows effects varying from person to person and group to group in a complex and contradictory fashion. This is true alike for the Christian, the humanist, and the Communist. Even though the last focuses toward "world revolution" as his objective, rather than the effect on persons, he is still caught in the same trap.

We speak of this colloquially as deciding, not between black and white, but between shades of gray. It would perhaps be more accurate to speak of it as a choice between two or more patchworks made up of black, gray, and white sections, according to the effect on various individuals, with the maximum public interest associating itself with that decision which has the greatest area of white and light gray! The concept "ambiguity" has also been used in this same connection, but I do not find it accurate in describing the foregoing.

We are now ready to close in on our Christian ethical definition of the public interest. It is to be identified with those consequences of intelligent, altruistically motivated collective choices within the governmental process which produce the situations most likely to stimulate subsequent intelligent altruistic choices among those affected. If this concept be divorced from the world as we find it, dare we settle for less as the ultimate goal—if not as contemporary criterion?

There remain some practical guide lines in spelling out the meaning of "intelligent" in such a definition. In setting forth these guide lines, one makes certain assumptions as to conditions which on the whole favor altruistic motivation. These are: First, freedom of religion, even to the extent of a favorable (though probably not a privileged) position for religions which bring their sanctions to the aid of altruistic motivation. Second, education for all to the limit of one's ability, but limited by the extent that a person will work at it and make sacrifices for it especially in the upper ranges. It is assumed that the selection and presentation of materials will be such that altruistic motivation is favored at the same time that the role of intelligence in carrying it out is clarified. Content therefore must include an analysis of the nature of society and its problems. Third, freedoms of speech and media of communication, with the usual safeguards necessary in a democratic society, involving such matters as "clear and present danger," "corruption of youth," etc. While freedom is no assurance of altruistic motivation, coerced behavior is a denial of motivation of any sort. Fourth, a standard of living which assures adequate nourishment and pleasant homes, but probably not so high as to involve the possibility of debilitating luxury. Fifth, this standard of living should depend upon individual and co-operative effort, and would be attainable by such effort (i.e., there should be constructive work available for all who desire it).

We come finally to some guide lines for decision makers including voters who seek to discover and act in the public interest. First, other things being equal, decisions should favor the consumer rather than the producer. This guide line may be modified by situations such as those of the artist of craftsman in which the work itself is an integral part of self-fulfillment, and the motivation thereof is implicitly altruistic. Second, other things being equal, decisions should favor the future generations rather than the present, long-term rather than short-term goals. This is especially true in conservation of natural resources. This guide line may be modified by the "insurance principle," under which we spend great resources in national defense to assure our survival, or in situations in which there is reasonable expectation that the discovery of new resources will keep pace with our utilization of the old. Third, other things being equal, freedom rather than coercion should be favored. This may be modified by the immaturity of those affected (e.g., children, insane, primitive people) or by the motivation of the coerced (e.g., the criminally inclined) or by considerations of convenience (e.g., in traffic controls). Fourth, decisions should assume a basic equality among individuals as "ends" or as "children of God" in matters of rights and justice. These need definition naturally, and in our frame of reference they involve the opportunity freely to behave altruistically—with as much intelligence (i.e., education, in this context) as they will sacrifice for and use.

I am aware that even within the assumed Christian context each of the assumptions is debatable and each of the guide lines is subject to further refinement. Additions to each are certainly in order. I am also aware, as indicated in my discussion of mixed decisions, that often two or more of these assumptions and guide lines stand in contradiction to each other. Whether these lists of assumptions and guide lines are accurate, complete, or the best that can be drawn up is not terribly important. Readers may draw up their own, doubtless better lists, based on either Christian, humanist, or other philosophies.

What is important is whether the case has been made out for a definition of "public interest" involving ethical terms and whether such a definition has both subjective and objective criteria. If this be granted, then it is of equal importance to judge whether the suggested formula, "intelligent altruistic decisions designed to maximize the likelihood of the same type of decisions among those affected," constitutes a description by which "public interest" may be identified at all levels of governance or group action including the international. It is in this light that the lists of assumptions and guide lines must be read. It is for this definition that one seeks to discover whether there are divine and human sanctions, intellectual, emotional, social, theological, scientific. If such be found, then the formula becomes endowed with the quality of an "absolute," toppling over ethical relativities and positivism in the process. Today, as never before in history, this search and its answer are vested with the urgency of a situation in time which involves physical as well as cultural survival for mankind.

A concluding word is in order. When one surveys the world as we see it today, it seems fantastic to suppose that any agreement on the public interest as quixotic as the one proposed can

ever be attained. Even lip service seems unattainable. Yet at least
once in our generation a code not far from this met with such
agreement. The Universal Declaration of Human Rights adopted
in the General Assembly of the United Nations, December 10,
1948, was built of this stuff. That the words were used—or must
have been used by many—either with differing meanings or in-
sincerely should not obscure the nature of the achievement. In
a saner, more relaxed world, the Declaration may even yet come
into its own.

*   *   *

COMMENT—by Edgar S. Robinson*

I, for one, would agree with your thesis that the quest
for the realization of values should focus above all upon *problems
of the relationship* between subjective intent and objectively
good consequences. In this respect, I interpret your nuclear
premise as reading that Christian absolutes are innately so suffused with social import and so susceptible of beneficial application that they can, more tellingly and regularly than some other
categories of absolutes, engender good consequences midst "the
relativity" characteristic of diverse and even singular circumstances. Here, you would seem to be contending that humanist,
utilitarian, etc., absolutes can not be as consistently or reach-
ingly productive of the public interest, as this must be identified
and effectuated in the vortex of facts and events, as is the religious
constellation of absolutes. The Christian vision and version of
the public interest are, in effect, alleged to surpass the other
world views cited in respect to the meritorious concordance of
intent and consequences. In gist, you would appear to be charg-
ing the other forms with infertile or obstructive absolutism—
absolutism betraying a dubiety or inadequacy of intent, a par-
ticularization or distortion of will and, hence, of horizon, that
militates against a truly embracing conception and reign of the
altruistically colored public interest. I agree with you that a

---

* Professor of Political History, The American University.

genuinely oriented good will, such as may be native to the Christian religion, offers an arterial route to a genuinely conceived of and implemented common weal. However, while you do elucidate the foregoing in regard to Christianity generously, I wonder whether or not you might care in a passage to hone to a slightly greater degree of acuity the qualitative distinction between Christianity and other candidates for ethical ascendancy—especially, a naturalistic humanism—from the specific standpoint of the nexus between "will and weal." If I may play the devil's advocate, such might, perhaps, also deserve consideration as a means of forestalling any assertion by empirically-pivoted-and-riveted humanists that they are *patently* best fitted to limn the functions and to undertake the exercise of intelligence as a "liaison officer" between personal will and public weal, tender values and hard events. To the extent that will is voluntary while weal harbors imperatives, one might add, the problem of the relationship between the two appears to be a most vital concern, and the Christian approach to intelligence as nexus might solicit a little further illustration through the medium of contrast.

If I may say so, your final paragraph seems to me to sum up the case neatly. And, even apart from the Universal Declaration of Human Rights, the quest for common ethical denominators among nations and peoples will intensify in our time of inevadable necessity, I am sure. Thus, I submit that you are performing an indeed valuable service in rendering some of the prerequisites so articulate and challenging. Did you wish to incorporate a word in the article that will *stress* the cogency of your enterprise in this particular era of human history?

3

PUBLIC INTEREST
AND ULTIMATE COMMITMENT

WILLIAM S. MINOR

The major purpose of this treatise is to make some contribution to the advancement of political and legal philosophy by critical analysis of relations between public interest and man's ultimate commitment. The raw material used by political and legal philosophy, like the raw material with which all philosophy begins to work, is neither analytic nor critical. This raw material is generally referred to in the vocabulary of philosophy as common sense data. The common sense data of political and legal philosophy are the multiplicity of unanalyzed and uncriticized publics including their unanalyzed and uncriticized interests within them. The basic purpose of political and legal philosophy, like all philosophy, is refinement of the raw material or common sense data by means of a continuing process of analysis and criticism in the interest of increase in the highest form of knowledge, called wisdom, which is intelligent guidance of life.

Public and private interests must be clearly distinguished. The distinction is based on the perception of two types of consequences as the outcome of human association and the effort to control human behavior in the interest of consequences assumed to be better rather than worse. Private interest functions in human associations which experience and control consequences directly. When consequences of human association cannot be experienced and controlled directly, public interest is generated. The effort to control indirect consequences calls for representatives of given human associations or groups whose office is to provide means which will yield better rather than worse consequences for the group including its representatives. This group with its representatives, organized to control indirect consequences which cannot be experienced and controlled directly, is a public or a political state. When political controls are fixated or focused upon maintaining some cherished past or present *status quo* of publics, the ever-changing, on-going, novelty-producing character of nature conflicts with the fixations which are not subjected to continuous analysis, criticism, and experimental reconstruction. The failure of common sense publics to keep this process of criticism alive is an invitation to violent revolutions within them.

Critical analysis of the multiplicity of common sense publics and their interests has become increasingly difficult. Many older publics were local homogeneous communities which, in the absence of special crises, tended to change less rapidly than current publics. With the growth of the industrial revolution, including the sudden displacement of people and the increasing mobility and fluctuation of their associations, a large number of the old publics have been so uprooted, divided, and dispersed that their presence, if they do exist, is indeed difficult to discover. In this context of a fluctuating dispersion of human associations it is even more difficult to observe with clarity the emergence of new publics which may appear. John Dewey observed that a new public comes into existence when a common interest develops in controlling "indirect, extensive, enduring and serious consequences of conjoint and interacting behavior." [1] Dewey also observed such increase in scope and complexity of these indirect consequences that the resulting situation amounts to the eclipse of the public and its interests. If Dewey's observations are ac-

---

[1] John Dewey, *The Public and Its Problems* (1927), p. 126.

curate, the publics become, more or less, myths of history cherished for the values they reflect from a distant past rather than values clearly expressed in the concrete present. From the context of these observations, it is easy to understand why some analysts of public interest dismiss as futile any philosophic treatment of publics, in which case impersonal relations are accepted and indifference to meaningful human association grows. In this predicament of the eclipse of public interest, urban political machines, economic corporations, military and business combines, and other special interest groups appear in that gap between the people and their would-be governmental representatives and take control of both. If no means can be provided to eliminate this gap between the people and their governmental representatives, legal and political philosophy which seeks for wise guidance of human conduct seems to be blocked; for the people with their representatives must be able to foresee the consequences of their own behavior in such a way that critical analysis of these consequences can be practiced; otherwise, intelligent guidance based on shared responsibility is impossible.

Without shared responsibility on the part of both the people and their representatives to analyze and criticize the consequences of their own behavior, there can be no public and no public interest. Consequently, irresponsibility is inescapable, and indifference to intelligent sharing of political and legal guidance is forced. The alternative appears to be the betrayal of philosophy and the return to common sense manipulation and dictatorial control of human life in the interest of political and legal order among men; but this alternative has not been accepted by philosophers of our time, including John Dewey, Alfred North Whitehead, John Herman Randall, Jr., Charles Hartshorne, Henry Nelson Wieman, George Axtelle, John Macmurray, Stephen C. Pepper, and George Herbert Mead—to mention only a few of them. They generally point to the advancement of communication, yielding meaningful community, as Dewey suggests,[2] and to the communication not only of

---

2 *The Public and Its Problems,* p. 142.

denotative but also of qualitative meaning [3] as necessary means to the development of publics in which responsibility of the people is shared with their political and legal representatives. The communication of denotative meaning in the most abstract scientific language of mathematics is mechanical and impersonal. In itself, this kind of meaning does not yield the growth of community; but if denotative meaning is supplemented and fulfilled by qualitative meaning, the growth of creative associations among men are stimulated and community as a necessary context for growth of public interest is created. However, philosophic transformation of common sense data of eclipsed publics is not easy. The blundering efforts of men to do this have yielded great and lasting tragedy. Some of these blunders may well be examined in an effort to prevent the repetition of them.

Men have blundered in their effort to understand the formation of intelligent policies and laws for the wise guidance of man. First, basic assumptions used to begin the policy-making process have often been treated as arbitrary assumptions without transforming these assumptions into hypotheses to be tested in the process of inquiry. The arbitrary assumption closes the inquiry before it begins and prevents inquiry from becoming self-corrective.

Second, men have blundered in failing to analyze and distinguish the differences and connections between descriptive and normative hypotheses. To report descriptively public interests which have occurred and are now occurring and to predict those which may occur does not yield knowledge adequate for wise guidance of human conduct. The purpose of that higher knowledge which we call wisdom is not merely to report and to predict but also to create. However, good reporting and predicting are especially useful in creating. Without careful analysis of causal relations by physical, biological, and social sciences there is no adequate basis for projecting the ends and determining the means necessary for creating better situations. Furthermore, the intentional quality resident in means-ends relations must be clearly distinguished from the intentional quality in-

---

[3] Henry Nelson Wieman, *The Source of Human Good* (1946), pp. 16-23.

volved in reporting as accurately as possible the nature of a
situation. The latter intention is the advancement of descriptive
knowledge, whereas the former intention is to increase the
knowledge of the wise guidance of life. In seeking both kinds
of knowledge, the effort is to attain positive correlations of the
data, in one case the causal relations, in the other case the
creative means-ends relations. Understanding of the nature of
publics and their interests depends on accurate descriptions of
them, but shared responsible political and legal guidance of
publics requires normative knowledge. Description of publics is
aided more or less by all the descriptive sciences, but more especially by the social sciences, whereas creative guidance of
publics is dependent on the basic normative science of axiology
and its use within ethics, including jurisprudence, aesthetics,
and religion.

Third, men have blundered by failing to understand that
positive correlation of descriptive and normative hypotheses
constitute the materials from which principles and policies are
formed. The two poles of a normative hypothesis used in political and legal guidance of public interests are (1) means, methods,
or technologies, and (2) ends, goals, or desired consequences. The
positive correlation of these two poles is what constitutes a
principle for the guidance of conduct. The major blunder in
this context has been to regard the development of means or
technologies as the work of the sciences, assumed to be merely
descriptive, and to regard principles as the projection of ideal
ends or goals and the abstract formation of these to be the work
of philosophy, especially ethics and religious philosophy. This
traditional bifurcation of the sciences and philosophy has been
most devastating to both, for technology divorced from ideal
ends must function mechanistically, and ideal ends divorced
from technical means become sentimental and useless. Only a
scientific philosophy which would include all scientific endeavor can possibly serve as adequate guidance for publics and
their interests.

A scientific philosophy would include the formal sciences:
mathematics, the languages, and logic. Their purpose is to make
and to reconstruct the tools necessary for gaining knowledge

on all levels: the formal level itself, the reporting or descriptive level, the predictive, and the normative or axiological level. It is significant to observe that the formal scientists, including language analysts, are studying the formal sciences with a newly awakened and fresh seriousness. Their basic contributions to the advancement of more intelligent communication as necessary for wise guidance of publics and their interests are instrumentally of fundamental value. Scientific philosophy also inincludes the reporting sciences: the science of history which endeavors to report the nature of past events as accurately as possible by making good use of the tools of the formal sciences in a wide and complex variety of combinations of technology; and also the physical, biological, and social sciences given to reporting the nature of current concrete events, again by use of tools made by the formal sciences, yet in a very different combination of methods from those developed and employed for the science of history. Without the reporting science of history and the sciences which report the nature of current concrete events, there is no basis for the science of predicting the nature of future events; for the discovery of the regularities and also the novelties within the behavior of past and present events is a prerequisite to prediction. Insofar as the great work of specialized scientists— who would give their lives to reporting past and present events and to predicting, insofar as possible, future events—is discounted, obstructed, or destroyed, there is no intelligent basis for the guidance of publics and their interests. Without these sciences to tell us where we have been, where we are, and where present trends are leading us, there is no analytic empirical basis for the development of the normative sciences. In the absence of descriptively analytic empirical knowledge, ideal ends projected and means supplied to attain the ends would be out of context and apart from the actual situations to be improved, making scientific normative endeavor impossible. The actualization of possible values necessary to the improvement of any situation, including publics and their interests, is located in the matrix of the concrete situation itself rather than in some transcendental ideal end separated from its concrete setting. A concrete public is the locus which carries the possibilities for the increase of value generated by shared responsibility in political and legal guidance of human behavior. Wise guidance is rendered impossible with total dependence on mere reporting and predicting of events. Not until the further purpose of creating improved situations by positive correlation of means-ends is recognized and accepted as our common and consummatory responsibility in attaining the higher knowledge necessary to the intelligent functioning of all the applied sciences, the arts, law, medicine, and religion, can we possibly develop a philosophy for wise guidance of publics and their interests. This is the emerging scientific philosophy which recognizes no bifurcation between the sciences and philosophy, since the quest for wisdom involves the formal tool-making, the reporting of past and present events, the predicting of future events, and finally the intelligent guidance of events. Philosophy is now being rediscovered as the analytic and synoptic discipline which defines and creatively co-ordinates education as intelligence functioning within human experience.

Fourth, men have blundered by cherishing and even revering principles as ends in themselves, with the result that the principles become fixed and held as eternally changeless. This blunder prevents principles from serving, as all principles are meant to serve, as tools of correlation within given concrete and changing situations. When a principle is abstracted from the material means-ends of the on-going situation the danger of its fixation arises. The completion of the abstraction of a principle is facilitated by assuming that mental constructs have a higher rank in the scale of values than any actual material means-ends data of a situation, such as concrete publics with their various conflicting interests in need of transformation and control by their people sharing responsibility through their official political and legal representatives. This abstraction and fixation of principles do more than render them useless for wise guidance of public interest. The focusing of attention on these abstract principles and the consequent rational exercises carried on in dealing with them creates the illusion that the work of genuine importance is being done, whereas the concrete publics with all their conflicts are forsaken in the name of reason and left to suffer whatever disintegration may occur when these publics are not guided and controlled by principles used as tools for transforming conflicting interests and activities by positive correlation of their means-ends behavior. However, when principles are accepted and used as fit tools to guide individuals and institutions, they are called policies. Further acceptance by custom, tradition, and legal procedure turns policies into laws.

When religious sanction is given policies and laws so that they become revered as sacred, new dangers arise. One of these is the danger of the fixation of habits of individuals and institutions, preventing the necessary modification of means-ends relations within the public in order for that public to continue to satisfy its genuine needs. Failure to prevent the fixation of principles turns principles into set rules which become the structures of dead habits. Unless principles and habits can be kept active, alive, and experimentally operative in yielding fresh dynamic correlations within the changing processes of nature, publics suffer eclipse and the people are tempted to regard the way of intelligence as a lost cause. Education becomes a superficial affair. The "disillusioned" see the quest for wisdom as the great illusion.

A second danger arises when laws are located in some realm assumed to be transcendent to nature's on-going processes, including causal and intentional operations within nature. One of these forms of transcendentalism locates the basic condition of law in an abstract realm of pure reason. In this context, laws, assumed to be sound or valid, tend to be regarded as eternal and changeless, rendering them incapable of operational quality necessary to positive correlation of causal and means-ends relations in the natural on-going world-in-the-making. This somewhat Platonic dualistic approach to the philosophy of law is one main source of the fixation of laws, rendering policies and principles incapable of continuous reconstruction for the intelligent guidance of life.

Another form of transcendentalism, not belonging to the tradition of philosophic Idealism as explained above, but to the philosophy of Supernaturalism, is equally effective in bifurcating law from the natural world in which laws are meant to operate.

In the supernaturalistic bifurcation, the laws, which are the outcome of man's efforts to describe or report, as accurately as possible, the causal relations within nature, are not bifurcated from
nature, but only the laws, which are the outcome of the intentional efforts of man to guide human conduct wisely, are bifurcated from the natural world of necessary causal relations.
This supernaturalistic bifurcation occurs because it is assumed
that these necessary relations are not a fit context for intentional
conduct, which requires some expression of human freedom.
The transcendental dimension appears in claiming that man
is not a victim of nature's necessities but is an intentional crea-
ture conditioned not only by natural necessities but more significantly by pure freedom from beyond history. When the effort
is made to locate the source of human freedom in an assumed
transcendental unconditioned realm devoid of natural structure,
it places the normative basis of laws in the context of a kind of
irrational mysticism which prevents critical analysis of them.
It is irrational because nothing devoid of structure can be
analyzed or known. Paul Tillich's approach to law is co-ordinate
with this view in the following respects. The ultimate basis for
criticism of natural human laws is the "positive law, posited by
God in his freedom which is not dependent on any given structure outside Him." [4] The "structure outside Him" is the structure of being, but this "being" is not "being-itself." According
to Tillich, various forms of theism have referred to God as
"being," but this concept "is wrong." [5] The term "God" rightly
refers to "being-itself" which, at best, is man's ultimate concern.
Scientific and philosophic truth which are about the structure
of "being" are contrasted with the truth of faith which is about
"being-itself" as man's ultimate concern. Tillich claims that
"scientific truth and the truth of faith do not belong to the same
dimension of meaning." Furthermore, he says, "Science has no
right and no power to interfere with faith and faith has no
power to interfere with science." [6] If scientific truth and the

---

4 Paul Tillich, *Love, Power and Justice* (Galaxy Book ed., 1960), p. 111.
5 Tillich, *The Courage to Be* (1952), p. 184.
6 Tillich, *Dynamics of Faith* (1957), pp. 80-95.

truth of faith are in such distinctively different realms of being, as Tillich believes, there is no basis for intelligent empirical analysis and criticism of natural human laws as expressed by publics and their interests.

A fifth type of blunder preventing philosophic transformation of common sense data of eclipsed publics and their interests may be observed in recent works of Logical Positivists and Language Analysts. Their general tendency has been to describe the intentional moral quality present in human behavior as basically emotive rather than cognitive. Typical of this approach are the works of A. J. Ayer, beginning with his *Language, Truth, and Logic*.[7]

Since it is commonly recognized that law is an outgrowth of what man believes man ought or ought not to do, we observe that law, functioning as an effort to control and to guide publics and their interests, has, at root, an intentional moral quality. If this intentional moral quality of law cannot be transformed from merely common sense emotive functioning to cognitive intelligent guidance of publics, there is no hope for development of the kind of criticism of legal efforts and political conflicts which would make possible the resolution of these conflicts by intelligent correlation of means-ends, yielding increasingly consistent continuities in human behavior. If man lacks the capacity to learn how to bring about this transformation, we may very well join the ranks, not only of the anti-intellectuals and the faithless participants in the educational process, but also the ranks of the military that have no commitment to the positive correlation of means-ends in their effort to deal with human conflict. Fortunately, there are resources emerging within the sciences, especially the axiological normative sciences, for correction and prevention of many of these blunders made by men.

Among these emerging resources are the critical and constructive studies being made of the principles now used to resolve human conflict and to open the way for a new growth of creative interchange among men, preventing the eclipse of publics and their interests. It is my purpose in the closing part of this

---

7 A. J. Ayer, *Language, Truth and Logic* (1936).

chapter to make a brief critical survey of seven main principles which are being used allegedly to serve this end. The first of these principles is commonly called punishment. When serious conflict among human interests develops within and among publics, resulting in failure of men to work together to get necessary work done, one commonly accepted means to resolve the conflict is to inflict upon the person or persons assumed to be causal agents in producing the conflict some form of functional and/or organic discomfort, pain, suffering, or death. Whether the punishment be administered primarily as a means to counter retributively the consequences of the conflict assumed to be evil or to deter further destructive conflict, the punishment is given as a means to resolve and to prevent such conflict. The degrees of punishment range from simple frowns and hand-slaps to fines, jail sentences, solitary confinement, prolonged anxiety of cold war, and military combat with its threat of the annihilation of man. The victims of punishment, if they survive it, may play the roles of the subdued and enslaved, or they may counter with the acceptance of the role of punishment itself and the effort to inflict it, not only on others, but also on themselves, at the opportune time. These more common responses of submission and rebellion tend to function ambivalently and to confuse publics and their interests so that creative interchange within and among publics cannot function effectively. Insofar as legal systems depend on punitive means for the enforcement of law, these systems are contributing significantly to the development and maintenance of attitudes and practices of both submission and rebellion. The wide scope of the practice of the principle of punishment within publics is clearly seen by observation of the use of punishment by parents to control conflicting interests in the family, by teachers and administrators of schools to control the conduct of students, by governments to enforce their laws, by military establishments to resolve human conflict in the interest of peace, and by churches to command obedience to the will of God who is himself frequently presented by spokesmen for the church as the source of eternal punishment for wicked and unrepentant sinners. The common acceptance of the principle of punishment within and among publics has caused men who have seriously qualified or rejected this principle to be regarded generally either as dangerous heretics not to be tolerated or as sinless saints whose ways cannot be followed by ordinary men. Meanwhile, public interests, as they arise and suffer control by means of punishment, are so obscured and blinded by the common responses of submission and rebellion that alternative principles for guiding conduct are rejected in favor of punishment as the last resort. In this context publics spend most of the public's money to finance the operations of punishment.

A second principle commonly used to control public interest is deception. This is an effort of representatives of a public to trick others into doing something presented as good for them when it really is not. The scope of this practice is wide indeed. Its use is common in the behavior of parents, the operators of business and industry as revealed in current advertising and price-fixing, in the behavior of politicians to operate the controls of government, in bureaus of secret investigation and spying agencies, and especially in military establishments where the science and art of deceit are studied, accepted, and practiced for purposes of military combat. Deceit may or may not be linked with deliberate punishment. Wherever it is used and detected it destroys and prevents trustworthy relations within and among the interests of publics. Deceit paralyzes publics, for no interchange of interests, communication, or human sharing can operate freely where deceit is present. Deceit yields, not only the eclipse, but also the death of publics.

A third principle used by publics to control human interests and activities is compromise. In conflict of interests each party agrees to give up something significantly desired in order that the job, which is inseparable from the work of both parties, may be done. This process may well be described as negative bargaining. This is a dangerous procedure, for it is difficult for each party to evaluate objectively what should be given up. Each tends to accuse the other of asking that too much be given up. However, the process is facilitated by the interest in getting some of the job done even at the cost of sacrificing a part of it. The principle of compromise is not given to gaining all-or-nothing for its public but rather to securing more-or-less. Compromise is one of the basic tools used in the operation of governments, especially English and United States governments. A public given to the compromising of its conflicting interests opens the way for increase of tension in that public because of what it gives up while the desires for what are given up are still strong. With this increasing tension, there is a long history of the forsaking of compromise and a turning to acceptance of the principles of deceit and punishment.

Positive bargaining is a fourth principle used by publics to control their conflicts of interest. Positive bargaining, at best, is a fair, just, or balanced exchange of goods and services by parties operating within and among publics. When each party, as in buying and selling economic goods, is interested in obtaining something which the other possesses, a fair exchange is possible. Our common experience with this principle leads us to believe that it is used to solve a multiplicity of the problems of publics. However, we observe that failure to agree on the nature of a fair bargain may lead the parties to use negative bargaining of compromise, and if that fails, to acceptance of deceit and possibly punishment.

In this brief survey of principles which are used to resolve conflicts of interest within and among publics, there are three more which are distinctively different from the four described above. These three, at best, are all modes of persuasion based on rational-empirical-experimental research methods increasingly refined by critically shared use of them. Only those publics which have representatives who have developed these research skills can use these modes of persuasion. The development of these research skills depends on the advancement of education within publics. Not only must the representative leaders of publics be well educated in the use of refined research methods, but also the people within publics must be so educated in order that representatives may receive intelligent support and constructive criticism from the people. When this kind of support and criticism is exercised by the people generally and increasingly, the gap between the people and their representatives is closed. The closing of this gap prevents representatives from being forced into the use of various forms of authoritarianism on the one hand, and it also prevents the people from developing both slavish and rebel attitudes and practices on the other hand. When the people, including their representatives, learn to appreciate and use the refined methods of research to gain knowledge at all levels—including the formal tool-making level, the reporting level of both past and present events, the predictive level, and the normative axiological level for guidance in the improving of present conditions—then it is possible for methods of persuasion to become increasingly effective in preventing the eclipse and disintegration of publics. Methodology of research is focal in order to gain knowledge necessary for intelligent persuasion and to resolve conflicts of interest within and among publics.

Personal persuasion is the fifth principle used by publics for the resolution of conflicts of interest. Personal persuasion, at best, is based on research methods, but the persuading is done by individual persons who try to persuade the people to follow the directives given by individuals. This creates an administrative gap between the representatives of publics and the people. The representatives have created a problem. It is the problem of bridging the gap or putting the plan across in order to persuade the people to follow their guidance in an effort to resolve conflicts of interest. This administrative bridge-building procedure in the context of confused and eclipsed publics has become increasingly difficult. The difficulties encountered have generated a new profession of public relations given to study and development of skills necessary to put plans across and thereby persuade the people within publics to follow the prescribed directives. Economic, political, military, and even educational institutions are depending increasingly on public relations agencies to do this persuading of the people for them. The rapid acceleration of expenditures for these purposes is a novel development within publics. However, the people are paying for them often without knowing much about it. The difficulties encountered in this persuading process cause many public relations workers to turn from high level research to bargaining and even deceit and punishment to get the job done.

Social persuasion is a sixth principle used for the control and guidance of publics. Social persuasion, at best, is democratic in that the people and their representatives share actively, and not merely theoretically, the responsibility for resolving conflicts within and among publics. This sharing is made possible by keeping the channels of communication open between the people and their representatives. When these channels are closed publics suffer eclipse. When they are kept open, effective criticism is possible. Criticism can be most effective only when it is an outcome of highly refined research methods, yielding evidence rather than mere opinion which does not necessarily involve any evidence. The shared responsibility necessary to the development and maintenance of democratic relations within and among publics depends basically upon man's sincere search for evidence, because it is evidence rather than mere opinion which is useful in resolving conflicts of interest. However, there are three main attitudes toward search for evidence. One is nihilistic and anti-intellectual, in which no significant evidence is expected. A second attitude is perfectionistic, in which absolute and complete certainty is expected. A third attitude is based on probability supported by whatever evidence may be attained by rational-empirical-experimental procedures. The third attitude fosters tentative rather than fixed conclusions, the open-searching-mind as opposed to any form of dogmatism. The third attitude recognizes that nature and human life within nature are adventures within a process context, a world-in-the-making. The perfectionistic attitude toward knowledge based on complete evidence generates the nihilistic attitude toward knowing, because the perfectionist attitude is controlled by the fallacy of all-or-nothing. Alternation between perfectionism and nihilism in man's struggle to know is common in our history of the epistomological quest. Growth in knowing through reflective-experimental procedures is a radically different approach. Unless this approach of intelligence is taken, publics are eclipsed by the destructive conflicts generated by ambivalent expressions of absolute certainty versus no certainty. Not until social persuasion is guided by intelligent experimental attitudes can we hope for the survival of publics capable of dealing constructively with their conflicts of interest.

Yet it is within the context of the effort to use the principle of social, democratic persuasion that publics have so greatly suffered eclipse. This is because rational-empirical-experimental re-search has been used to date mainly in the formal tool-making, the reporting, and the predicting levels to gain knowledge, while the effort to create improved conditions through axiological, ethical, aesthetic, and religious guidance of publics by critical transformation of their conflicting interests has been largely ex-cluded from the domain of research done by these rational-empirical-experimental methods. The value disciplines have not been studied until very recently by other than merely intuitive and rationalistic speculative methods for learning how to guide human conduct. Therefore, the value disciplines have provided a happy hunting-ground for both nihilists and dogmatists with the result that social persuasion is commonly based on common sense. Furthermore, research aiming at mere tool-making, re-porting, and predicting does not fulfill the function of rational-empirical-experimental guidance of publics. The inability to use this high level research in the value disciplines is the supreme tragedy of the twentieth century, because without intelligent guidance in a technological age which requires it man cannot inherit the earth. Man cannot live on. Man cannot survive.

A seventh principle is needed to supply social, democratic per-suasion with an axiological normative basis for intelligent criti-cism, transformation, and guidance of the conflicting interests of publics. Lacking such a principle, these controversial conflicting interests are commonly presented to publics in such a way that the outcome is a cancelling-out process, yielding no significant transformation of them and no intelligent guidance even though the clashing opinions were vividly expressed. This kind of situa-tion leads either to a stalemate with a growing sense of futility regarding constructive guidance or, finally, to a return to the use of the principles of deceit and punishment, even though the transition from the former to the latter may have involved a struggle to discover and rely upon (1) a leader with effective power of personal persuasion, (2) positive and negative bar-gaining.

The emergence from merely intuitive and speculative value theories to scientific axiology as normative for the guidance of conduct is facilitated first, by distinguishing clearly the effort to report and to predict events in the quest for knowledge from the effort to create improved situations in the quest for the higher knowledge of intelligent guidance, called wisdom, as discussed above. Second, the facilitation of this emergence depends on distinguishing impersonal causal relations from personal intentional relations involving positive correlation of means-ends. A third contribution to this facilitation is the discovery that the principle of objectivity as formulated traditionally for reporting events scientifically must not be confused with the principle of objectivity used to guide events intentionally. The principle of objectivity for reporting events includes the aim of eliminating all subjective and personal elements insofar as possible. Since the aim of creating improved situations clearly includes personal elements, it is commonly assumed traditionally that an objectively scientific effort to guide events is impossible. Many have overlooked the fact that interests are not basically subjective because interests have objects which can be dealt with operationally and experimentally. The objectivity of intelligent criticism of interests of both individual persons and publics is based on the observation that not just any means-ends can be correlated positively, yielding continuity rather than self-blocking activity. Inquiry to discover why this is so leads us to a fifth precondition for the facilitation of axiological guidance of persons and publics. Positive correlations of means-ends relations yielding continuities of activity, however limited, are observed to have within them an integral quality or a quality of integrity which is not only formative in nature, including human nature, but also normative for human nature. This integral quality is what makes it possible for intentional human activities, within the context of nature generally, to be correlative. It is this correlative quality of intentional human activities which makes wisdom as the higher knowledge of intelligent guidance possible. In order to observe the functioning of this quality, the correlations in the context of mere immediacy must give way to the context of continuity. The discovery and facilitation of these continuities are not bound by the traditional philosophic quest for abstract rational consistencies but are released by the quest for operational consistencies in nature itself, including human nature as an inseparable functioning within nature as a whole. The integral correlative quality of nature, however limited, is normative for scientific axiological guidance of persons and publics. Rational-empirical-experimental research reveals increasingly the nature of those activities which are and those which are not correlative. A by-product of discovery of and respect and reverence for these activities by increasingly intelligent adjustment to them is human freedom, for human freedom means basically self-facilitation rather than self-blockage of activities. These self-facilitating activities have within them the quality of creativity which involves the continuous emergence of novel qualities with a kind of balance between their expansiveness and their cohesiveness. These creative, correlative qualities within the continuities of nature's activities may well be designated by the traditional term, "divine," for the genetic historic function of divine activity is the basic normative quality which it provides for human judgment and criticism. This is the judgment of God as a factual normative process empirically observable within nature. God, in this factual and naturalistic use of the term, is basically normative for the criticism and transformation of conflicts of interest within and among publics. The seventh principle is, therefore, the principle of God, the principle of divine persuasion. Intelligent worship of God by man is done by rational-empirical-experimental research. Man, at best, lives his faith within the development and experimental practice of this research. It is through this kind of research that God does reveal his ways to man. These ways are not man's ways until man experiences ultimate commitment to God. Within this commitment, human interests, desires, ideas, beliefs, habits, customs, mores, laws, cultures, and all philosophies of living are continuously subject to the transforming power of divine persuasion.

THE PUBLIC INTEREST
IN POLITICAL ETHICS

C. W. CASSINELLI

Politicians, governmental officials, journalists, and professors of political science have long used the phrase "the public interest" without visible embarrassment and presumably with every expectation of being understood. Recently, some writers have questioned the propriety of this uncritical attitude; they have asked for a definition of the public interest, and occasionally they have suggested that it cannot be defined. Scrutinizing common and overworked phrases is, of course, a principal responsibility of the academician, and in the long run it leads to increased understanding. Nevertheless, I believe that these recent critics have overlooked certain fundamental characteristics of the concept of the public interest, and that consequently much of what they say is misleading or beside the point.

Although the usual references to the public interest are uncritical, the political scientists, political "commentators," party leaders, administrators, and judges clearly have something definite in mind when they make them. The task of the analyst is to discover what this something is and then, if it makes any sense at all, to define it more or less precisely and explore its implications.

44

I

The expression "the public interest" normally occurs in statements about the actions of men believed influential in public affairs—governmental officials, leaders of political parties, officials of great private organizations, and any others who influence public policy or have power over many people. The actions of these men are linked with the public interest in judgments of consistency; ordinarily it is said that they are—or are not—in the public interest. When an action is in the public interest, it is worthy of approval; when an action is not in the public interest, it deserves our disapproval. Men of public affairs will often meet or try to forestall criticism by saying that they have acted in the public interest.

When one says that a given action is in the public interest, he usually intends to convey some information other than his own approval of the action; he means more than "This action, hurrah!" or "I like this action." The phrase "the public interest" is supposed to convey certain reasons why the action is approvable, and the words "public" and "interest" are definitely intended to retain their ordinary meanings. The meaning of "the public interest" is not necessarily affected by insincerity in its use. Some writers seem to have condemned the concept to meaninglessness simply because it has so often been abused by charlatans and tyrants. Manipulative misuse, however, need not destroy the meaning of a word, although it usually tends to reduce its usefulness. The word "healthful" has suffered in contemporary advertising, but it still means "helping to promote health," and it would be ineffective if it did not have this meaning. Even if this meaning were lost after years of constant abuse, there would still be things and actions that promote health.

The public interest is a standard of goodness by which political acts can be judged; action in the public interest, therefore, deserves approval because it is good. It has been suggested that the concept is useless as a "tool of analysis" or an "aid to scientific study," and that thus it should be abandoned. This statement is quite irrelevant. The public interest, as an ethical concept, has functions quite different from those of analytic models, such as bureaucracy and federalism, and standards of measurement, such as efficiency and popularity.

The word "public" means that the ethical value in the standard of the public interest applies to every member of the political community; it is a value to be distinguished from something advantageous to one person and disadvantageous to another.[1] The word "interest" indicates the evaluational meaning of the standard; it refers to something we should be "interested in," even though we may not be, and it could be replaced by "profit," "welfare," or "benefit." Therefore, to say that an action is in the public interest is to judge it consistent with a political situation that is beneficial to everyone, if not immediately at least in the long run, and whether or not everyone realizes it.

The public interest is the highest ethical standard applicable to political affairs. Those who use the expression are always referring to the ultimate moral goals of political association, even though they may not be sharply aware of it. The whole point in talking about something that is good for "the public," rather than good for only a part of the public, is to contrast the higher with the lower good. When the advantages resulting from government are fairly distributed among all members of the community, the best possible political situation has been achieved. The public interest need not imply that all men are entitled to identical or equal benefits, but it always implies that everyone should receive his due, no matter how modest it may be in comparison with the due of others. When everyone is benefiting in his proper—and perhaps special—way, when the public's interest is being met, then the most desirable type of political association has been realized.

I have thus far dealt with the public interest only as a standard for specific political actions, or at most for general patterns of public policy. This standard, however, cannot be separated from correlative standards for governmental institutions and procedures, and for the traditional, social, and economic founda-

---

[1] This does not mean that the "public" interest is opposed to "private" interests. See my essay, "Some Reflections on the Concept of the Public Interest," *Ethics,* LXIX (1958), 48-61, where the relationships between the two are described.

tions upon which governments rest. Foundations, institutions, and policy are always mutually interdependent; for example, the consistent protection of civil liberties depends upon a certain kind of government, and a parliamentary government requires a special environment. To praise or condemn a pattern of public policy is unavoidably to praise or condemn the institutions producing it and the society underlying these institutions. Because of this interrelationship, the ethical standard of the public interest can be applied to all phenomena relevant to politics.

II

The concept of the public interest has, I believe, the essential and practically invariable core of meaning described above. It has frequently been criticized as ambiguous and occasionally as meaningless, but this criticism either confuses the clear general meaning of the concept with its many interpretations or denies that we should evaluate our political life. There is obviously no unanimity regarding the ultimate moral goals of political association, but this disagreement does not undermine the concept of such goals. The critics often say, in effect, that since we have difficulty in deciding what is most desirable in politics, we should stop discussing the issue.

Social scientists cannot ignore the fundamental issue of the final political good: this is the principal lesson to be learned from examining the concept of the public interest. The phrase itself is expendable; even though men of political affairs continue to use it, it could disappear from scholarly prose with no effect whatever on the existence and significance of the idea to which it now refers. The preference of many social scientists for dealing with human behavior on levels that require only limited (and usually suppressed) value judgments ought not to tempt them to condemn the discussion of broader evaluations as futile or meaningless. The simple fact that men distinguish between good and bad obliges us to think and write about problems of ethics, and the ultimate goals of political life are unquestionably among the most important of these problems.

Some political scientists have recently taken the interesting

position that in contemporary democracy the public interest—
or its equivalent—is the "process of group accommodation" or
the "democratic method." The motivation behind this identification seems to be a desire to retain some elements of the concept
of the public interest and at the same time to eliminate others.
They appear to be unwilling to say that politics has no goal at
all, but reluctant to risk the charge of simply contributing to
the endless list of arbitrary and incompatible interpretations of
the public interest.

This attempt to avoid the difficulties of evaluation by adopting a presumably modest and minimal value is necessarily unsuccessful. No matter how thin it is, an interpretation of the
public interest is subject to all the questions raised by the problem of "grounding" value judgments. Identifying the public interest with the democratic method is precisely comparable, in
its status as a value judgment, to identifying the public interest
with the terrestrial realization of God's will: neither can be
"proved" to a skeptic. The only way to avoid this unsettled (and,
to some, unsettling) situation is to deny that the ideas of good
and bad make sense. One cannot wash his hands of the problem
by saying "Let every man be the judge for his own case," or
"One man's opinion is as good as another's." This relativism is
helpless in the face of conflicting preferences, and, like other
value statements, it is confounded when the skeptic asks for
"proof." Maintaining a practical or theoretical interest in politics
implies taking a stand on some "unprovable" interpretation of
the public interest.

III

The fear of committing themselves to "forcing their personal values on other people" is apparently an important reason
why some writers have said that the public interest is a meaningless concept and why others have reduced the political goals
of democracy to a minimum. Almost all social scientists have a
healthy aversion to the principles of the Platonic Republic and
a healthy attachment to the liberty and equality of the modern
democratic state. They may have concluded from Plato's argu-

ment that anyone who takes any kind of definite stand on the content of the public interest is logically required to support governmental institutions of unchecked power and public policy of thorough regimentation. Fortunately, however, this conclusion is incorrect. The fear that the concept of the public interest is in itself somehow "undemocratic" is unfounded, because in certain familiar situations men habitually judge other men's actions undesirable without trying to force them to behave correctly, and because interpreting the public interest in terms of political freedom logically excludes forcing men to conform to it.

On the psychological level, we experience no difficulty in everyday life in evaluating the behavior of our families, neighbors, political allies and rivals, and great segments of our fellow citizens without having, or desiring to have, control over them. On the social level, modern democracy is famous for the coexistence in harmony and independence of many men with many conflicting opinions and preferences. The mutual tolerance of the democratic society does not depend upon an "equilibrium of power" that prevents some men from dominating others; it derives from a widespread feeling that, no matter how strongly one holds a particular belief, the other man is entitled to his own opinion on the issue—that, in other words, he has a right to be wrong.[2] This feeling is perfectly normal and understandable.

In ethical theory, as well as in practical life, we can adopt goals that apply to the whole community and at the same time maintain that they are not to be realized by the use of force. When we interpret the public interest as the "maximization of freedom," with its corollaries of "liberalism" and "constitutionalism," we cannot force people to abide by this interpretation without preventing the achievement of the very goal we seek. With this interpretation of the public interest, and no doubt with it alone, the goals we wish for all men must be pursued willingly and voluntarily by all men. It makes no sense to say that we must force them to be free.

Despite the fact that a self-appointed elite cannot force a peo-

---

2 See C. W. Cassinelli, *The Politics of Freedom: An Analysis of the Modern Democratic State* (1961), Ch. 8, for the reasons behind this attitude.

ple to adopt a constitution, respect civil liberties, recognize civil rights, and provide for social welfare, the utilization of force has its place even in an ethics of political freedom. People must be disposed to value freedom in its various manifestations, and this disposition is not accidental but associated with certain definite characteristics, such as a high standard of living and a high degree of education. Since we cannot assume that everyone will always work for the extension of these characteristics, or that those who desire their extension will adopt the correct means, anyone committed to freedom must also be committed to overcoming opposition in order to improve levels of learning, physical and mental security, and opportunities for leisure. Although force must be used very carefully and sparingly in order to prevent the whole program's being frustrated by resentment, the point to be stressed is that it may well become necessary to adopt the method of coercion to overcome the opposition of elites or masses to the realization of the public interest interpreted as political freedom. It is instructive that programs of material amelioration have generally been considered humanitarian duties rather than arrogant attempts to shape the world according to one's private prejudices. Even those writers most apprehensive of inadvertent Platonism are usually reluctant to say that a man's preference for poverty, illness, and ignorance is sufficient grounds for leaving him in this condition.

In theoretical politics as in practical life, indifference, humility, and relativism eventually become inappropriate; there is always a place where a firm stand must be taken. The ethics of freedom has the great advantage of implying that this stand be taken at the right place. The provision of security and opportunity is very likely to be approved both by those who have them and by those who lack them; and in the event that one's commitment to the public interest as freedom requires the application of force, it occurs at the ethically least distasteful level, where it resembles the normally approved practices of checking exploiters or disciplining children. The time spent trying to avoid accusations of pontification could be more profitably devoted to exploring the conditions that make the open society possible.

IV

I have argued that in examining political life we cannot avoid referring to some interpretation of the public interest; and that even when we adopt freedom as our most fundamental political value, we may have to sanction coercion as a means of protecting and promoting it, even though we cannot "prove it to be correct." The concept of the public interest, in any of its interpretations, comprises only phenomena directly related to governmental policy, and thus it has the additional characteristic of dealing with only part of human life. Because of this, it cannot stand alone when we raise the issue of ethical desirability; for example, public policy promoting civil liberties and civil rights must be supplemented by a family structure providing security and an educational system encouraging honesty and generosity. To be meaningful, each of these goals must be instrumental to general human excellence; each must contribute to what has traditionally been called the "good life." To put this another way, the political values that come within the scope of the public interest are values only because they are deducible from a general conception of human excellence.[3]

Most discussions of political ethics must as a practical matter be limited. It is perfectly reasonable to talk about the desirability of a certain policy-making procedure without reference to the public interest, and to argue in terms of a specific interpretation of the public interest without reference to the "good life"; everything cannot be said on every occasion. Nevertheless, the logical connections among these levels of evaluation remain. When we approve of a detail of governmental organization, we commit ourselves to an interpretation of the public interest; when we interpret the public interest, we bind ourselves to a conception of the "good life." When we choose "freedom," or the "accommoda-

---

[3] It has been argued that right action cannot be deduced from general moral principles; a cogent example is Maurice Mandelbaum, "On the Use of Moral Principles," *Journal of Philosophy*, LIII (1956), 662-670. Since this position fails to relate rightness and goodness, it seems unacceptable; see Oliver A. Johnson, *Rightness and Goodness: A Study in Contemporary Ethical Theory* (1959), Ch. 6 and *passim*.

tion of group demands," as the ultimate goal of political life, we obligate ourselves to justify this choice by reference to a conception of human excellence.

V

A final important characteristic of the concept of the public interest is its status as the standard of evaluation that gives meaning to the idea of political rights and political duties. Faithful execution of the laws, voting in general elections, nominating the best available candidates, making sound legislative decisions, and obeying the law are duties only when implied by an interpretation of the public interest. The official and the citizen have political obligations only because the best possible political system cannot be realized unless their actions meet certain standards. No one, for example, has an intrinsic duty to govern according to the constitution or to pay taxes according to the law.

The relation between the public interest and the responsibilities of governmental officials deserves special emphasis. Although references to the public interest usually contain references to the actions of officials, the "responsibility" of the officials is not always seen as dependent upon the public interest. No one wants "irresponsible" officials, but the usual standards of responsibility—the constitution, norms of honesty and efficiency, the people—are not always recognized as justifiable only in terms of some specific interpretation of the public interest. Some writers seem to fear that accepting the public interest as the ultimate standard for governmental responsibility commits one to giving each official the right always to act according to his own momentary conception of his society's final political goals. This fear is baseless; every properly organized polity has a constitution that defines functions and allocates authority, and that thus makes impossible a class of officials who alone understand the political good. The immediate and normally overriding responsibility of every official is to exercise his authority to the best of his ability; but the public interest is still the final justification for this authority and for the constitution that confers it.

Even though institutional stability should relieve the official of most calculations of ultimate political desirability, his formal authority cannot possibly encompass every eventuality he will encounter. He cannot avoid exercising discretion, and in doing so he often must act according to his own interpretation of the public interest.[4] I hope he is prepared to do more than defer to the group that protests most vigorously.

Finally, the concept of the public interest can help retard the worrisome tendency of the citizen, with apparent encouragement from some academics, to believe himself possessed of many rights, while denying or ignoring any concomitant duties. This attitude is arrogant and socially dangerous; it undermines authority, and it could lead to the predominance of what Ortega y Gassett called the "mass man." When the public interest is kept firmly in mind, the political duties of the citizen can be properly stressed, and his political rights can be put in their proper perspective as necessary conditions for his ultimate duty of living the kind of life befitting a human being. Once again, the public interest, no matter what it is called, is seen as a concept indispensable to political ethics.

---

4 See Carl J. Friedrich, "Authority, Reason, and Discretion," in *Nomos I: Authority*, ed. Friedrich (1958).

5

THE PUBLIC INTEREST:
PROPOSING PRINCIPLES OF
CONTENT AND PROCEDURE

HAROLD D. LASSWELL

I

We begin by locating ourselves as scholars in the processes of decision and choice in the life of man in society. For analytic and comparative purposes it is convenient to adopt seven categories to describe the several phases of decision in the activities that are variously called political, governmental or legal. We begin by showing how these categories can be used to describe the activities that are conventionally recognized as governmental in the United States. We might have begun with the smallest units of government, such as town or township, and moved upward to the national community. However, there may be readier communication if we select examples at the national level.

The seven categories are intelligence (and planning), recommending, prescribing, invoking, applying, appraising, terminating. Intelligence is the principal role of fact gathering and future estimating agencies like the Census and the CIA, or planning organs which are authorized to propose, not to push, policy

54

programs. By recommending we mean active promotion of policy proposals. In the United States we identify quasi-official bodies like the political parties as especially influential recommenders. To prescribe is to lay down constitutional provisions, statutes, and the like. To invoke is to make a preliminary characterization of concrete circumstances in terms of conformity to prescriptions. This is the conspicuous role played by the Attorney General and by arresting officers. Application refers to relatively final activities within the frame provided by prescription, and includes the disposal of controversies by judicial and regulative bodies and most routine operations of administrative services. To appraise is to explore and assess the degree to which official policies have been realized. Congressional committees spend much of their time examining the success or failure of executive and administrative organs in giving effect to legislative and constitutional policy. Many categories of inspectors are specialized to the task of providing fiscal and other data bearing upon appraisal. Termination puts an end to legislative or treaty prescriptions, for instance, and also to arrangements, such as contracts, made within the prescriptive framework.

As private scholars it is obvious that we may become officially involved as consultants in connection with all seven functions. However, the intelligence and appraising functions seem especially appropriate to our skills. The role that we play in intelligence and appraisal, at least, is further emphasized if we go beyond the official to the unofficial activities which are engaged with each function. We have done this in the case of political parties in connection with recommendation, and undoubtedly should add the entire network of pressure organizations. The intelligence function in our society is unofficially served by the public press and by private research agencies, notably universities. Although strictly speaking no private entity is authorized to prescribe rules of conduct, it is a commonplace of scholars of the law that prescriptive norms are continually appearing or disappearing in the customs of the marketplace and other private sectors of society. Private citizens as well as prosecutors or police are active in the invocation of prescriptions; indeed, an overwhelming number of complaints in many jurisdictions are initiated by private individuals and associations. The applying functions of society are in a bad way unless private organizations and individuals conform themselves to the articulated prescriptions. The appraisal function is especially dependent upon the fact gathering and interpretative operations of crime commissions, tax bureaus, and the like. The terminating of obligations goes perpetually on in the social process.

We have been referring to official and unofficial activities at the national level of politics, and we might with equal validity consider the role of private scholars in local or world affairs. Nor would a comprehensive statement stop with political institutions, formal or informal. It would systematically consider all activities in any given social context. Such a check list would identify institutions devoted to wealth, production, and consumption; family and friendship relations, health, safety, and comfort; the cultivation and exercise of skill; religious and ethical activities; enlightenment; respect. We reserve the term decision process for political, governmental, and legal activities, and refer to the choosing process in any other institution. All choosing as well as decision processes are amenable to examination in terms of the seven phase analysis.

II

Our problem is the clarification of public interest. In common with all problems five intellectual tasks need ultimately to be performed: (1) What is the *goal* of this investigation of the concept of public interest? (2) What *trends* in contemporary of modern affairs lead us to conclude that the problem is significant at this time? (3) What *factors* in the social process must be taken into account in comprehending these trends? (4) If we *project* developments into the immediate or long-range future does it appear probable that the significance of the problem will increase or decrease? (5) In the light of the total context what conceptions do we *propose* for the specification of public interest?

1. The objectives to be accomplished have been formulated by the various members of the Society of Political and Legal Philosophy in various ways. I shall postulate the following goal,

believing that it is in varying degree parallel to the conceptions current among us. My overriding objective is to clarify the conception of public interest in a way that contributes to the realization of human dignity on the widest possible scale. It is not intended to lead discussion toward the theological or metaphysical postulates from which a commitment to human dignity can be derived. Rather, the thrust of the present inquiry is toward the specification of goal in reference to the social and historical process, with a view to the possible improvement of strategies appropriate to its fulfillment. This is a consultation among persons who willingly entertain the general objective, whether they regard it as derived from Christianity, Judaism, or another religious tradition, or from one of the metaphysical schools, and whose broad interpretation is approximately equivalent.

Perhaps it is worth saying that I do not intend to present an idiosyncratic conception of human dignity. What I have in mind is widely understood since it is the dominant theme of the Declaration of Independence in American tradition and of the recent Charter of Human Rights.

As living beings men and women seek to bring about outcomes that they desire. Hence they seek to maximize the net result of participating in human affairs by improving their position in regard to every value (preferred outcome).

Individuals do not typically pursue values in utter disregard of the values of at least some other human beings. This comes about because the most important effect of home and education is to enable each individual to develop a "Self". A Self is composed of the "Ego" (the "I", "me") and all recognitions of every ego with whom the Ego is identified. Usually the Self includes members of the family, locality, nation—in fact, every individual and group with whom one is "we" rather than "they." For every component of the Self there are somewhat distinctive expectations and value demands.

What are the value demands? If we were to name each specific outcome desired by human beings the list would be impossibly long. Hence we use a brief list of terms in the classification of values. In the following list the order of mention is not important; nor, for that matter, is it important whether everybody

uses the same terms or not. The significant point is that labels
are needed to refer to all valued events.

Wealth:	Wealth and income
Well-being:	Mental and physical health, comfort and safety.
Affection:	Family and friends; attachments to larger groups.
Skill:	Excellence in the arts, crafts, professions.
Rectitude:	Worship and sense of responsibility.
Respect:	Recognition, social standing.
Enlightenment:	Information; interpretations of past, present, and future.
Power:	Governmental and legal relations.

When we look at a city, a nation, or any other community
we find variations in the degree to which everyone participates
in the shaping and sharing of values. In some countries a few
people are very rich and a multitude is very poor. Middle income
groups are missing. Some localities are healthy and well looked
after; others breed disease and neglect. In some nations the ruling
regime tries to break up family solidarity by putting its members
into separate work camps. Educational opportunities are denied
to millions of young people who are thereby prevented from
achieving excellence in the arts, crafts, or professions. Worship
is interfered with and a single system of ideology is imposed upon
the population. In many countries, the stigma of social caste
stands in the way of acknowledging individual merit and the
stream of public enlightenment is dimmed by censorship and
discolored by propaganda. Government and law are conceived as
the privilege of the few.

In sharp contrast to the situation in which great differences
separate a privileged caste from the community as a whole, the
commonwealth that harmonizes with the philosophy of human
dignity achieves widespread rather than narrow participation in
value shaping and sharing. The following statements spell out
some specific details of what is meant by a commonwealth of free
men. Although far from exhaustive these items are representative of the interpretations that are currently given to the funda-

mental goal of human dignity; they are taken from the Charter of Human Rights.

In politics, law, and government power is shaped and shared when there is right to "take part in the government," to "recognition as a person before the law," and to "effective remedy by competent national tribunals." There is a right to "a social and international order."

In economic relations benefits are shaped and shared when there is "right to own property" and to a "standard of living adequate for the individual and his family."

In enlightenment matters there is shaping and sharing when "freedom of opinion and expression" exists, and the right "to seek, receive and impart information and ideas through any medium regardless of frontiers" is effectively implemented.

Skill shaping and sharing imply the "right to education" and "the right to participate freely in the cultural life of the community, to enjoy the arts and to share in scientific advancement and its benefits." Included are the acquisition and application of socially acceptable skills in arts, occupations, and professions; hence the "right to work, to free choice of employment," and "to protection against unemployment."

In regard to well-being, shaping and sharing signify the "right to life, liberty and security of person," and condemn "torture," as well as "cruel" or "inhuman" treatment or punishment. There is "right to rest and leisure" and a general "right to social security."

In reference to affection, shaping and sharing include the "right to marry and to found a family" and to engage in congenial association with others ("peaceful assembly and association"). And there is the right to be identified with a national community ("right to a nationality").

In matters pertaining to respect, shaping and sharing make it imperative to affirm that "all human beings are born free and equal in dignity and right." "Everyone is entitled to all rights and freedoms—without distinction of any kind." Obviously, there must be no "slavery or servitude," no arbitrary interference with "privacy, family, home, or correspondence," and freedom from attacks upon "honor and reputation."

A community in which rectitude is widely shaped and shared provides for "freedom of thought, conscience, and religion." "Everyone has duties to the community," and there is no right to destroy the rights and freedoms of others.

The foregoing indications show that the ideal of human dignity takes the entire body politic into consideration. It is not a matter of giving a privileged few their freedom of choice but of striking a balance among the claims of all.

How is the discussion of public interest connected with realizing the goal of human dignity? It is apparent from our statement that the fundamental objective puts a heavy burden of emphasis upon the role of individual choice. But the usual connotations of "public" are "collective" with overtones suggesting that collective modes of choice are desirable. How do these connotations conflict or integrate with one another? If we provide formulations that offer guidance to ourselves and others in connection with these issues it is possible that we have contributed to the grand design that we have in mind.

2. But is this attempt timely? Granted that questions centering around public interest are always with us, can we say that contemporary and modern developments indicate that this is a relatively propitious time to deal with the problem? I believe the reply is affirmative, since there is much evidence of confusion in considering the issues of internal and external policy now before us. It is not necessary to argue in a presidential campaign year that contradictory interpretations are prevalent concerning the public interest, or that individuals who profess intense devotion to serving public interest often appear as special pleaders for projects of dubious validity. The vast public issues of modern and contemporary times bring these contradictions of doctrinal interpretation and behavior into great prominence. Hence scholars are appealed to in the hope that they can aid public navigation by providing clearer intellectual charts than are presently in general circulation.

3. Even a cursory review of factors that condition present confusions will call attention to the fabulous increase in the scale and diversity of the world community and of all its component communities and pluralistic associations. The explosive develop-

ments of the techno-scientific age hold us in their grip, a grip that may prove fatal in view of the anarchic structure of a world arena obsessed by the expectation of violence and the demand at the highest levels to make as few concessions as possible to external control.

4. To project the present into the future is in no sense to alleviate the gravity of the human condition. There is serious question whether the challenge of totalitarianism will be held in check or overcome by bodies politic that succeed in sustaining the vitality of their aspirations and approximations to freedom. Whether one militarizes the garrisons or civilizes the military is in doubt; there is also doubt of the continuity of life itself.

5. If recommended formulations of the public interest are to be helpful to ourselves and others, I suggest that they must propose two sets of closely interconnected principles. I refer to principles of content and principles of procedure. The generalizations relating to content put forward definitions and criteria of the public interest; they are guides to what needs to be thought about. Generalizations relating to procedure deal with the order in which matters of content can be considered with the best chance of arriving at results that harmonize with the criteria.

As the complexity of modern society increases we are ever more aware of the importance of procedure. Unless group leaders—like legislators—who lay down high level definitions are aware of the cruciality of providing bridges between initial generalization and concrete circumstance, definitions are likely to be distorted or nullified at the phase of application. Suppose that a statute has been duly enacted in which the public interest is particularized as "public necessity and convenience." Has the intellectual task of providing guidance in clarifying the public interest been satisfactorily performed? The answer is emphatically negative. By what procedures are the events to be identified in concrete circumstances which are eligibly designated as in harmony with "necessity" and "convenience"? More pointedly, what are the qualifications most likely to produce a decision maker —an event designator—whose decisions will be most in harmony with the definition? By what modalities of selection and training are qualified persons most likely to be at the "right place at the right time"? If we assume that an adequately prepared decision maker is at hand, how can the concrete circumstances be best presented in order to increase the likelihood of a decision in harmony with the original definition?

In the legal system of the United States statutes are enacted in the expectation that a matrix of procedural practices can be taken for granted for the implementation of a new prescription. However, it is often recognized by legislators and chief executives that extra attention must be given to "who does what how." Hence we find that much contemporary legislation seeks to anticipate issues that will arise at the application phase. For instance, provision may be made for administrative boards of appeal in order to relieve the regular judiciary from the burden of making various determinations.

The foregoing references have been to official action by groups or in the name of groups. The importance of building bridges between generalized principles and concrete opportunities for application is equally pertinent to individual choices. The findings of modern social and behavioral sciences have added to the sensitivity of our perception of these points. The most prominent examples, perhaps, are afforded by individuals who are deliberately seeking to conform to a general norm of conduct, yet who in many circumstances act in ways that violate the norm—violations, indeed, attended by subsequent remorse. We recall at once the alcoholic who tells himself and others that he is through with alcohol, yet succumbs time after time. Or the morphine addict who tries and fails with monotonous regularity. Obviously, if norms which are fully adopted at the conscious level are to affect conduct more is needed than generalized (and neatly subcategorized) formulations of the norm. The individual or the group that adopts the norm needs also to adopt procedures that make them fit to live up to it. Persons who have strong unconscious objections to the norm can only live up to its requirements when they are subjected to procedures that liquidate the compulsions that control their behavior. Sometimes the procedures of free association and interpretation—as in clinical psychoanalysis—are able to free the individual from his inner contradictions sufficiently to reinstate freedom of choice. Often procedures that employ chemicals as well as communications are potent enough to break the vicious circle. In many cases the essential point is to modify the social strategy of an individual so that he interacts frequently with a supportive environment from which he obtains the specific indulgences needed to enable him to overcome deprivations.

The so-called "pathological extremes" do not exhaust the procedural provocations or techniques that we have in mind in connection with verbalized norms of the public interest. If an individual intends to make a viable contribution to the clarification of the public interest it is probable that he will be disappointed unless he becomes familiar with the setting in which the problem is relevant. What, for example, is the public interest of the United States in the emerging world of outer space? Or, for that matter, the much better known area of degrees of permissible market control ("antitrust" and the like)? The problem solver (or tackler) in these areas must employ procedures by which his ignorance of outer space is reduced and his knowledge of market factors is enlarged. In the course of our discussion of the public interest it is to be hoped that we discover principles that aid in constructing the many bridges between articulated norm and concrete circumstance that require building and rebuilding in our historic epoch.

III

We begin by emphasizing the fact that whether we like them or not *value consequences* follow from any act within the social process. Moreover, as scholarly observers we can describe these consequences with varying degrees of comprehensiveness during any period of time and in any social context. Our description will depend upon the procedures that we employ in formulating the theoretical models to use as exploratory guides, and upon the modes of data obtaining, processing, and fitting the theoretical models of which we make use. In the discussion to follow we refer to an *alpha* statement as a definition or principle of content. By a *beta* statement is meant a formulation of procedure.

By *common interest* is meant that in a given social context a specified activity has inclusive value effects (*alpha*), as ascertained by stated procedures of inquiry (*beta*), which are compatible with the goal of human dignity. In terms of the perspectives of participants in a social process, common interest refers to shared demands about value effects (*alpha*), supported by expectations regarding conditioning factors (*beta*). The statements about these perspectives and conditions made by scholars also involve procedures (*beta*).

There is ample room for scholarly observers who describe any given context to differ with one another in identifying common interests. To some extent these are matters of taste in definition and need give rise to no problems of interdefinitional translation if terms are clearly set forth. Possible differences also arise from the choice of procedure used in empirical examination of the context. Here, too, there need be no insuperable difficulty in understanding if the methods are lucidly set forth. One observer, for instance, may rely upon the results obtained by a controlled interview sample; another may have intensively interviewed a very small number of participants whom he regarded as particularly well-informed insiders. The technical task of calibrating results obtained by procedures of varying degrees of intensiveness is always with us. We must also take cognizance of differences in the skill with which a recognized procedure is employed, making appropriate discount for lack of excellence.

We need a term to designate value consequences which are incompatible with the common interest. For this purpose we introduce the label *special interest*.

When we spoke of common interests as inclusive we were reiterating the point that social consequences always follow from any act; hence social consequences are relatively common or special.

By *public interest* is meant that the common interest is sufficiently great to warrant the use of inclusive procedures of choice or decision (as viewed by an observer employing *beta*).

By *private interest* we refer to value effects which are common interests of insufficient magnitude to warrant the use of inclusive rather than exclusive procedures of choice or decision (*beta*).

In the world community as a whole actual or potential effects may be judged insignificant by a qualified observer. He has no trouble in concluding that a barroom quarrel between farmhands in the Middle West is less consequential than an altercation between officials at a diplomatic reception at the United Nations. However, if a Middle-Western neighborhood has been taken as the context of inquiry, the quarrel may loom large enough to be put into the public interest category. Hence inclusive procedures of decision or choice are involved; this means, for instance, that community leaders may appropriately intervene in the situation.

It needs no elaboration to say that scholarly observers are likely to differ from one another in whether the common interest is "sufficiently great" to warrant calling it public interest. It is also probable that the observer's conceptions of public interest will differ from the conceptions current among participants in the context referred to. In some United States communities where the religious tradition is strong clergymen or church elders consider it part of their obligation to intervene in any situation that deviates from religious and ethical norms, as they interpret them. You and I may adopt conceptions of public interest which deny that the common interest is sufficiently great in many circumstances to warrant intervention by a community spokesman. (It is not a question of gossip "behind the backs" of the parties, but of face-to-face relationships.) Hence we conclude that intervention by a local clergyman or elder is a coercive act of a "busybody" who unconsciously pursues a special interest (a recurring problem modeled upon the Elders and Suzannah at the bath).

I do not want to engage in the discussion of a specific case at the moment, but rather to defend the role of the scholarly observer in confronting "conventional" perspectives and operations with his own "functional" definitions, principles, and procedures of empirical study. My position is that the intellectual serves the public interest when he confronts conventional images and conformities with functional conceptions and empirical findings. In some instances . . . the observer does not differ with definitions or principles which are articulated in the conventional perspectives. His contribution is to provide data about conformity between proclaimed norms and actual behavior. In other instances the observer adopts unconventional definitions and principles regarding the content of public interest, and also reports the results of investigation. The scholar may not be part of the procedural process by which inclusive choices or decisions are made in a given context. But his proposed interpretations, if communicated to the community, rest upon methods which are in principle capable of being comprehended and checked by anyone who acquires the requisite skill.

Note that we have set up the definitions so that private interests are also common interests; and they are not necessarily limited to the interests of an individual (acting as a whole person) rather than a group (individuals acting for collective objectives). What is labeled public or private in a given context depends upon what is warrantably left to inclusive or exclusive judgment. In the United States we recognize that some of our common American interests are sufficiently great to be dealt with on a national scale; by contrast, we leave other common interests to the States or other local entities. Hence (in our terms) we identify the public interest of America and the private interest of the States. Within each component community, however, there are parallel distinctions. At the state or municipal level we identify public interests which are settled by inclusive procedures and private interests which are exclusively disposed of by counties or wards. These distinctions are applicable to pluralistic associations which are relatively specialized to the pursuit of distinctive value outcomes. Some churches provide for the public interest of the church to be settled by national or international assemblies; other matters are within the private realm of exclusive settlement by local congregations. Corporations typically distinguish between questions requiring the action of the Board, and those in which the common interest is advanced by being left to the exclusive judgment of the President. In family matters it is possible to distinguish, in any case, the family public interests requiring all-family action (or nearly all-family action) from family private interests left to less general channels.

By *public civic interest* we refer to public interests best effectuated by inclusive procedures which employ mild sanctions (*beta*).

By *public order interest* we refer to public interests best effectuated by inclusive procedures which employ severe sanctions (*beta*).

It is not necessary to conclude that since common interests are sufficiently great to warrant inclusive procedures the procedures must be part of the legal order and hence sanctioned by potentially severe value deprivations. All sorts of common interests are conventionally recognized in local communities which are effectuated through civic "drives" managed unofficially by churches, business and fraternal organizations, private welfare agencies, and the like. It is taken for granted that the consensus of common demand is so high that only a few crackpots—or people "down on their luck"—will fail to go along by contributing money or labor.

When we refer to the public interest we have in mind the basic pattern of value participation and the established institutions which are protected and fulfilled by the legal order. Since the legal order protects itself it is, of course, part of the total system of public order. A systematic examination of the public order of the United States would lead us to inquire into all value-institution patterns in order to discover the degree of protection afforded by the legal system.

In this connection we underline once more the difference between what is conventionally called law or the legal order in a given social context and the meaning that we assign to the term for functional purposes. We define law as part of the decision process, which we have characterized above according to the expectation that severe sanctions are available for use against challenges. Law is not identical with the entire decision process; it refers rather to decisions that are both authoritative and controlling. When decisions are controlling though not perceived as authoritative, they are instances of naked power. When purported authority is not controlling, it is pretended power. Lawful power conjoins both.

Conventional and functional conceptions, when applied to the

United States, lead to identical results in describing many phenomena. Consider the prescribing decision made by Congress when it enacts a statute. This is a law in the conventional sense in this country; and if it is expected that the requirements laid down in the statute will usually be enforced in the circumstances where it is presumed to apply, and if the measures of enforcement include prison terms and heavy fines, for example, we also classify the statute as law in the functional sense.

I referred above to community chest drives as outside the legal order (as conventionally described). It is worth noting that a competent investigator may show that in some communities, at least, these drives are part of the political (power) process as functionally defined, and perhaps come in the category of naked power. If so, they presumably should be brought within the discipline of legal order. The observer's conclusions may rest upon the severity of the negative sanctions imposed upon non-contributors to be drives. Research may show that most of the population conforms on the basis of an expectation system which includes the likelihood of job loss, consumer boycott, denunciation from the pulpit, and similar deprivations.

Assume that we have identified public interests among the common interests of a church, a trade union, a hospital, a family, or any similar group. Is it useful to distinguish between civic and public order interests in the internal process of these pluralized associations? Note that one objective of our definitions is to foster the examination and comparison of social contexts, however large or small. If we limit the discussion temporarily to a church, does it make sense to ask whether some norms are expected to be enforced by extreme sanctions? I propose that the reply to this question is in the affirmative, since we can define mildness or severity according to the perspectives of the church membership. If we shift the frame of reference and examine the social context of the metropolitan area in which the church is located, all the sanctions employed by the congregation may appear mild in terms of the percentage of the metropolitan population involved, or the magnitude of deprivation imposed upon individuals. If the social context is kept explicit and the content and procedures of inquiry are fully disclosed, comparisons can be made in equivalent terms. In the analytic and procedural system outlined here it is sensible to explore the public order interests of a family, or a trade union, for instance, or, indeed, of any group.

IV

We propose a few principles of content designed to clarify the criteria of public interest, and deal subsequently with procedural principles.

Any definition of human dignity that we would accept seeks to make clear that the ideal goal is a social context in which choice rather than decision is cultivated on the largest possible scale. Decisions are expected to be coercively sanctioned; hence our aim is to reduce the frequency of coercion to as near the vanishing point as we can bring it. This, of course, is a long-range objective, and for much of the immediate and middle-range future at least most of us would join in projecting a world community in which the chronic expectation and cultivation of violence and other extreme measures of coercion continue. Since any policy proposals that we make are estimates of how our long-run objectives can be brought nearer to realization, we must often propose short- and middle-range measures that themselves diverge from measures appropriate to the terminal state. Scholarly observers, like everyone else, are likely to differ among themselves in the degree of immediate conformity to ultimate norms which they are willing to endorse. But scholars have the obligation of laying out in frank detail the principles of content and procedure upon which they rely at any given cross section in time.

Because of the severity of the sanctions involved we are especially concerned with criteria of public order interests as distinct from public civic and other common interests. However, it is in harmony with our long-range goal to begin with a principle that positively affirms the *probable creativity of voluntary participation in the life of society, and hence supports a presumption in favor of freedom of choice in the pursuit of common interests.* This principle is more accurately described as a comprehensive hypothesis, an hypothesis so sweeping that it is not practicable in a short presentation to do more than allude to the grounds of inference upon which it is based. For example, I am impressed by the remarkable fact in connection with human creativity that we cannot forecast in detail where great native ability will emerge or under what circumstances talent will mature into socially contributory skill. Creativity is a many-sided relationship that depends upon the coming together of innovation and the capacity to recognize that an innovation is of potential significance. We know of climaxes of creative explosion in many ethnic aggregates, civilizations, and classes. In the light of the record we have every confidence in the wisdom of relying upon the initiatives of humanity as a whole rather than attempting to cultivate a super-caste of human beings with power to domineer permanently over their fellow men.

We start therefore with a strong presumption in favor of a competitive social process in which human beings are left free to induce one another to engage in the accumulation of one social value rather than another, or to enjoy a given value rather than to accumulate it further. The theoretical model is that of a variety of situations in which the pursuit of one value is relatively more prominent in the perspectives of the participants than another, and in which each outcome situation is characterized by free offers and counteroffers of values (thus affording opportunities to maximize preferred events). The prototype for this mode of analysis has been provided by economists who conceived a speculative model in which goods and services are sought in a free market. Inducements may be such that an individual participant accumulates wealth; or he may choose consumption enjoyment.

A parallel mode of analysis is applicable to each of the value-institution processes to which we have referred above, though these analyses have not yet been carried out with the degree of acceptance that has attended economic studies. I shall furnish a few hints of what is meant. In some societies excellence in music is highly valued, and many individuals devote themselves to accumulating (improving) their proficiency in singing or instrumental performance. In situations relatively specialized to demonstrating prowess in music the accepted norms of excellence are applied and an individual is appropriately evaluated by himself and others. In other social situations the top value sought is health, culminating in outcome situations in which the accumulation (improvement) of health is certified by the self and others.

Analytic models are important means of describing concrete circumstances, since circumstances are characterized according to the degree of conformity, or deviation from, the models. When we examine social contexts with the aid of such analytic constructs it is possible to identify the degree to which the specific context conforms to, or diverges from, a "pure type" market or other situation largely focused upon one value. In varying degree we expect all values to be involved, and in a relatively competitive society it is practicable to describe the way in which conventionally labeled business situations, for example, are affected by inducements having to do with outcomes specialized to skill, health, affection, or other value categories.

Looking at an entire social context we discover that in highly competitive cultures the free play of inducement patterns reflects and in turn modifies the aggregate flow of human activities into production (wealth shaping, accumulation), the acquisition of skill, the improvement of health, the cultivation of rectitude, the formation of family and friendship associations, the expansion of knowledge, and the enhancement of respect (which are value shaping or accumulating activities in categories other than wealth).

Instead of saving and investing, however, individuals may consume more. In place of improving the excellence of artistic and professional skills, individuals stay at the same level or deteriorate. Instead of considering the consequences of all their acts for human dignity, individuals discontinue moral self-appraisal in new problem situations. In place of cultivating old and new friendships, individuals reduce their affectional involvements. Rather than engage in inquiries that advance the available supply of enlightenment, individuals live off accumulated knowledge of man and nature. A similar disinvolvement may also show itself in regard to health and respect.

Viewing the whole of any social context we may find that the relatively free adjustment of value inducement patterns modifies aggregate as well as individual balances between the accumulation and enjoyment of any category of value.

The immediately preceding discussion included no examples from politics in order to emphasize that we were referring to situations comparatively free of coercion. In the long run it is proposed to do away with coercive sanctions; we commit ourselves in the meanwhile to the practice of competitive management of whatever coercions cannot be eliminated. Hence we endorse popular participation in elections, freedom to form political bodies and pressure groups, freedom to campaign (without coercive pressure) against rivals, and freedom to form and re-form coalitions.

As a guide to the search for public order interests we propose as a criterion *the prospect of achieving a minimally coercive result in the social context. Thus an inclusive procedure supported by the potential use of severe sanctions is indicated when alternative procedures are likely to result in even greater coerciveness.*

I surmise that we all agree that such a public order interest should be fully recognized and applied in the world political arena. It is asserted by some scholars that such an interest is already recognized in what is described as the universal legal order. Presumably these scholars are speaking correctly within the jurisprudential definitions they have adopted. Undoubtedly, however, they would agree that the global order which they allege is *not* presently characterized by the expectation that disputes are likely to be settled peacefully. The arms race makes it only too evident that the world arena is military, not civic.

Within the definitions that I accept there is at present no universal public order sufficiently well developed to deserve the name. Rather, there are rival systems of public order, also of varying degrees of completeness. Hence we do not say that there is a presently recognized universal public order interest, although we affirm that such an interest ought to be fully perceived and provided for. It is closer to present fluid transnational arrangements to say that universal, or at any rate very comprehensive, public civic interests are recognized, and that special interests abound.

In describing the social context of many communities the distinction between recognized public order interests and recognized civic interests is helpful in calling attention to the significance of many activities which are administered through community-wide organization conventionally called government. Many activities have been loaded upon modern governments because of expected economies of large-scale operation. Many of these activities are almost unanimously agreed to, and present negligible enforcement problems. Or agreement is so general that conformity is obtained with very mild sanctions. Also in some communities the government makes no effort to enforce conformity in neighborhoods where sentiment is averse to an operation. Hence the government serves as an administrative agent for part of the community and refrains from attempting to impose the majority view upon dissenting minorities. One advantage of such public civic interests is that they forestall adverse consequences that would follow if the public interest in a given value effect were incorporated into the legal system.

Many questions arise once we have identified an eligible public order interest, whether or not it is so perceived in the context. Can we further categorize the principal public order interests of a body politic?

We speak first of the *supervisory* interest within a public order system. Our commitment to voluntary choice has been emphatically stressed above. However, disputes over private agreements and alleged private wrongs so frequently lead to private acts of coercion that most of us concur in the view that government is the appropriate agency to provide facilities for the settlement of private controversies. This requires clarifying the prescriptions to be applied by community decision makers when they are brought into the picture. It calls also for the encouragement of noncoercive procedures of private norm setting and settlement in the hope of keeping the role of government at a minimum in competition with public civic agencies of mediation, conciliation, or arbitration. Despite the presumption we have stated in favor

of civic channels, the qualified observer will not generalize about
a given social context without taking into account the possibility
that the failure of government to act may result in increasing
the coercive hold over individuals—and especially over modern
minded minorities—who are victimized by traditionally conservative elders who act in the name of kinship, feudal traditions of
suzerainty, traditional chieftainship, magical potency, and such.
Where folk societies are in process of transition to membership
in a modern state these complications are typical rather than ex-
ceptional. We sum up the public order supervisory interest by
saying that it is directed toward the accommodation of private
interests.

We further identify among the principal public order interests the *regulatory* interest. The object of regulation on behalf
of our preferred goal is the protection of basic patterns of value
distribution and of all fundamental practices compatible with
the goal, and further the guiding of social interaction toward
more perfect fulfillment of the overriding aim. There is no question here of waiting until private controversies are brought to
the notice of community decision makers. The initiative lies with
government in the light of aggregate events in the social process.
In metaphorical terms the object is to keep at the focus of judgment the shape of the channels cut by the stream of social life
and to act for the purpose of keeping some channels intact while
deepening and strengthening others.

Among pertinent criteria for the regulatory interest we can
mention *the support of policies that limit the degree of permissible inequality in value position.* It is not compatible with
the conception of human dignity to allow individuals to sink
in the competitive struggle to the lowest depth of value deprivation. Examples of the minimum guarantee (or "floor") principle
are such programs as "protection against unemployment," no
"cruel" or "inhuman" treatment or punishment, no "slavery or
servitude."

The regulative interest also requires *the establishment of upper limits ("ceilings") upon permissible inequality.* Consonant
with this are "antimonopoly" policies designed to forestall the
possibility that creeping autocracy will transform free institutions

before it is generally recognized that freedom is undermined. Limitations upon inheritance and graduated income levies are well-known policies which may be appropriate to concrete circumstances.

We also identify among public order interests an *enterprisory* interest. The value effects sought in this connection require continuing and highly monopolistic administrative activity by government, on pain of relative increase in coercion or in the undermining of other basic features of the public order system. The administration of defense and police forces is an enterprisory policy of the kind; so, too, is the administration of staff and facilities for supervisory, regulative, or other public order interests.

It is helpful, further, to clarify the public order interest in sanctioning and *corrective* processes. Strictly speaking sanctioning arrangements are part of the prescriptions specialized to supervisory, regulatory, or other major interests, since every prescription is composed of *norm setting* and *sanction stating* propositions. We define "sanctions" in a functional sense to refer to prescribed and enforced consequences following upon breaches of norm; further, these arrangements are directed at targets who are expected to be able to modify their conduct by taking risks into account. That is to say, sanctions are formulated and applied with participants in view who *can* conform or not on the basis of calculated net advantage. The corrective interest differs from this, since it is aimed at locating and transforming participants who are *not* able to make these calculations or to make them effective in their conduct. Perhaps the explanation in the case of individuals is that they have not been educationally exposed to the culture so that they are ignorant of norms. Or it may be that the individual is ill and thereby incapacitated from the standard level of choice expected for adults in the culture. In the case of large communities, the transformation required is from folk society to civilization, or from totalitarian to nontotalitarian structures. We can further specify public order interest in sanctioning to include *deterrence, withdrawal* (or termination of active norm violation), *restoration* (of values destroyed), and *prevention* (removal of incentives to violation within the limits of existing structures). The corrective interest involves the *reconstruction* of personality structure or the social structures of groups.

It is convenient analytically to identify the *constitutive* public order interest along with supervisory, regulative, enterprisory, and corrective interests. The immediate social consequences at stake in constitutive interests concern the decision process itself. The constitutive task is to establish and maintain an arena composed of participants whose perspectives are compatible with the fundamental aim and to provide for an allocation of decision roles, recruited by appropriate methods of selection and qualification, empowered with requisite jurisdiction, employing pertinent modes of action to achieve the necessary flow of decision.

Although in one sense of the word all steps toward realizing an articulated basic goal can be called procedural, it is useful to give the term a more limited meaning, and to think of norms as expounding content and implementive statements as referring to procedures. Since both dimensions are invariably involved at all phases of problem solving, it is most clarifying to employ these conceptions flexibly for purposes of relative emphasis. Every public order interest requires formulation content-wise in terms of the value consequences sought and, procedurally, according to the practices specialized to the inclusive determinations required to give effect to formulated content.

V

It will be expedient to limit our discussion of procedural principles to a set of proposals which it is believed can presently be applied by scholars who are concerned with articulating the public interest and, ultimately, to more active participants in decision and choice. At every step it is appropriate to ask whether the procedures used are the most contributory to outcomes consonant with the common interest, and especially the public interest. The technique of choosing has become a major focus of theory and investigation in recent years owing to the development of the theory of gaming and the extension of gaming procedures from war games (and exercises) to diplomatic, economic, and communicative instruments of policy. The free association innovations of psychoanalysis and the experimental advances in the study of small group communications have had their part to play. So, too, have the information net theories originated by engineers. Decision technique is also affected by the audio-visual-print devices now available for the storage and recall of information, especially in the environment of continuing decision or choosing groups or individuals. Outcomes are affected by procedures that bring to the focus of attention the several tasks to be performed in problem solving (or tackling), referred to earlier in terms of goal, trend, condition, projection, alternative. Procedures that fail to bring these dimensions of a task to attention, or which do not succeed in mobilizing the most pertinent, reliable, and concise formulations, are to that extent prejudicial to good judgment. Students of decision seminar techniques are actively occupied in exploring and assessing the methods referred to here. It is not only a question of university seminars for the advancement of knowledge but also of procedures best adapted to the performance of consultative and advisory roles throughout modern society. Eventually it is to be anticipated that final decision makers will themselves be more ready and able to take direct advantage of such techniques.

The fundamental principle in problem solving, it appears, is to follow an agenda that provides for the consideration of every problem in ways that expedite the performance of the basic intellectual tasks involved. Within this broad mandate there is ample leeway for the phasing of events at the focus of attention in ways that take fully into account the time available for the solution of a problem and the probable contribution and cost of accessible sources and strategies.

In the clarification of possible value gains and costs formal models of decision making can sometimes be specified in sufficiently precise terms to enable the outcome to be determined by the processing of quantified variables. However, in confronting many matters an individual or group is unable to use such precise methods of weighting and indexing the values at stake. The appropriate procedure therefore includes an experience of exposure to more heterogeneous formulations, in the course of which evaluations are "discovered." The decision seminar technique, though adaptable to the most rigorous rules, is likewise adjustable to the needs of those who are predisposed to operate less selectively. It is evident that a continuing question concerning decision choosing technique is under what circumstances one pattern is more effective than another.

The following comments touch upon some procedural points pertinent to each task. First, in regard to goal clarification, it is important to challenge any confusion between an "absolutely" formulated commitment to a basic value pattern and "relatively" formulated statements of institutional practice. We are expressing our commitments to "human dignity" and "shared power" absolutely. They are long-range goals and we are on guard against "absolute" commitment to "presidential" versus "parliamentary" government, or "proportional representation" versus "single member districts." Similarly, our absolutely phrased commitment to "shared economic benefits" (shared wealth, for short) is separable from a relative commitment to "the stock market" or even to the "capitalistic" or "democratic socialist" system of institutional devices. As we have indicated it is to the public interest that scholars challenge conventional images—and especially absolute commitments to specific practices—by subjecting such images to disciplined revaluation in functionally formulated inquiries. The Berle-Means confrontation of the accepted image of American capitalism as "owner managed" with the image of "manager management" is a case in point.

So far as the scholar's access to comprehensive trend and factor knowledge is concerned it is exceedingly difficult for any private scholar to obtain enough knowledge of any social context to build bridges between his absolutely held abstract commitments to human dignity and the proposing of institutional practices appropriate to their realization. It was this precise difficulty that led, during the last two centuries, to the growth of so many specialists from the mother matrix of philosophy. Today we are aware of the need for intellectual tools and procedures by which more philosophically—that is, configuratively—oriented thinkers can play a creative role. To some extent we must build continuing decision seminars in our universities, and elsewhere, to pro-

vide an ever more selective, comprehensive, and reliable reminder of the context.

The critical projection of future developments is today playing a role of increasing importance in anticipating the shape of
things to come and in modifying our choice of problems relevant
to the common and the public interest.

It is significant, too, that we are devoting more time and
attention to discovering and applying techniques of creativity,
including the invention of policies designed to maximize long-
term or more immediate objectives. I referred before to highly
formalized or relatively heterogeneous methods by which alternatives are evaluated in the light of images of the whole.

VI

By way of brief summary: I have underlined the importance of formulating principles of content, whereby criteria
of public interest can be provided, and principles of procedure,
whereby the likelihood can be increased that content criteria
will be correctly employed in concrete circumstances. Common
interest has been distinguished from special interest, public from
private interest, public civic from public order interest. Content
principles have been proposed with particular reference to public
order; a few principles of procedure have been suggested. The
present sketch is chiefly oriented toward the role of private scholars in confronting conventional images of the self with images
that have received definition in functional terms and benefited
from the discipline of empirical inquiry by appropriate methods.

6

THE CHANGING CONTENT
OF PUBLIC INTEREST:
SOME COMMENTS ON
HAROLD D. LASSWELL

W. FRIEDMANN

Time permits no more than highly selective comments on the many points and suggestions contained in Mr. Lasswell's paper; but I must also confess to a rather basic difference of approach. Perhaps because I am essentially a lawyer, or perhaps because of personal inclination and temperament, I look for solutions to problems, however difficult, however shifting. The "Public Interest" makes me think of some of the burning problems of our time, such as the distribution of resources in this country, the respective spheres of public and private initiative, the clash between national security and freedom, problems that not only dominate the presidential election or the writings of leading economists, political scientists, and lawyers, but also stand out almost daily from the decisions of the Supreme Court. And, most directly pertinent of all, the growing power of massive and highly organized groups, of industry, labor, farmers, retailers, veterans, advertisers, and many others struggling to secure their interests, raises the burning question whether there is a public interest, expressing the aspirations and values of the community, and rising above these pulls and pressures. Lasswell's paper shows awareness of, and touches upon many of these questions. It is, however, primarily concerned with categories and methods of procedure. Because of this difference of approach it may be that my very brief summary of the points that I consider most important in Lasswell's paper does not do justice to his thought.

Let me say first of all that I do not think that discussion is needed on the often formulated "value demands" which we can find in various forms in all the juristic discussions of the balance of interests, nor do I propose to take up Lasswell's emphasis on the importance of procedure as well as content, because this is an elementary consideration for the lawyer, and especially for the common lawyer. The history of the common law is one of emphasis on forms of actions and procedures, and it is only in the last few centuries that principles of substance have been developed and have to some extent displaced the pre-eminence of procedure. In the United States, the due process clauses of the constitution have been the most important and fertile source of constitutional protections, and the rapidly developing science of administrative law—primarily concerned with the protection of the citizen against arbitrary encroachments by public authority —is so much weighted on the side of procedure that I for one believe that it has neglected the principles of content, i.e., the formulation of the principles by which the relations of public authority and the citizen should be governed.

What appears to me to be the most important aspects of Lasswell's paper are: (1) what we may call his "Grundnorm," his basic hypothesis that the public interest lies "in favor of freedom of choice in the pursuit of common interests"; (2) his classification of "special," "public," and "private" interests; (3) his rather casual reference to the position of group interests; and (4) his classification of what he calls "the principal public order interests of a body politic."

As to the first, most, perhaps all of us, will, like Lasswell, accept as the basic norm of contemporary American and Western society the principles of the Declaration of Independence and

of the Charter of Human Rights. We will accept the preferability
of choice to coercion in the attainment of stated goals, but exactly how far does this take us? The United States has lived
under a constitution implementing the Declaration of Independence for nearly two centuries. Has this prevented a drastic
shift in the scale of values symbolized by what we call the "public
interest"? Think of the dramatic, though partly still unac-
knowledged, transition from the pre-eminent emphasis on
freedom of property, contract, and enterprises, which dominated
the Supreme Court for the half century roughly beginning in
1885 and ending in 1936, to the highly regulated welfare state
which is contemporary America. Has it prevented the deep conflict over the existence and scale of "preferred freedoms" which
still splits the Supreme Court? Has it prevented a drastic increase
of controls not only over the economic but over the personal
activities of the citizen to cope with the clashing claims of freedom
and security in a troubled and neurotic world? And what about
the very notion of coercion which Lasswell seems to take as
having a clear and fixed meaning? He seems to me—although I
am not sure—to take the view of the analytical positivist in jurisprudence that sanctions are the physical sanctions imposed by
the authority of the state in the name of the law, "legitimated
power." But does he, a student of political science, psychology,
and sociology, really wish to ignore the subtler and often in-
finitely more powerful forms of coercion that do not fall within
the category of official legal sanctions? To come to a poignant
and typical illustration, do we as scholars, political scientists, or
jurists have to ignore the ubiquitous forms of psychological coercion that pervade contemporary American society from Madison
Avenue, whether dubbed with pseudo-scientific names such as
motivation research or not? Of course when we hear of brainwashing by Soviet or Chinese authorities we have no doubt that
this is coercion. But surely there are many intermediate forms of
conditioning the mind, many roads that lead to 1984. Kenneth
Galbraith has formulated some of the questions connected with
this in his *Affluent Society*. The present pattern of accepted
values, with its attendant distribution between public power
and private freedom in matters of allocation of resources, means

that a vast proportion of the nation's resources and energies is not only allowed to flow but is directed into conspicuous consumption, while public tasks in the field of education, housing, even defence remain unfulfilled. Does the public interest demand that we keep hands off this problem because it would mean coercion, and if it does not who should be entitled to apply a degree of coercion to effect a partial redirection of resources? Here, of course, we get into the subtleties of democratic procedure on which Lasswell wisely warns us we should not plump for one or the other, cabinet or presidential system, direct or indirect voting, and so forth. Do not let us forget that many forms of coercion "in the public interest," regarded as atrocious and "un-American" even half a century ago, such as compulsory educacation, minimum social security, multitudes of statutory or administrative compulsions for the protection of health, safety, etc., are now all but universally accepted. Do we have to rest at this point, or do we not have to go further in the readjustment of values in the light of new challenges of undreamt magnitude?

The scale of what Lasswell calls "public order interests" does enumerate supervisory, regulatory, and enterprisory interests. In the last category, somewhat surprisingly, he does not touch upon the question of the state as economic entrepreneur, but only mentions "the administration of defence and police force," in other words, the traditional minimum functions accorded to the state for centuries, not as enterprisory but emphatically as protective order functions. Hardly anyone would think of defence and police as "entrepreneurial" interests. In fact, Lasswell's scale of "public order interests," especially when seen against these illustrations, looks to me rather like an abstract from the existing order of things. The state may supervise by providing courts and other official agencies for the settlement of disputes; it may regulate, perhaps by the Securities and Exchange Commission (SEC) or the Federal Communications Commission (FCC), and it may "enterprise" by providing defence and police forces. Perhaps the—to me somewhat obscure—reference to "permissible inequality in value positions" means the legitimation of antitrust law and possibly social security legislation, but what is perhaps the cardinal problem, namely the possible readjustment of public power and private enterprise in the light of the contemporary challenges from abroad, finds no mention.

I also believe that Lasswell's paper is permeated by a methodological confusion between the "public interest" and the various methods to implement and enforce whatever the public interest may be at a given time. Surely regulatory, supervisory, enterprisory, corrective, and other processes are not public interests but *methods* of ensuring and protecting them. This is more than a matter of terminology. It seems to me that Lasswell's methodology—and his paper is overwhelmingly one of methodology— tends to obscure the fact that the public interest cannot but be a constantly shifting composite and balance between the values that direct a particular society at a given time—unless we accept a rigid natural law position, which I am sure Lasswell does not wish to do. Yet the pattern of values, processes, and interests as he construes it seems to me to be pretty much a legitimation of the order of things as it is, or has merged over the past half century.

And now a few words about what I regard as the major gap in the paper. Surely one of the outstanding—perhaps the pre- eminent—problem of contemporary industrialized society, and most particularly in the United States, is the position of group interests between the state and the individual. The most important and evident social phenomenon of our time is the power of the highly organized interest group struggling to advance its own interests through the official organs of the state. As the state is still the repository of legal sovereignty, the formal expression and the visible symbol of the "public interest," the question arises whether, in Earl Latham's words, it is merely a "cash register, ringing up the additions and withdrawals of strength, a mindless balance pointing and marking the weight and distribution of power among the contending groups." [1] If that is the position, then the public interest dissolves itself into a mere struggle for supremacy between highly organized groups, it becomes absorbed in the struggle between pressure groups, while

---

[1] Earl Latham, *The Group Basis of Politics* (1952), p. 37.

the individual is crushed between them.[2] I have argued elsewhere [3] that there is a genuine public interest which we might
call the "reserve function" of the state, an embodiment of values
and interests that bind together the many conflicting and contending groups. Most of these cluster around basic national
loyalties, and this reserve function therefore usually becomes
conscious and articulate only in times of great emergency such
as wars and economic or natural disasters. We may be near to
one of those periodic articulations at this time. When presidential candidates and leading politicians and scholars speak of
"national goals," of the need for better education, better scientific training, conservation of national resources, more financial
and personal sacrifices for defense, and altogether some change
in the accepted standards of contemporary American society,
they do transcend the mindless balance of conflicting group pressures, even though in practical conduct they may yield to the
one or to the other. When it comes to the implementation of
some of these drastic readjustments—as is very likely within the
next few years—we will be confronted with a direct clash between
the still currently predominant equation of the public interest
with traditional ideas of "freedom of enterprise" and the new
national goals which only public power as the articulate repository of a public interest transcending the clash of conflicting
group pressures can implement. It is therefore of cardinal importance for us to realize—and here Lasswell is probably not in
disagreement—that the public interest constantly needs redefin-

---

[2] I may remark in passing that I consider Lasswell's classification of "special," "public," and "private" interests as unfortunate. We can, of course,
adopt any nomenclature we like, but quite overwhelmingly, in the literature
of law and political science, private interests are considered as those of special
groups or individuals, as opposed to the interests of the community as a
whole. In Lasswell's terminology the "public interest" is a common interest of
greater, and the "private interest" a common interest of lesser, magnitude. On
the other hand, Lasswell's "special interests" are apparently what most other
people call "private interests." I believe that such a change of accepted meanings is deplorable, unless demanded by overwhelming reasons of logic or the
introduction of new concepts. But I submit that the changing around of accepted notions and terms is merely confusing.

[3] W. Friedmann, *Law in a Changing Society* (1959), pp. 301ff.

ing and reassessment in a never-ending readjustment proceeding through many channels: public discussion in universities, press, and other media of public communication leading in due course to legislative changes. No less important is the continuous process of official reappraisal through the decisions of the Supreme Court on basic constitutional problems. Here I agree entirely with Lasswell on the role of the scholar.

Let me briefly mention in conclusion that the constant redefinition of the public interest—sometimes, though not always, expressed by lawyers as "public policy"—is one of the paramount tasks of the student of jurisprudence. It is only a few weeks ago that I had occasion to discuss these matters in some detail with some twenty-five Appellate Court judges from all over the United States. Although legislation now takes charge of a growing number of problems formerly left to the practical lawyer, the function of the judge in assessing the public interest in a given situation remains immensely important. The public interest is not identical with public policy, but it forms an important part of it. Current discussion or summings up of public opinion through radio, press, Gallup polls, scientific congresses, and other media translate trends of current thought into generally understandable language. The judge can seldom be a pioneer in social progress. He must not walk either too fast or too slow. He cannot consider a single bold social innovation undertaken by a radical government as being an assured part of the social thinking of his generation and country. But he is no more justified in regarding principles accepted a century ago as being fixed for all time in the interpretation of the law. In trying to translate social evolution into legal judgments, the judge must look for aid not only to jurisprudential thought but also to the multitude of other sciences which influence the law. This he cannot do unaided. He must, for example, weigh the state of modern medical research before deciding whether to accept blood group tests as evidence in maintenance actions, or other actions in which the proof of parenthood is relevant. He will also have to take into account medical and psychological research in decisions on mental instability or insanity, in both civil and criminal suits. The research of modern economists and statisticians on business cycles and national income curves has long been accepted as evidence of decisive importance in such matters as the fixing of a basic wage by the Australian Commonwealth Court of Arbitration. But in all these matters, the judge must tread carefully; he cannot follow his own economic or political or scientific views in advance of what he regards as reasonably well established in the light of current public opinion, the legislative policy not of a particular political party but of the major political parties of the country, and of contemporary scientific research.

7

COMMON AND PUBLIC
INTEREST DEFINED:
COMMENTS ON
HAROLD D. LASSWELL'S PAPER

GEORGE NAKHNIKIAN

Harold Lasswell's paper, "The Public Interest: Proposing Principles of Content and Procedure," is comprehensive and condensed. It suggests certain questions which are central in the sense that any relevant response to them is likely to stimulate an exploration and clarification of the main themes and logical structure of the paper. I propose in short to raise questions which are within the competence of the analytic philosopher. Other sorts of questions, though not necessarily unphilosophical, are posed by Friedmann. I shall begin with a brief summary of the relevant context surrounding the issues that I want to raise.

Lasswell's specific concern in this paper is the contribution scholars can make "in the processes of decision and choice," the former (i.e., processes of decision) relating to political, governmental, and legal institutions, and the latter (i.e., processes of choice) relating to the remaining institutional practices. Lasswell holds that the scholar's unique contribution is to provide "functional" and "unconventional" models for the critical appraisal of the "conventional" ways of thinking characteristic of nonscholars.

As regards the public interest, Lasswell finds that there are two main types of problems to which scholars can direct their thinking. The first he calls definitions or principles of content. In familiar philosophical terminology these are formulations of ends or standards. The second he calls principles of procedure, and, again, in familiar terminology, these are propositions about means appropriate to antecedently determined ends.

The citizen embroiled in his daily affairs, the man who holds political office, the practicing lawyer and the run-of-the-mill judge are to be distinguished from the scholar. The scholar is an intellectual. His two distinguishing marks are (1) that he is equipped to employ intersubjectively communicable methods and their results, and (2), because of (1), he is equipped to act as consultant to those who want to put into order the congeries of their values and the means of realizing them. This is what I take Lasswell to be saying.

Now let me turn to the things that puzzle me. The first of these has to do with the status of, and interconnections among, principles formulating ends and empirical (scientific) propositions. On page 61, Lasswell says that principles of "content put forward definitions and criteria of the public interest." Inasmuch as Lasswell construes public interest as a species of common interest and inasmuch as he defines "common interest" in terms that refer to the ultimate standard of human dignity, it would seem that principles of content should be straightforward value judgments, principles formulating ends. Yet one instance of such a principle, given on page 69, is said to be an hypothesis, and it has all the earmarks of being an empirical hypothesis at that. For it says that the probabilities are in favor of creativity coming out of voluntary participation in the life of society. I am at once reminded of what I take to be the big issue Dewey was struggling with in his ethical theory. Having correctly recognized that value judgments are not identical in their logic with the propositions of the special sciences, Dewey tried to show that nevertheless there is an intimate connection between them. But Dewey never fully succeeded in spelling out exactly what that connection is. When dealing with this most important problem, Dewey either gives the impression of reducing value judgments to scientific propositions or he gives the impression of reducing scientific propositions to value judgments. So my first question is: what is the logical status of principles of content—are they value judgments or are they scientific hypotheses?

The next set of questions arises out of focusing attention on two sentences on page 64, the second of which is the crucial one: "There is ample room for scholarly observers who describe any given context to differ with one another in identifying common interests. To some extent these are matters of taste in definition and need give rise to no problems of interdefinitional translation if terms are clearly set forth." Notice the phrase "identifying common interests." This, which appears in the sentence immediately preceding the crucial sentence, carries over into the crucial sentence. For the matters in which Lasswell allows that scholars may differ are matters of "identifying common interests." What does it mean to say that identifying common interests is (to some extent) a matter of definition? An obvious answer, the one I imagine Lasswell would give, is that the expression "common interest" may be defined in one way by one scholar and in another way by another. There is here no problem of communication if both set forth their definitions clearly. But this would leave the substantive questions in abeyance. If I decided to define the word "electron" to mean a pixy that causes engine trouble in airplanes, am I then in a position to differ from a physicist in identifying electrons? A common interest is the sort of thing that we *ordinarily mean* by the locution "common interest." And if the locution has no ordinary meaning, then two scholars can neither agree nor differ in identifying common interests unless they use the *same stipulated* definition of "common interest." Otherwise, they can differ only in that one *calls* a common interest what the other does not. But that is not a substantive difference, either scientific or valuational.

Moreover, it seems that Lasswell's model makes it logically impossible for anyone to use the locution "common interest" in the sense defined by him unless he happens to agree with Professor Lasswell that human dignity and the *summum bonum* are analytically identical. Let us see why. Lasswell seems to take it for granted that common interest is by definition a function of the *summum bonum*. Moreover, he defines common interest to mean "that in a given social context a specified activity has inclusive value effects . . . as ascertained by stated procedures of inquiry . . . which are compatible with the goal of human dignity" (page 64). As a direct consequence of this definition, "*x* is a common interest" entails "*x* is compatible with human dignity." But what Lasswell seems to take for granted and the articulated definition together imply that the *summum bonum* is analytically identical with human dignity. Hence, Lasswell is committed to the inference from "*x* is compatible with human dignity" to "*x* is compatible with the *summum bonum*." Therefore, he is committed to inferring "*x* is compatible with the *summum bonum*" from "*x* is a common interest." But no one would be committed to making the last inference who did not agree with Lasswell that human dignity and the *summum bonum* are analytically identical. Therefore, no one could be using "common interest" in Lasswell's sense if he did not agree with Lasswell's view of the *summum bonum*.

These queer consequences would remain even if we were to give up the assumption that common interest is definitionally a function of the *summum bonum*. Without this assumption it is no longer true that "*x* is a common interest" entails "*x* is compatible with the *summum bonum*." Lasswell could so formulate his position as to leave no doubt that he *judges* human dignity to be the *summum bonum* as a matter of (moral) fact and not as a matter of definition. However, the concept of common interest would still be an evaluative one in that *compatibility with human dignity,* which is part of the *definiens* of the concept, is roughly equivalent to saying that certain (moral and legal) rights, privileges, and immunities are not violated. So that anyone who believed that something is a common interest would be believing that the thing in question is (morally and legally) permitted. But it follows that only those who in fact happen to agree with Lasswell's moral commitment to human dignity would be in a position to use the locution "common interest" in his sense. Only they would be in a position to assert, judge, or believe that something is or is not a common interest. For in so judging, they would necessarily be making an evaluation. They could not be so judging if human dignity were of no value to them.

This has paradoxical consequences. First, it implies that no one can be a scholar who does not accept human dignity as an absolute standard. This comes about as follows: Lasswell asserts that his theoretical model is one that any scholar can use. But anyone who cannot in principle use the language of the model cannot use the model. Hence, he is no scholar. This is hard to swallow in that it makes it logically impossible for anyone to be a scholar if he does not adopt human dignity as an ultimate standard.

The second paradoxical consequence seems to be a formal contradiction. For earlier in the paper, unless I have misunderstood him, Lasswell characterizes a scholar as one who (1) has mastery of intersubjectively communicable methods and can apply them to obtain intersubjectively communicable results, and (2) because of (1), he is equipped to act as a consultant to those who want to find out the best means for achieving their goals. A man of that description can act as a spectator of a value system foreign to his own, and to those within the system who have hired him as consultant he can say such things as: *As* such and such is what we have scientifically established to be your preferences, then for their realization so and so is the means that we have scientifically established to be the most efficient, least costly, least fraught with what you would regard as troublesome. A man who can make such assertions may, for all we know, be a Plato; but insofar as he can make them, he can, *in principle,* be a scholar, although *in practice* he may be inhibited by unconscious factors from giving good advice to those whose preferences are repugnant to him. But, according to the first consequence, the one that seems hard to swallow, a Plato cannot *in principle* be a scholar because he would not identify human dignity with the *summum bonum.* Because these contradictory consequences seem to follow from different parts of Lasswell's model, it would seem that the model is formally inconsistent.

These difficulties, if they are indeed real, would disappear if it could be shown that the absolute goal of human dignity is universally shared. But no argument is given that this is the case, and there appears to be weighty evidence against it. It might seem that another way out is to say that in the sentence on page 78, "We are expressing our commitment to 'human dignity' and 'shared power' absolutely," the "we" is meant to include those and only those who in fact are committed to these absolutes. But this is not wholly satisfactory because it still leaves us with the counter-commonsensical conclusion that a man who does not subscribe to the standard of human dignity cannot *in principle* be a scholar.

A more satisfactory way of avoiding these paradoxes is to modify the definition of common interest. Stipulate that "*x* is a common interest in society *S*" is to mean that in the social context of *S* a specified activity *x* has inclusive value effects . . . as ascertained by stated procedures of inquiry . . . which are compatible with the basic goal or goals prevalent in *S* in the light of the most feasibly complete intelligent comprehension of the reality surrounding the life of *S*. So modified, the *definiendum*, "common interest," can be used by any scholar regardless of his own normative preferences. The only common requirement here is that the scholar be committed to employing methods of inquiry characteristic of the sciences, whenever these are appropriate, and to methods of conceptual analysis or reconstruction, whenever these are appropriate. But this poses no special problem, inasmuch as the employment of such methods, one would suppose, is a logically necessary condition of being a scholar. Then the only methodologically interesting question has to do with the usefulness of the stipulation relative to the purposes of scholars who deal with the explanation and control of institutional practices.

The addendum to the suggested modification to the effect that the basic goals of *S* be adopted in the light of fully intelligent comprehension of the factors in the life of *S* would require a further modification of Lasswell's manner of characterizing values. On page 57, he identifies values with preferred outcomes. But this will not do because not every preferred outcome is worthy of being preferred. Here it is in order to recall Dewey's distinction between objects that are *valued* (liked, enjoyed, prized, preferred) and objects that *have* value (are worthy of being liked, enjoyed, prized, preferred). To be capable of being valued is a necessary but not sufficient condition of having value. There is a valuable insight in Dewey's suggestion that we construe the value or goodness of things in terms of their capacity to be desired (actively sought) by those who have an intelligent comprehension of their nature. This suggestion is squarely in the tradition of the best in Greek philosophy, and it is one which I have no reason to believe is not the one intended by Lasswell. What I am proposing here is that he formulate his intention with greater precision.

Lastly, I submit that Lasswell's exposition could be much improved if he were to abide carefully by a distinction which, I believe, every scholar interested in understanding and controlling institutional practices would do well to observe. I mean the distinction between advocating norms, goals, ends, and the specification of the practical means of implementing them, on the one hand, and on the other, the conceptual problem of clarifying what "public interest," "common good," "common interest," and related expressions mean. We might add that the working out of a theoretical model for empirical application may call for stipulated meanings pragmatically defended, if there are no useful concepts in existence to elucidate. (Einstein's proposal to define "simultaneous" with "operationally" is a good case in point.) On page 56 Lasswell says: "Our problem is the clarification of public interest." Had he observed the above distinction, he would have seen that the quoted expression has at least two senses. One thing it can mean is: my aim is to propose certain moral and procedural principles in conformity with certain overriding standards which I share with many others and which, in the present context, are to be treated as ultimate moral standards. Accordingly, he should have presented his paper as an essay in normative ethics. This is a perfectly respectable procedure characterizing important elements in the work of the classic social and political theorists from Plato to Marx. According to the second possible meaning of the expression, the paper could have attempted to clarify relevant existing concepts, or it could have argued that no workable concepts of the sort needed exist, and it could have gone on to propose conceptual conventions suitable for scientific work. Or the paper could have been divided into two main parts, each devoted to one of these principal tasks, and inasmuch as these two activities, that of the moralist and that of the logician, though distinct, are not unrelated, the two parts might have been made to cohere in an illuminating way. Such a structure is intended in the paper, but, as written, it fails to fulfill its purpose mainly because the proposed definition of common interest involves the confusion between the task of the moralist and that of the logician. And this confusion is one of the root difficulties in "natural law theories," of which the position taken in Lasswell's paper seems to be a species.

8

THE PUBLIC INTEREST: SOME OPERATIONAL DILEMMAS

STEPHEN K. BAILEY

During the few minutes it takes to read this essay, several hundred thousand people clothed in the garb of governance will make or sanctify decisions affecting millions of their fellow human beings. Many of these decisions will have an imperceptible emotional fallout (as when a State Highway Commissioner adds three feet to a design of the shoulder of a new road or an African Prime Minister decides to fly to the United Nations by chartered rather than by commercial airplane). Yet even low-voltage decisions such as these may set in motion events which could change the lives of millions. The widened shoulder may some day save the life of a motoring dignitary; the chartered flight may explode in mid-air.

But many public decisions—besides being pregnant with consequence—have an immediate and widespread emotional impact. Things said and done by public officials often stimulate in countless fellow human beings emotional reactions ranging from joy through smugness through discontent to violent anger. The confections which emerge from the kitchens of government are as bittersweet as life itself. A new highway destroys livelihoods along an old; victory on Normandy Beach is defeat for parents or wives of the dead; low bid to General Motors is less money for Chrysler; the Norris Dam floods a boy's favorite cave; schools cost money.

The phrase "the public interest" is the decision maker's anchor rationalization for policy-caused pain. Without such a concept, most presidents, congressmen, governors, commissionners, managers, and mayors—and, I should hazard, commissars, premiers and generals—would become unnerved. The moral buffer between social gains and losses consequent upon public decisions would disappear. The wounds incurred in the strife of policy battles would fester and rankle. Retaliations would become certain in their uncertainties.

There is perhaps no better example in all language of the utility of myth than the phrase "the public interest." It is balm for the official conscience. It is oil on the troubled waters of public discontent. It is one of society's most effective analgesics. But to have this phrase serve this purpose over time, public servants must be able to give it a rational content anchored in widely shared value assumptions. The more that a society is built upon consent rather than upon threat and constraint the more this is true. Happily for policy makers, the public is often quite easily satisfied. I have watched fence-mending congressmen explain with astounding success an unpopular vote simply by leading untutored constituents down a garden path rich with flowers marked "fair," "just," "decent," "good," "brave," "clean," "reverent." The most discouraging aspect of totalitarianism is not the power-lust of its leaders, but the ease with which people adjust to losses in political freedom when that loss is explained in terms of public necessity.

So the tranquilizing effect of the phrase "the public interest" may in fact not be in the public interest. The timid and the trusting alone never created or sustained a free society. And the timid and trusting are numerous in all societies. The test of the public interest can never be uncritical majority acceptance. Majority acceptance is relevant only when the majority is free to act politically, is in a critical and soul-searching mood, and when contending advocates before the bar of public opinion defend their "truths" in terms of academic canons of truths (i.e., evidence which would be acceptable to a panel of the most highly admired professional scholars in the field). The true test of the public interest, then, is something beyond its analgesic utility. The true test is the freedom of the individual men and women who constitute society. In short, the essence of the public interest cannot be far removed from Cicero's "right reason," as applied to the dilemmas of freedom in the modern world.

But even if one accepts an appeal to the bar of "right reason" as the essence of governing in the public interest, little dent has been made on the operating dilemmas of conscientious public servants. The ethical dilemmas of policy making in the modern world are complex beyond description. The internal dialogue of the decision maker, on those rare occasions when he has the time for ethical reflections, is fraught with paradox, anomaly, and the imponderable. Not acting in the public interest is normally far less a question of malevolence than of conceptual inadequacy; far less a question of fact than of meaning. And when a conceptual breakdown occurs, conscience often becomes paralyzed. For the decision maker, the result is hunch—hunch rationalized after the fact into the dignity of thoughtful deliberation.

Perhaps the simplest way to bring these generalities to life is to record in slow motion the internal dialogues of two different levels and categories of decision makers each wrestling with an issue peculiar to twentieth century America. These two will be (1) an American President trying to think through what should be done about revolutionary subversion in a nearby Latin American republic, and (2) a Catholic majority leader of a state senate asked by his governor to shepherd through the legislature a school aid bill for public schools only.

These will be made to seem like difficult questions. Inherently they are. Contextually, they may not be at all. The internal dialogue is never smooth and uninterrupted. It is intermittent. It is made lumpy by the weight of immediate circumstance, by rationalizations of self-interest on the part of the decision maker, by an unfathomable will to believe one set of facts or advisers over another.

It is difficult to make hypothetical what is so poignantly real at the time of writing. But this is not an exercise in current events or modern history. There is no way in which I can get inside the mind of John F. Kennedy as he deals with the problem of Castro's Cuba. But I can, and do, assume that any American President confronted with a Cuba-like issue is caught on the horns of a most vexing dilemma. The President wishes to serve the public interest. Respecting treaty obligations, in his view, is in the public interest. But so is a Western Hemisphere free of Communist subversion. But what if there is a conflict between these two goals?

Let us picture an American President, sitting perhaps in a rocking chair, occupied with an internal dialogue on the question of what to do about a neighboring Latin American Republic which we shall call Habuna. He first reflects upon the fact that the Habuna problem is not new. At least ten Presidents have been confronted with an "Habuna issue." The "issue" has in fact been many issues compounded of alien and domestic mismanagement and exploitation—political and economic, a local population divided into frivolous privilege and grinding poverty, a one-crop economy, and a church culture rich in moral ambiguities. Not the least important historical reality has been the dominant economic and military position of the United States in Habuna, and the uneven record and effect of its economic and military forays. Dictators have been supported or broken according to the economic interests of American companies, or the felt security interests of the United States Government. Even allowing for differences in diplomatic style over the past half century, the President reflects that American intervention in Habuna has had its ugly aspects from the very beginning. There is little wonder, therefore, and considerable justice, in the fact that the most recent revolution in Habuna has used *"Yanqui"* imperialism as one of its points of attack. The United States has frequently not used its economic or political power morally: that is, with due calculation of the interests, aspirations, and sensibilities of the people of Habuna.

On the other hand, muses the President, American exploitation of Habunans has been nothing alongside of Habunan exploitation of Habunans. And in recent years, through membership in and support of the Organization of American States, the

United States has taken the leadership in attempting to create a community of law and interest which would ultimately feed benign antibodies into the wracked bodies politic and economic of small countries like Habuna. But this solemn treaty commits the government of the United States not to use force "for any reason whatsoever" against the internal or external affairs of another country.

Unfortunately, this treaty was signed before there was clear evidence that international communism would attempt to involve Habuna in the international civil war which seems destined to plague mankind for the balance of the twentieth century. Infiltrating the recent revolutionary movement in Habuna, Communist agents have exploited the social and economic and political injustices of the people of Habuna and have identified these injustices with "*Yanqui* imperialism." The unquestioned goal of the Communists is to use Habuna as a base for the subversion of all of Spanish America. As the President ponders all this, it becomes clearer and clearer that Communist domination of Habuna would be a direct threat to the national security of the United States.

But at what point is it clear that Communists are, in fact, dominating the situation in Habuna? The Habuna leaders claim *not* to be Communists. They are friendly with Communist nations; they trade with Communist nations. But this may be nothing but a normal symptom of revolutionary sovereignty—a desire of a little fellow to express his independence of one big fellow by playing with another big fellow. To be sure, intelligence sources suggest that a known Communist seems to be the *eminence grise* behind the revolutionary leader. But has the leader himself *really* been subverted? Can a great nation attack and control little nations on the grounds that the little nation *may* be *becoming* subverted by another great nation unfriendly to the first great nation? And what if the real subversion is ideological rather than national? Suppose the known "Communist" who serves as the *eminence grise* is a confirmed Marxist who is sympathetic to the Soviet Union (or Communist China) because he believes in the principles of world revolution. His real interest is to lead Habuna into a new day. He is as blind to the evils of Communism as most Americans are to the historic evils practiced under the name of democratic capitalism. Have we the right to stop distasteful internal revolutions which parallel external ones? Can we assume that all Communist revolutions are dangerous to our *military* security?

And even if the "nature" of the top Communists in Habuna involves distinctions more precious than relevant, how does the United States combat the Communist virus?

A wholesale use of American arms? We thereby violate a treaty. We also risk provoking an uncontrolled international war. We also face the certain hostility of large blocs of world opinion. All this can lead either to an immediate disaster for the world, or the promotion of world cynicism about international agreements. International justice becomes, to paraphrase Thracymachus, the interest of the stronger nation. Even if the United States should succeed in winning to its side other Latin nations, is the military intervention of a bloc of nations any more or less risky than unilateral action in terms of the dangers suggested above?

But what is the price of *not* taking action? Exploiting the real injustices of Habuna and of other Latin countries, skillful Communist propagandists and agents might start a prairie fire of revolutions which would exploit anti-American feelings and ultimately leave the United States and Canada isolated in an otherwise hostile hemisphere. The peace, safety, and prosperity of the American people would then be in constant jeopardy.

Can action be taken which does not violate the letter of treaties, protocols, and unilateral promises of nonintervention, but which can destroy the Communist influences within Habuna? Would promises of massive economic aid to the new government wean it away from Communist influence, or would Communist aides simply subvert American aid for Communist purposes?

Is the clandestine arming, supplying, and transporting of anti-Communist refugees and rebels a possible answer? But what does this do to the faith of other nations (to say nothing of the faith of the American people) in the word of the United States government? How many ex-colonial nations, fresh with memories of "indirect rule," would either see or accept a distinction between

"military intervention" and military and logistical help to those
who *do* intervene? Would the great new nations of South Asia
or the wobbly novitiates of Africa accept such a distinction—
especially when the propaganda from Habuna is that the revolutionary leadership has succeeded in effecting land reforms and
labor reforms which touch responsive chords in all lands where
expectations are rising?

The President rocks on all this for a while. He cannot afford
to become unnerved by the complexity, so he allows himself only
one more question. What if the overwhelming majority of the
people of Habuna do not *want* the responsibilities of freedom?
What if self-determination has no effective meaning for Habunans except to be ruled by their *own* tyrants—including Communist tyrants? What if the Grand Inquisitor was right: that
most people cannot stand freedom? What if the *real* appeal of
communism is its promise of superimposed order—substituting
for the miracles and mysteries of the church, the miracles and
mysteries of science and the state? Can people be "forced to be
free"?

The President shakes his head vigorously. He knows he would
not entertain such thoughts if he were not weary. He reaches his
arm firmly toward a telephone which has two buttons—one
marked the Secretary of Defense, the other marked the Director
of the Central Intelligence Agency. Without further hesitation
he presses one of the two buttons.

New Rhodecut ranks forty-eighth in area but fifteenth in population of the fifty-one American states. Bordered on the west
by the Hudson River, on the east by Massachusetts and Con-
necticut, New Rhodecut has a great historical tradition and a
large number of second generation immigrants. It is 45 per cent
Catholic. The lower house of its legislature is strongly rural and
Republican. The state Senate is marginally Democratic but 75
per cent Catholic. The Governor is Democratic and Protestant.
Two years before, he had signed a bill providing for the public
transportation of parochial school children. This year, he has
backed a bill which would provide a ten per cent increase in
state aid for school teachers' salaries in public schools only. The

majority leader in the state Senate is a Catholic. The Governor
has asked him to take the leadership in the legislative fight for
the new school aid bill. The majority leader does not approve
of the bill as written, but has been unsuccessful in moving the
Governor toward a bill which would also aid parochial schools
in some way. (The Governor contends that the church was considerably benefited by the bus law, and that direct financial aid
to parochial schools is prohibited by the state constitution.)

What course of action by the majority leader is in the public
interest? As he sits by himself in the Capitol cafe and stirs his
morning coffee, the majority leader reflects upon his reputation
as "Mr. Democrat." He is where he is today because of party
loyalty. His friendship for the Governor goes back to the mid-
thirties when they both were freshmen assemblymen from adjacent districts. This would not be the first time the majority leader
would have supported a bill he did not like, but it would be
his first break with the Governor if he refused to support the
school aid bill. The difficulty this time is that the issue is nothing
more or less than the future of "equal opportunity" in the
Commonwealth of New Rhodecut—or so it seems to the majority
leader.

Long years in public office had made the majority leader a
"realist" about his own church. He found some church fathers
dedicated, many quite unbelievably naive, and some completely
obnoxious. But in the field of education, all of them were in
trouble. In New Rhodecut twenty-five per cent of all school children between the ages of seven and fourteen were in parochial
schools. Whether this was a good thing or a bad thing was not
the point at issue. The majority leader was dealing with a fact
not a theory. The fact about parochial schools was that they
were strapped for funds, and that their educational product was
inferior. The effect of further state aid to *public* schools would
be to weaken still further the competitive position of parochial
schools. Years ago parochial school needs had outstripped the
supply of qualified Sisters. So, in addition to meeting rising
building and equipment costs, church fathers had had to bid in
the open market for lay teachers. Every time public school
teachers' salaries were raised, parochial schools found it that

much harder to attract or hold an adequate instructional staff.

Perhaps the answer is to starve the parochial schools into dissolution. Perhaps the public interest would be best served by a monolithic, nonsectarian, nonreligious, public school system. But surely, thinks the majority leader, this is no answer. American pluralism is something to be valued. Furthermore, the "faithless coldness of the times" argued for more rather than less emphasis upon values in education—especially moral and religious values.

And even if these values were not at stake, the cold truth was that institutions never die painlessly. The passionate and militant in the clergy would attempt to keep the Catholic schools open even if no observable educational standards remained. Even if dissolution could be forced within a decade, what of the children who had been the innocent victims of these vast societal clashes?

The majority leader squints at the morning sunlight pouring in the cafe window. Through the trees in front of the Capitol he could barely make out the fluted columns of the state Supreme Court building. The law. What of the law?

The state constitution says in unequivocal language that "no funds of the Commonwealth may be appropriated for purposes of aiding or supporting in any way or manner any but public educational facilities and instructional staffs." But the majority leader is a lawyer, and he knows how flexible and creative an instrument the law can be. The school bus law was passed, and had been supported in the state Supreme Court (three to two) on the grounds that citizen safety, not aid to parochial schools, was the issue. What if the state paid a per pupil grant to parents of school-aged children allowing them to send their children to any school which met minimum standards set by the state? This would not be aiding private "educational facilities and instructional staffs" any more than was the case with the G. I. Bill of Rights. Young citizens would simply be given equal opportunity for a decent education. And would not "state standards" make all private schools essentially public? Is this not the goal of the American society? To give every child an equal chance to maximize his own potential. Even twenty-five years of friendship for the Governor should not be allowed to stand against this great principle.

A Negro bus boy stops to fill the sugar bowl at the majority leader's table. Reluctantly, the majority leader lets his mind move to the most vexing of issues. If a state makes available per pupil grants to parents, what saves the desegregation movement in the American South? If Catholic parents can send Catholic pupils to Catholic schools with public funds, what stops white parents from sending white pupils to all white schools with public funds? On the other hand, New Rhodecut is not the South, is a long way from the South, and the parochial schools of New Rhodecut are fully integrated—more fully in fact than many of the *public* schools in the commonwealth. Perhaps the example of flourishing, integrated parochial schools would be helpful throughout the nation. But. . . .

The majority leader struggles to his feet, drops a dime on the counter, and walks hesitatingly toward the restaurant door. There he suddenly throws back his shoulders, sets his jaw, and strides resolutely toward the executive chambers.

Anyone familiar with public policy making will realize how unreal these sketches are. Alternatives are almost never as open as these vignettes imply. Psychologically, few men could stand the whip-saw of options which conscious deliberation opens up on most issues—public and private. Sanity demands a high degree of stereotypic behavior. Furthermore, most men are not as self-less as these internal dialogues suggest. Men rarely divorce their own personal advantage and future from considerations of public policy. There is almost always present a calculus of precedent and of anticipated reaction relating to the future of the actor as well as the action. One of the key arts of administration and of politics is to discover decisional formulae which bind together private and public interests. Finally, the sketches do not furnish sufficient information about the political and administrative context within which these decisions would have to be made. Without a rich contextual definition, any portrait of decision making is bound to be misleading and jejune.

But if these sketches are inadequate as models of reality, they are even less adequate as guides to principles of the public interest. For in both cases, no clear doctrine guides the ponderer. Tossing values back and forth is hardly a substitute for the establishment of value priorities which can guide the searching mind in its quest for rational judgments about the public interest. In both cases it is possible that if a system of value priorities had been clearer, the perception of alternatives would have been simpler and in many cases quite different from what was outlined. In the first case, for example, suppose that the President's top value was the physical security of the United States, and his second value the rapid improvement in the social and economic conditions of the Habunan population. Would not an unperceived alternative have been joining the year-old revolution, using American public funds to recompense those legitimate American industrial and commercial interests injured by the revolution, and ultimately channeling rather than obstructing the revolutionary stream? In the second case, is it in the public interest to attempt to resolve an issue before it is ripe for social acceptance? Should a majority leader accept an advocate's role when the time calls for astute brokerage? Is the public interest often not best served by postponement of conflict until a new and unifying perception of options becomes clear?

And yet, inadequate as they are, the two sketches are not without meaning. The public interest is not self-evident. The observable options before the decision maker are frequently harsh. The stakes are often enormous. Substance and process are frequently at war. It is my guess that few citizens have any idea of the moral complexity of the problems which come to the attention of our political leaders and officials.

It is no more than an act of faith, but I cannot help but believe that—in spite of operational dilemmas—"the public interest" is the central concept of a civilized polity. Its genius lies not in its clarity but in its perverse and persistent moral intrusion upon the internal and external discourse of rulers and ruled alike.

9

THE PUBLIC INTEREST: EFFICIENCY IN THE CREATION AND MAINTENANCE OF MATERIAL WELFARE

R. A. MUSGRAVE

My purpose here is to outline briefly what economists have to say about "The Public Interest" or, as they call it, the problem of welfare economics. While less satisfactory and successful than other branches of economics, it is nevertheless one to which much thought has been given, and for which specific tools of analysis have been formed.

The tradition of economic analysis anchors in the hedonistic proposition whereby individual interests, by courtesy of the invisible hand, coincide with the public interest. More specifically, economists have argued that given the state of income distribution and the principle of consumer sovereignty—the rule that individuals should be free to use their income as they see fit—the play of free competition will result in the most efficient use of resources. The outcome will be most efficient in the sense that scarce resources are used so as to maximize consumer satisfaction. Factors of production will be used in the best way to produce what people want most. Certain "welfare conditions" are derived which must be met if this efficient resource allocation is to prevail.

These conditions, interestingly enough, will be met by a perfectly competitive market economy, as well as by socialist planning, provided that the socialist state recognizes consumer choice. This line of reasoning is still the backbone of normative economic analysis. Over the years, economists became increasingly aware, however, that the market need not function in this way, and that certain difficulties could not be solved by even a competitive market. The argument had to be qualified to meet these problems.

PROBLEMS OF ALLOCATION

Accepting the assumption that the state of income distribution is given and that consumer sovereignty is to be respected, certain situations exist in which the market on its own does not satisfy the conditions of efficiency. Under such conditions, the public interest, still defined in essentially the traditional way, requires corrective measures through public policy. Some situations of this sort will now be examined.

In certain areas efficient resource use could be achieved through competition but does not come about because the market is "imperfect." Hence the public interest requires controls to restore or to maintain competition. Public policies of this type include such matters as antitrust legislation, regulation of public utilities and other "natural monopolies," financial regulation, control of advertising, etc. While such policies of control encounter all sorts of practical difficulties—e.g., how to define "competition," or the absence thereof, in a workable way—conceptually these cases are relatively straightforward. The standard of public interest is provided by the results which would be obtained under perfect competition. Policy measures to come closer to these results, therefore, are in the public interest.

A more difficult set of issues arises when the nature of the economic problem is such that it cannot be solved efficiently by simply assuring competition. Such is the case with diminishing cost industries, where the efficient solution may require that firms operate at a loss. Technically speaking, marginal cost must equal price or average revenue, but average cost is above marginal cost. Thus a subsidy is needed. The problem is how to finance it, and how to determine the proper amount thereof.

A related problem arises in the case of goods which involve "externalities." These may take the form of benefits or costs. For instance, a shopping center may raise adjacent real estate values, or a factory located near a beach may create a smoke nuisance and reduce the value of beach property. Such external benefits or costs are not accounted for in the market calculations. The real estate owners are not called upon to pay for benefits received, so that the value of the shopping center (if estimated from cash proceeds) is set too low. The factories causing the smoke nuisance, similarly, do not have to pay for the damage, and costs charged (to the consumers for the factory's product) are too low. Efficient resource use would require that these benefit and cost components be considered. The problem is to determine what costs or benefits to assess, and on whom, and who is to be paid or charged, and how much.

An extreme case of such externalities is encountered with regard to those goods and services which must be satisfied through the public budget. National defense, for instance. Here the entire benefit is external. The same services are enjoyed by everybody, and protection enjoyed by *A* does not reduce that enjoyed by *B*. (Technically speaking, demand curves of individuals are added vertically rather than horizontally in obtaining total demand.) Since the benefits derived by any one person are independent of their own contributions, individuals are not willing to declare their preferences. This is quite different from the satisfaction of private wants, where the market acts as an auction system. No benefits are received unless payment is rendered. This auction system breaks down in the case of social wants. Here some sort of political voting system is needed to reveal preferences. Moreover, even if preferences are given, there is no single optimal solution, such as applies in the ordinary case of private wants. Since *A* and *B* share in the satisfaction of social wants, any rearrangement of *A*'s outlays thereon also affects *B,* and vice versa. There will be some solutions which both *A* and *B* prefer to others, but no single outcome which both like best. The traditional definition of efficiency vis-à-vis the pattern of demand resulting from a given distribution of money income breaks down. The final solution must involve a determination of the relative real income positions of A and B, thus linking the allocation and distribution aspects of the problem.

A further situation in which decisions can not be left to the market arises in connection with time preference. The relative value of present as against future consumption may differ greatly from the point of view of the individual and the society. The individual's life is short, whereas society continues. Hence, there may be a need for public control over exploitation of raw materials. Or, more generally, public policy may be called upon to determine the rate of economic growth, and the underlying strategic decision of how output should be divided between consumption and capital formation.

SOLUTIONS TO ALLOCATION PROBLEMS

How have economists handled these and similar situations where public policy is needed to correct market forces? What criteria have been used to decide which solution is efficient and thus in the public interest? Traditionally, economists have tended to answer these problems by arguments involving interpersonal comparison of utilities. The efficient solution was that which maximizes total utility, where A's gain in utility exceeds B's loss. The best known illustration of this is taxation according to "ability to pay," where, under the principle of least total sacrifice, progressive taxation is deduced from the assumption that marginal income utility curves are declining and equal for all people. The "new welfare economics," dating to the thirties, has rejected the possibility of interpersonal utility comparison. Indeed, it has become a mark of sophistication among economic theorists to reject interpersonal utility comparisons as unscientific.

Instead, the rule is used that a rearrangement is "efficient," i.e., in the public interest, if *someone* gains while *no one* loses. Recently, even this has been criticized as overlooking gain or loss from change in relative position. If this principle is accepted, there remains the question whether a rearrangement is efficient only if the rearrangement includes actual payment of compensation, or whether it is efficient even without compensation being provided, provided that the rule could be satisfied if compensation were paid. Most people now hold that compensation must be paid. If we assume that people's preferences are known, this principle permits us to solve at least some of the previously noted problems.

However, preferences are not known in most of the cases, and circumstances are such that people are not forced to reveal their preferences. Yet, unless these preferences are known, we can not determine what taxes should be charged and what compensations should be paid. Such is the case especially for determination of the public budget. A political process, involving compulsion in application of group decisions, is needed in order to force people to reveal their preferences. But in conducting this process, how is the right to vote to be distributed, and what voting rule (majority, qualified majority, plurality, and the like) is to be applied? One voting rule may be more efficient than another in the absence of political strategy. Thus, given "true" voting, the results of point voting will be preferable to those of majority rule. But this picture may change greatly if due allowance is made for the imperfections introduced through strategy in voting. Here welfare economics becomes interlocked with the theory of games, and a web of new difficulties arises.

PROBLEMS OF STABILIZATION

Since the thirties, emphasis has shifted from problems of allocation to problems of stabilization. Classical economists thought in terms of a system where full employment is established automatically, and price levels remain stable, lest they are disturbed by foolish monetary expansion. The essence of the "Keynesian revolution" has been recognition of the fact that this is not the case in the real world. The desire to save *more,* if not matched by a corresponding desire to invest, may lead to lower national income, unemployment, and *less* saving. The invisible hand crosses itself and produces the opposite result from that which was intended. "Stabilization policy" is now needed in the public interest to obtain the desired outcome. If done properly, this can be handled without interference with the state of income distribution or an efficient allocation of resources.

More or less similar problems arise with regard to inflation. Traditionally, this was thought to be due to excessive expansion in money supply, but it may be caused also from within the system by changes in velocity, or the rate at which money is used. In either case, prevention of inflation may be accomplished without serious interference with other objectives. Recently, there has been much concern with the problem of cost-push inflation, and this poses a more difficult policy issue. If unions insist on a higher money wage, or if management insists on higher prices, a full-employment output requires a higher level of aggregate expenditures. The government, in conducting its monetary and fiscal policy, may now have to choose between underwriting this required increase in demand, thus condoning inflation, or denying the needed expansion and thereby tolerating or creating unemployment. Such, at least, may be the case unless some degree of direct control over wages and prices is applied.

Further problems of monetary and fiscal policy arise with regard to economic growth. Given the imperfections of the economic system, it is difficult to argue that the rate of growth should be left simply to determination by the automatic forces of the market. While the market functions efficiently in determining the allocation of resources between red and blue hats, it may not do so equally well in setting the growth rate. The public interest thus enters in setting the appropriate rate of growth, not only as a matter of cold war, but also in the interest of efficient resource use.

THE PREMISES RECONSIDERED

Once one discards the traditional assumptions of a given distribution of income and of consumer sovereignty, a quite different set of problems arises about which economics has little to say.

In the earlier analysis, which accepted interpersonal utility comparisons and took the income utility curves to be known, it could be argued that the optimal income distribution is that which maximizes aggregate utility. Once the interpersonal comparison was rejected, the welfare concept of maximizing aggregate satisfaction by transferring income from people with low to people with high marginal utilities became meaningless. Economists can still analyze the effects of changes in distribution on economic incentives, but this is all. Nor is the difficulty solved by holding that the proper state of distribution must be determined by the political process. The essential problem is merely shifted, since now the question is how to distribute votes. We are thrown back on the old problem of the natural laws on which the social contract is to be based.

Most economists, today, would say that economics does not tell us which particular state of distribution represents the public interest. Economists have tried to formulate principles of consistency which must be complied with in setting up various rules of social ordering, but the choice between them is a matter of value judgment. And this, of course, economic theorists must avoid!

Next, consider what happens if the assumption of consumer sovereignty is discarded. Everyone agrees that there should be some instances in which society interferes with consumer sovereignty—i.e., the sale of narcotics to minors. While these are exceptions, the practice could be extended to all goods, and an authoritarian preference pattern could be substituted for individual choice. This would be distasteful as a value matter, but economic analysis would not be affected greatly. Though developed on the basis of a free-choice assumption, much of the argument may be applied readily to a state with authoritarian choice. In fact, matters would be simpler. However, economic analysis as such does not tell us which system of choice is better, or in the public interest. This is a value judgment and again precedes application of traditional economic analysis.

Indeed, economic analysis has traditionally stopped short of certain noneconomic implications of economic processes. Thus it might be argued that a continuous increase in the standard of living may be demoralizing, that pursuit of the profit motive harms the trader's soul, and so forth. Economists will not deny that the concept of the public interest must be broadened at some point to include such matters, but they would hold this to be outside their province. This province, and the corresponding concept of public interest, is defined more narrowly as efficiency in the creation and maintenance of material welfare.

. . . that vague, impalpable but all-controlling consideration, the public interest.

Justice Felix Frankfurter

THE PUBLIC INTEREST: ESSENTIAL KEY TO PUBLIC POLICY[1]

GERHARD COLM

I

In political debate, judicial practice, and economic policy discussions the term public interest plays a dominant role. The term lends itself to convenient use—partly because it resists, by its nature, precise definition. For this very reason, however, the idea of the public interest has been viewed with suspicion by those who try to formulate a rigorous "scientific" theory of political science or economics, especially public finance. Thus the recent literature in these fields has revived earlier efforts to do without a concept which so stubbornly defies neat and precise formulations and mathematical equations of political and economic behavior. A philosophy that denies the term any genuine

---

[1] This essay is an outgrowth of a letter written on request of the Committee to Advance Original Work in Philosophy; see its publication, Wayne A. R. Leys and Charner Marquis Perry, *Philosophy and the Public Interest* (1959). I am not here concerned with differences in the meaning of the terms public interest, general welfare, national interest, and similar phrases. This article was originally published in *Social Research,* Vol. 27, No. 3 (1960), 295-307, and appears here with an emendation.

meaning not only has a methodological appeal to theorists in political science and economics but is welcomed also by those who are tired of hearing the term in campaign oratory or in the pretenses to idealism made by those who advocate particular interests.

The most brilliant and most persuasive exposition of a theory of democracy based on the assumption that there exist only individual self-interests is that by Anthony Downs. In the market economy, according to classical theory, entrepreneurs are motivated only by the desire to make profits, and goods and services are supplied as an unintentional by-product. Downs contends that in a comparable manner democratic government renders public services as a by-product of the politicians' desire to be elected. "The government . . . is interested in [each adult citizen's] vote, not his welfare." [2] There is only a passing reference to those queer politicians who "act as they think best for society as a whole. . . . The politicians in our model never seek office as a means of carrying out particular policies; their only goal is to reap the rewards of holding office per se." These rewards are defined as "income, prestige, and power which come from being in office." [3] According to this model the voters too are exclusively motivated by self-interest. They try to satisfy their self-interest by buying divisible goods and services through the market with dollars and indivisible goods through the government with votes.[4]

Thus a structure of political and economic theory has been erected which has as its foundation only one assumption: that all people—whether entrepreneurs or consumers, politicians or voters—are motivated only by their own interests. Robert Dahl puts it in these words: "If one rejects the notion that public interest is some sort of amalgamation of private interests, there is

---

2 Anthony Downs, *An Economic Theory of Democracy* (1957), p. 18.

3 *Economic Theory of Democracy*, pp. 27-28.

4 I have elsewhere criticized the view that the market supplies only divisible goods, the government only indivisible goods; see "Comments on Samuelson's Theory of Public Finance," *Review of Economics and Statistics* (November 1956).

little philosophical mileage to be gained from using the term at all." [5]

Like the hedonistic and utilitarian philosophers of an earlier epoch who sophistically made allowance for social values, the present-day theorists of self-interest occasionally permit the public interest a kind of incognito entrance through the back door. Thus Anthony Downs says that "by attributing all human action to selfishness . . . we also include a broad sense which may call for great self-sacrifice." [6] He also comes close to recognizing such a thing as a general interest when, at various points of his analysis, he speaks of "social goals" or "unequivocally good acts." [7] Similarly, Richard Musgrave states that "while social preference must be anchored in individual valuation, it does not follow that people are selfish monsters. Altruistic or social motivation may be imbedded in the structure of individual preference patterns." [8] In basic intention, however, these theorists of political science and economics appear to be bent on eliminating as an operational concept the "vague, impalpable" idea of public interests or social goals.

In contrast to these views, I wish to argue here that we can deal more adequately with problems of economic and social policies, public finance, and judicial procedures if we face up squarely to the meaning of the term public interest than if we deny this concept or let it in only by the back door. There are four levels on which I wish to examine its meaning, but first I shall enumerate several considerations which appear to me to demonstrate the need for the concept and the inadequacy of the back-door approach.

First, policy is concerned not only with the welfare of the present but also with that of "our posterity," as the United States Constitution calls it. In Downs' treatment of the time

---

5 Robert Dahl, "Letter to Committee," in *Philosophy and the Public Interest.*

6 *Economic Theory of Democracy*, p. 88.

7 *Economic Theory of Democracy*, pp. 160, 173,

8 Richard A. Musgrave, *The Theory of Public Finance* (1959), p. 11. Musgrave, too, when speaking of "merit wants" (p. 13) comes close to recognizing the public interest.

factor in government decision making [9] the government is not
concerned with the future beyond the next election. Certainly
it is true that the "political clock" affects time preferences in
policy decisions; unstable governments, in particular, are often
forced into poor policies because of the need to show quick results—a constraint on their policies of which they are usually
painfully aware. But in Downs' view such a policy is the norm
and not a compromise of what is required in the public interest.
According to his approach a policy of conservation of national
resources, for example, would not make political sense. I contend,
on the contrary, that the time dimension of the public interest
is identical neither with time as calculated with the aid of the
discount rate nor with time as measured by the election cycle.
The nothing-but-self-interest school makes some allowance for
the time factor by saying that the self-interest of the voters includes an interest in the needs of their born or unborn children
or, if they have none, the children of their neighbors. In contrast
with this back-door approach I maintain that the time problem
in public policy can more adequately be dealt with if we grant
the existence of a public interest that extends the future and is
a genuine concern of the government, including the voters.

Second, the tremendous importance of functions related to
the United States position in the world makes it especially artificial and labored to interpret all international and defense activities as designed to meet individuals' self-interest in national
security and prestige. It is true that many local government activities can be interpreted as related to the individual benefits
of the residents, but the same kind of interpretation makes no
sense for the large national programs. There the public interest
may to some extent even transcend the national interest and
begin to be concerned with supranational groupings and with
humanity as such.

Third, the satisfaction of many self-interests has indirect beneficial effects for society as a whole. To be sure, individuals benefit
from good education, but good education of the individual is
also a requirement of a good society. Our theorists have inter-

---

[9] *Economic Theory of Democracy,* pp. 174ff.

preted this as a "spill-over" effect, through which a service performed primarily for individuals has indirect secondary results. I regard this again as a highly artificial and unworkable approach, which uses a complicated structure only to avoid a departure from the principle that everything has to be explained in terms of individual self-interest.

Finally, in a democracy many specific interests are shared by only a minority of the voters (such as the interests of farmers in adequate prices of farm products). Therefore, in order to obtain legislation in support of their interests, the minority group must persuade others that the pursuit of its special objectives is not only in their particular interest but also in the public interest. Also in this case, circumlocutions are possible. It may be said, for example, that in appealing to the public interest the representatives of the farm interests are "in reality" appealing to the particular interest of the specific individuals or groups of individuals. Once more, however, I regard this as a "back-door" approach that makes it much harder to come to grips with the issue.

II

Against this background of general considerations I want now to suggest four levels, or points of view, from which the concept of the public interest may be usefully analyzed: meta-sociological, sociological, judicial, and economic.

The Meta-Sociological Level. Where only one ultimate system of values is recognized, as in a theocratic or monolithic society, the concept of the public interest is clear and indeed self-evident: it is the expression of the unitary system of values. This highest value may be the establishment of God's Kingdom on Earth or the ultimate triumph of communism. In any case there is a presumably unambiguous criterion for formulating the public interest, difficult as it may be to apply the criterion in practice. Since there is an identity between the ultimate value and the public interest, the latter concept has in this case no importance. In a pluralistic society, however, various individuals and groups have different ultimate value systems. Some have a religious concept, others a biological one (such as survival of the race), others

a cultural concept (permitting the development and manifestation of such genius for creative achievement as is latent in the
society), others a nationalistic political concept ("manifest destiny" or defense of a particular "way of life"). The denial of
any values beyond the desires of individuals can itself be regarded as an ultimate or meta-sociological value.

But even in a society of greatly divergent ultimate values there
is a considerable common ground in the proximate objectives.
While their substance is subject to change—to more rapid change
than the ultimate values—these objectives themselves are clear
and recognizable. Healthy and well-educated individuals of the
present and future generations, political independence, stable
social institutions, a desirable degree of self-initiative and self-
responsibility are some of the penultimate values on which people with different ultimate values can agree. It is this area of
intermediate objectives that may be called the public interest.
It is not necessarily identical with the tasks for public operations.
Either private or public activities may or may not serve the public interest. Thus a reasonable standard of nutrition of the people is in the public interest. This does not mean that all nutrition
must be provided by government operations. It means only that
if private operations fail to achieve the desirable result (as in
case of natural catastrophe or war) the government will step in
because the public interest is involved.

One might say that an essential condition for the existence of
a democracy is some degree of common conviction that certain
achievements serve the variety of ultimate values. In other words,
the public interest is the life hypothesis of a pluralistic society
—enabling people with different religions, different philosophical
convictions, or different subconscious value systems to have a
common ground for promoting their various ultimate values.
Without this common ground, representing more than an accidental coincidence of individual interests, a pluralistic democracy could not exist. In a theocratic or monolithic society, there
can never in principle be controversy about ultimate objectives,
only about means. In a pluralistic society, there can and will be
controversy about ultimates, but the controversies will not become disruptive as long as there is some common ground with

respect to the penultimate values, the public interest. There will never be unanimity about their exact definition; indeed, without some controversy about the changing meaning of the public interest, democracy would not be alive. But without some common ground concerning those changes in meaning, it could not survive.

The Sociological Level. The meta-sociological value systems and the related concepts of the public interest become manifest only through sociological articulations—the expressions of individuals and groups. This is far from saying that these values must be only individualistic values. In each individual or in each group of individuals, the personal interests and the concept of the public interest are present in varying degree. Each emphasizes this or that aspect of the public interest in accordance with his own perspective, which is itself largely influenced by his own position in society and his own interests. Thus the mixture of personal and general interests differs in various groups and individuals, but from these varying emphases a consensus emerges as to what constitutes the public interest within the frame of reference of the particular society and culture. One of the main functions of the political processes in a democracy is to hammer out this common understanding of what is accepted as constituting the public interest.

We have had experience with all kinds of dictators who arrogated to themselves the right to determine what the public interest is, or rather, should be. It is a misunderstanding, however, to contend that the concept of the public interest presupposes a totalitarian philosophy. Totalitarianism refers to the manner in which decisions are made in a society. What is to be regarded as the public interest can be determined in a dictatorial manner, or it can result from democratic processes.

Many people today fail to recognize the function of leadership in a democracy because they confuse leaders and dictators. The nature of the public interest, as perceived by millions of voters, must be articulated by political leaders, even though the leaders' interpretations cannot become reality except by the vote of these millions. Many voters would not have a clear notion about their own concept of the public interest, but have a clear preference for leaders who "stand for" their concept of good government, which implies their interpretation of the public interest. This is why the content of the public interest or general welfare cannot be ascertained by some improved voting system or even by some sort of Gallup sample poll, as has been proposed. It is through the political "debate," the vote, and the influence of pressure groups that the public interest evolves as a set of concrete objectives to be pursued by actual policy. Through these "sociological" articulations of the public interest the value systems are transformed into power structures.

As I have mentioned, Downs' "economic theory of democracy" construes the voting mechanism as a parallel to the market mechanism. Even in regard to the market mechanism there is oversimplification in contending that consumer purchases determine what is to be produced. The entrepreneur is the one who takes the initiative in developing, producing, and advertising new products. The consumer, through his purchases, gives or withholds approval, but the entrepreneur's function is more than that of a mere agent responding to individuals' wishes. Correspondingly, it cannot properly be said that citizens' votes determine the government's activities. Political leaders take the initiative in developing the programs that are required by their understanding of what is needed in the public interest. The voter rarely has an opportunity to vote on the national issues directly, but by voting for candidates and parties he approves or disapproves the programs for which they stand.

The model of the so-called economic theory of democracy would have us believe that the voter merely "buys" certain benefits with his vote. Actually, he also participates, through his vote, in the process of government. He votes not merely in accordance with his self-interest but also in accordance with his concept of a good society and in favor of men whose image of government appeals to him.[10] Thus the politicians who have the highest vote-

---

10 Downs introduces the appeal to ideologies in an ingenious but, in my opinion, inadequate manner. Voters, he contends, take principles and ideologies into consideration when they cannot find exactly how a candidate will act on a specific issue. Thus ideology serves mainly as a stop-gap for lack of knowledge.

getting appeal for national office are those who in appealing to the voters' personal interests can also convey the conviction that they act in the best interest of society as a whole.

Basically Downs' model is best suited to depict not a democracy but a paternalistic government in which the politicians try to keep the people happy in order to stay in power. No allowance is made for the value of participation in government, which I believe is the essence of democracy. Just as it misses the essentials of a dynamic economy to regard the entrepreneur simply as an agent responding to consumer demand, it misses the essentials of a vital democracy to regard political leaders simply as functionaries responding to individuals' wishes. If that were the nature of a democracy we could save a great deal of money and energy by simply installing an electronic computer in lieu of our whole complicated political machinery.

The Legal Level. Reference to the public interest has always played an important role in the justification of government regulation of private business, and also in the self-regulation of certain occupations.[11] In many cases either government regulation or self-regulation must restrict personal or corporate activities. The restrictions are given legal sanction by reference to a public interest which in the event of conflict is presumably superior to the particular interests. This concept is of basic importance in spite of, and even because of, the fact that the requirements and the interpretation of the public interest are fluid and changing. The use of the public interest concept in this connection permits considerations that are superior to particular interests, and yet permits the judicial interpretation of the statutes to move in step with actual developments in the content of the concept.

The Economic Level. Until a few decades ago the government was recognized as a supporter of the public interest mainly through these regulatory functions just discussed. In recent years, however, a more affirmative concern of the government in the public interest has developed, largely through the evolution of

---

11 For many examples and citation of literature see Leys and Perry, *Philosophy and the Public Interest,* Appendices A and B.

such operational concepts as high or full employment. When the inevitably vague concept of the public interest is translated into specific objectives to be accomplished to a specified extent and within a specified time period I propose to speak of "goals." These goals give us yardsticks by which the results of private and public activities can be assessed, and which can be of use in the formulation of public policy programs—for a program states a goal and also the means by which it will be pursued within a given time period.

We may perhaps distinguish two kinds of goals that are related to the public interest. In somewhat arbitrary terminology I have called one kind the performance goals, the other the achievement goals.[12] Performance goals refer to the smooth operation of the economy, as evidenced by low unemployment, reasonable price stability, and and adequate rate of economic growth; in a democracy, good performance also implies a maximum use of oppressive government regulations with difficult and demoralizing methods of enforcement. Achievement goals, on the other hand, refer to the specific content of the public-interest concept, such as an adequate standard of living for the people, adequate education, defense, conservation and development of resources, a proper contribution to underdeveloped countries. The multitude of these specific achievement goals must be pursued in a manner that results in a satisfactorily performing economy. This means that productive resources should be allocated to the various purposes in a manner corresponding to their relative urgency and assuring full, but not excessive and therefore inflationary, use of resources.

National economic budgets have been developed as tools for appraising the pursuit of the various achievement goals and for appraising the performance of the economy as a whole. These national economic budgets thus represent, as it were, a quantified expression of the public interest. Developed by the government, they can reflect the interpretation of the public interest in the views of the highest elected officials in the executive and legisla-

---

12 Gerhard Colm, "National Economic Budgets," to be published in German in *Handbuch der Sozialwissenschaften*.

tive branches. They can serve as the basis for public debate to ascertain to what extent there is agreement or disagreement with respect to the proposed interpretation of the requirements of the public interest. Once they are confirmed, they can provide a frame of reference for the formulation of the government's policies. Thus through the national economic budgets the vague concept of the public interest can be transformed into an operational instrument.

The national economic budget represents not only goals but also to some extent forecasts. For instance, it includes estimates for private consumption of a magnitude that appears adequate in consideration of potential total production and the amount of resources needed for governmental purposes, gross investment, and net export; in regard to the details of consumption, however, the budget estimates only what consumers are likely to spend if they have the total consumer income posited in the budget. Similarly in regard to investments, the detailed figures represent hypothetical forecasts rather than exact goals. Thus the national economic budget is not a blueprint for precise enforcement but a guide for appraising actual economic performance and for deciding on changes in public or private policy that may be required in the public interest.

As I have said, the public interest not only refers directly to public operations but also includes the adequate satisfaction of individual wants. Only where these individual wants cannot adequately be satisfied by private operations is there, in the United States economic system, a reason for government action. There are hardly and social functions, however, that have not been performed at one time by private, at another time by public, operations. Thus there is no absolute and permanent distinction between "private" and "public" wants. Nor can public and private activities be distinguished by the criterion of divisibility. While the government performs many indivisible services it is also concerned with the provision of an adequate supply and distribution of divisible goods, such as nutrition or housing.

In his article "An Economist's View of the Public Interest," Musgrave discusses the reasons why the market process does not always assure an allocation of resources which results in the best satisfaction of individual wants under a given income distribution. The allocation of resources through the market can be unsatisfactory (from the individuals' point of view) when competition is imperfect or when full utilization of capacity in diminishing cost industries calls for a subsidy or when production involving "external benefits or costs" calls for pricing below average costs of production. In all these cases Musgrave sees public action justified "in the public interest." He also sees the public interest involved when decisions are made concerning the division of resources devoted to the satisfaction of current needs and the building up of capital for the satisfaction of future needs. Here he sees the public interest protecting the continuing life of society versus the limited life of the individual. All this is in complete agreement with my own views.

Musgrave feels perplexed about the role of "normative" economics in answering the question concerning what the public interest requires if questions of distribution of income, free consumers' choices, and public morale are involved. Because he cannot see that economics as a science can give the answers he proposes that the economist be concerned with the public interest only to the extent that it is defined as "efficiency in the creation and maintenance of material welfare." Musgrave perhaps asks for too much when he wants the economists to determine what the public interest requires. I only want the economist to provide tools for aiding the decision makers and appraising the consequences of the decisions. In other respects, I believe Musgrave's approach is too restricted if it suggests that the economist should be concerned only with the "material welfare." The approach outlined in my article deals with the development and allocation of resources for all national and individual goals. In that respect, I am suggesting a broader approach than Musgrave does.

Briefly, then, in our society government economic action is called for with respect to functions that must meet a double requirement: first, that they are in the public interest; and second, that they cannot adequately be performed by private operations. Hence two interrelated but separate judgments are reflected in national economic budgets: judgments about the public interest, and judgments as to which activities should be pursued by private and which by public operations. Much of the controversy that purports to be a dispute about the existence of the public interest is actually an argument over whether, in a specific case, the public interest is better served by private or by public operations.

The vague concept of the public interest loses much of its vagueness as a result of political debates, judicial interpretations, and translations into specific goals of economic performance and achievement. As a matter of fact, it is difficult to imagine that politicians, statesmen, judges, and officials concerned with the formulation of government policies could do without this concept. Even a person who is wholly agnostic with respect to the public interest as a meta-sociological idea may find that the concept is needed at least as a working hypothesis, regardless of whether it corresponds to a "reality."

The skeptics are of course right in pointing to the fact that the public interest concept is often used to rationalize or glorify the particular interest of a minority. Then it has to be "debunked." Determining whether the claim is or is not justified in any particular case is one of the purposes of debate and analysis in the democratic process. Without a concept of the public interest, however, even the debunking of particularistic claims is not possible.

A politician who appeals only to the self-interests of the voters will not win their respect. A voter who considers only his personal interests will lose his self-respect as a citizen. Politicians and voters alike can promote their self-interests only by reconciling them with the requirements of the public interest.

I would like to conclude with a metaphor. Producers and actors who present a play and the people who come to see it are all motivated by self-interest, be it the desire to earn money or to gain fame or to be entertained. Nevertheless, the varying self-interests of all of them will not be satisfied for long unless the producers and the players and the audience find a common ground under the spell of the play as a work of art. To satisfy self-interests, those concerned with a play and those concerned with the conduct of government must in some respect transcend their self-interests. Hence we cannot have a meaningful theory

or successful practice of government or of government economic
and fiscal policy without "that vague, impalpable but all-controlling consideration, the public interest." [13]

---

[13] Frankfurter, *Felix Frankfurter Reminisces,* ed. Harlan B. Phillips (1960),
p. 72.

11

THE PUBLIC INTEREST: THE PRESENT AND FUTURE OF THE CONCEPT[1]

DAVID BRAYBROOKE

"The public interest" is not the *supreme* goal of public policy and administration. Nor do all things that are morally required of government fall under its head: it is not a *comprehensive* consideration in public policy. It is not even—and it never has been—a *goal* of public policy; and though it is not—and never will be—obsolete as an *occasional* consideration, it cannot be counted on to indicate more than a range of possibly suitable policies, and its helpfulness is in fact currently in suspense. Yet there are many familiar cases in which it is a straightforward consideration with a stable meaning, and operates with impressive force and clarity.

---

1 I have tried out some of the ideas contained in this work on Professors Stuart Hampshire, H. L. A. Hart, and Charles W. Hendel; and I thank them for their reactions and comments. I owe a substantial debt, in my refusal to treat "the public interest" as a transcendent or all-embracing standard of policy, to Brian Barry, now of the University of Birmingham, and the line which he takes on this subject in his D.Phil. thesis "The Language of Political Argument." Barry has since supplied some helpful criticisms of this work as originally presented, which I have taken into account in revising it.

INFLATION OR DEFLATION?

I shall justify all these paradoxes in due course. It is, however, only fair to say straightaway that these justifications depend on taking as standard one pattern of usage which the phrase, "the public interest," seems to exhibit and rejecting another pattern. I shall call the pattern of usage which I accept, "The Deflated Pattern," and the pattern of usage which I reject, "The Inflated Pattern." Choosing between them is arbitrary to a degree, since neither pattern is firmly established in language to the exclusion of the other. There is evidence for both; and evidence, consisting of cases which might be assimilated to either, that the two patterns overlap.

Nevertheless, the advantages of the deflated pattern seem to me compelling. If the concept of the public interest throws any special light on discriminations of policy, it is light that is generated within the deflated pattern. Inflated to the point of taking in every consideration, the other pattern ends up by meaning no consideration in particular. The deflated pattern does not have this defect of perfect indistinctness; among its advantages, it has the advantage of being specific enough to repay analysis, and it is to an analysis and critique of the deflated pattern that I shall devote this paper.[2]

The deflated pattern limits the use of the concept of the public interest to cases in which the three following features are prominent: first, a person or firm or relatively small group of

---

[2] This means that I shall be addressing myself throughout to the conceptual problem, what "the public interest" means, rather than to the institutional or organizational problem, how (given that it means so-and-so) it is to be advanced or safeguarded. Though both problems might be broached by the question, "How do we determine the public interest?", which is ambiguous; they are different problems. They are at any rate sufficiently independent to invite a division of labor, and substantial enough on either side to be worth the effort. Explicating the meaning of "the public interest" is not the same thing as carelessly moralizing in its name. On both these points—the difference between the problems, and the interest of the conceptual problem taken separately—Glendon A. Schubert, Jr.'s article, " 'The Public Interest' in Administrative Decision-Making," *American Political Science Review*, LI (June 1957), 346-368, useful and provocative though it has been, seems to me to have spread some confusion.

people with special interests is arrayed against "the public"— a body open in membership to anyone who does not belong to the special group, and a body which therefore varies in identity as the special group changes from case to case. Second, though government action may be neither expected nor asked for, the question whether the government shall act or not act will be raised if other measures for assisting the public should fail. The existence of the government is therefore presupposed. Third, the issues debated in these cases are approached as issues of domestic and internal concern, even when they have some connection with foreign policy.

It follows immediately that the public interest is not, as used within this pattern, a comprehensive consideration, for there are obviously many possible disputes over policy from which one or more of these features are missing. But it is not a supreme and insuperable consideration, either, even among the cases that do have all these features; for while no one ever *comes out* against "the public interest," [3] there are plenty of cases in which it is displaced and superseded by other considerations. Desegregation, for example, is not an issue for which the consideration of the public interest is decisive; it is an issue that turns on direct considerations of humanity and justice and freedom.

How far does the deflated pattern extend? I am not claiming that it covers the whole field over which the phrase, "the public interest," is used; but it covers a good deal. For example, politicians pledge themselves to champion the public interest. Admittedly, this is meant to be a very comprehensive and elevated claim, but even so, it may often fall within the deflated pattern, since it can be interpreted as meaning, "Whenever there is any need of defending 'the public' against groups with special interests, we shall leap to the defense." Again, the deflated pattern

---

[3] People in authority sometimes encounter circumstances in which it would be "in the public interest" to do something—e.g., seize a man's land for redevelopment—but in which it seems to them (as they will say) best to put off doing it—the man is an aged pensioner who will feel dreadfully victimized. But even here it would not be said (in so many words) that postponing the seizure, or taking up another plan, was "contrary to the public interest." The people responsible would not want to pronounce upon the action in these terms.

can accommodate the fact that professional bodies, and sometimes business firms, profess themselves to be acting in the public interest when they set up codes of ethics [4] or voluntarily cease doing something objectionable. They may or may not feel under pressure to act before the government does.[5]

Questions in which the public interest figures as a clear and decisive consideration are at the same time leading examples of cases in which "the public interest" has a stabilized—and deflated—meaning. For a topical example, consider the question whether the F.B.I. should disclose the names of its informants in "security" matters, exposing these people to subpoena and cross-examination. Let us assume that the question is approached on the supposition that the special group against whom the public is arrayed consists of the people denounced and their counsel. Even when approached this way, the question may be disputed without referring to the public interest; for it may be argued that it is *unjust* to penalize anyone because of information that has not been tested by confrontation and cross-examination. The moral dilemmas into which the safety of the state leads us may be much more excruciating than anything that will come up in connection with the public interest.

If the question is to be answered on the basis of the public interest, however, it seems to me quite clear how an answer will be reached. One will have to balance the dangers of refusing people the protection of normal legal procedures against the dangers to the whole complex of public institutions of inhibiting action against suspected subversives. The police must have power

---

[4] See Appendix B, "Self-Regulation in the Public Interest," in the helpful recent survey of literature and opinions about "the public interest" by Wayne A. R. Leys and Charner M. Perry, *Philosophy and the Public Interest* (1959).

[5] There is at least one possible use of "the public interest" which falls outside the deflated pattern without falling into the objectionable inflated pattern. One may speak of street lighting or water purification as being in the public interest without implying that there is some special group which stands to lose from these things. In the absence of statistical evidence, one can only guess how frequent this use of "the public interest" is; I choose to regard it as infrequent, especially as an unmixed case. I also think that the phrase does no distinctive work in this use. It is readily supplanted by speaking of street lighting or water purification as being in *everybody's* interest, a simpler and more powerful notion.

to protect the state; on the other hand, if they have too much power, they are liable to subvert public institutions themselves. The question then is to be settled by assessing the comparative risks of either policy. If normal legal procedures are threatened with disuse in the face of spreading administrative tyranny, while the possibility of effective subversion is very remote, then it is in the public interest to maintain and extend normal legal procedures. Contrariwise, if subversion were rampant and spreading, it might be in the public interest to tolerate, temporarily, and in strictly defined circumstances, the omission of various devices of legal protection.

A second topical example offers itself in the question whether drug houses should be allowed to make markups much higher than those normal in consumer's goods—to take a round number, say ten times as much as is normal with wholesale prices. Here, the survival of the state and public institutions is not in question; but it is clear that the public interest is not invoked gratuitously, because such extraordinary markups are possible only through the favor of a specific public institution—namely, patent laws— and the public is affected in matters of vital necessity—namely, health and medical care.

Again one may sense in the background the possibility of raising considerations that would supersede in moral force any reference to the public interest. One may feel a certain moral uneasiness about making *any* profit from sickness and distress. This, however, is not at present in our society the sort of consideration that would be decisive. The arguments actually given are, on the one side, that high prices prevent people from getting the medical care which they need, or, at the very least, exact undue expenditures from them on goods which they are not free to forego. On the other side, it is contended that high markups on successful drugs are necessary to cover losses on unsuccessful ones, and that this is the means of financing research.

The solution seems quite straightforward. If there are alternative ways of financing research, which—without upsetting our general political and economic arrangements—would be equally productive in discoveries of effective drugs, then it cannot be in the public interest to allow drug houses to make extraordinary markups; for then, by hypothesis, there is another policy which has all the advantages of the present system in the way of promoting health and providing medical care, and more besides.

For a third example, we may turn to the question of whether nationwide strikes in a given industry, say the steel industry, should be allowed to run on indefinitely, when neither management nor the unions desire government intervention. The public interest—that is, the interest of people outside the steel industry —is here affected in two ways: people outside the industry stand to suffer loss of business and employment; they are liable also to be deprived of goods and services, the need for which cannot perhaps be easily postponed.

The issue is complicated by the question of precedent. There may be some industries where the effects on the public of a strike would be trivial, others in which they would be intolerable; and it may not be desirable that the government should intervene, except in the latter cases. The search for a solution, therefore, is likely to be a search for a rule. One might imagine in the case of each industry plotting adverse effects on the public against possible durations of a strike, and attempting to draw a line somewhere between effects amounting to death and destitution and effects not rising above inconvenience. The rule would be that strikes in any industry must be prevented from going on long enough to push the effects beyond the tolerable level so established. Sometimes, however, no search for a rule would be necessary; it would be immediately clear—even allowing for the habitual exaggerations of the press on this subject—that the effects of not intervening would be disastrous for the public.

The last example also serves to show how the concept of the public interest tends to fill with air, break away from the moorings of the deflated pattern, and soar off into the cloudy sky. Either the union concerned or the companies, or both, often do desire government intervention; and whether they do or not, either or both sides might benefit from it. So their interests tend to be merged with the public interest. Again, the members of the union may be so numerous as compared with the members of the public who are immediately affected that it may seem invidious to treat them as a special interest group. Though they are not in fact part of the public themselves on this occasion, their preponderance in numbers may induct the same sort of caution in observers as is due the notorious fallacy of excluding them and other union members from the people, the reservoir from which the public, however differently constituted, is on every occasion drawn. In the third place, intervention in industrial disputes is frequently thought of nowadays as a matter of national defense, involving "the national interest and safety" (though again, to do so is seldom very realistic); and it is easy to see why the concept of the public interest would tend to coalesce with this other concept (which touches the relative position of our country among international rivals), for both the public interest and the national interest are responsibilities of the government.

There are further temptations that invite adopting the inflated pattern for invoking the public interest. People desire to have a way of referring simultaneously to all the things that they believe should be achieved in politics, and the phrase, "the public interests," may not sound so idealistic or moralistic as its putative rivals, "the general welfare" and "the common good." Furthermore, people readily fall in with the conception of politics currently favored by political scientists, which dissolves the activities both of parties and of the established branches of government into the activity of interest groups, and they wish to use "the public interest" to signify the way in which the struggle between interest groups *ought* always to be resolved.

I think these temptations to inflate "the public interest" so that it envelops, loosely, everything that ought to be achieved in politics should be resisted. The assumption which accompanies the temptations, that all moral and political values are compatible and can be reduced (if we could only discover how) to one criterion, simple or complex, has little evidence to support it; and the pursuit of such fancies may lead us to discard the virtues of the language that we have, with its many possibilities of firm discriminations. If we set "in the public interest" equal to "the optimum policy," it will cease to give us any special light. How ironic it would then be to complain that the concept is too vague and shifting and out of focus to help in choosing policies!

EXPANSION WITHOUT INFLATION

The impulse to generalize the concept of the public interest does not rise solely from sources external to the deflated pattern. Even as used within the deflated pattern, "the public interest" has a special susceptibility to expansion. It is meant to introduce a variety of subordinate considerations, and though this does not mean every consideration, new considerations appear from time to time and establish a place for themselves in the repertory. The full dimensions of the deflated pattern cannot be discerned until its mode of expansion has been described.

The best way of representing this mode of expansion is to arrange the disputes in which the deflated concept of the public interest figures in a certain continuous order or spectrum. At one end (the stabilized end) of the spectrum there are cases in which to say, "P is against the public interest," is to refer to the dangers which P involves for specific going public institutions, whose advantages for the public outside any special group are taken for granted. Next, there are cases in which specific institutions (for example, the patent laws) are under attack, and the question of the public interest turns on the dangers involved for more fundamental and comprehensive institutions (for example, the laws protecting private property in general and encouraging private enterprise).

These cases would merge with those in which the evidence is pushed deeper than the consequences for any specific institutions, and the issue becomes one of whether the public requires protection (against the special group) with regard to a recognized list of vital needs. In a rough order of accepted urgency, these are food, shelter, clothing, sanitation, medical care, education, recreation. However, as we run through this list, we approach the other end (the unstabilized end) of the spectrum. The list of vital needs is protean in expression; more important, it is perpetually unfinished.

With equal chances of recognition, the list might be given as "Health, safety, education, and recreation"; or as "Property and livelihood, sanitation, safety and convenience, traditional amenities"; and in many other ways. The variety of possible formulations facilitates the expansion of the concept of the public interest and its adaptation to particular circumstances. A person who invokes the public interest may choose the formulation best suited to his requirements—one that gives prominence to his chosen subjects and puts least strain upon public recognition. This freedom of variation, however, has at any moment its limits. Sanitation was once not a recognized subject of remedy on any version of the recognized list. The position of education on the recognized list of needs demanding government attention is not yet entirely firm in every respect and in everyone's view. Recreation is only beginning to make a large place for itself; it is one of the points at which we can most easily see the list expanding.

Considering the spectrum, one can easily see that the public interest is not simply a question of what the public happens to prefer, whatever sense we choose to give to the idea of public preference; much less, a question of what self-designated champions of the public interest happen to prefer. Whether or not a given institution can survive certain supposed dangers is something for economics or political science or sociology to tell us. The fact that people want it to survive will make no difference if they also insist on pursuing a policy that undermines it.

Similarly, when health or education or recreation are at issue, the consequences for the public in these connections are to be objectively investigated. The ultimate, decisive form for such an investigation is that of a comparative census.[6] One attempts to discover how may members of the public will suffer deprivations, say of food and sanitation, if the special group is allowed to operate without interference, and how many would suffer similar

---

[6] The census-notion, whose workings in ordinary discourse about policies deserve more than cursory attention, cannot be treated in detail here. Its importance, for instance, to the interpretation of utilitarianism, will be exhibited in a forthcoming book about policy evaluation which C. E. Lindblom and I have written together.

deprivations if action were taken against the special group. If more members of the public suffer under a policy of nonintefer- ence than would suffer otherwise, then interference is in the pub- lic interest. It is true that more than one vital need may be af- fected, and if there is more than one census to take, on different subjects, there is a possibility of conflict between their results. But such conflicts, when they threaten to appear, are generally avoided by redesigning policies and providing for compensation, so that no one loses in one vital need what he gains in respect to another.

There is, more often than not, no need to resort to a full, person-by-person census; the results of one can be approximated closely enough by various short cuts. Sometimes (as in the drug case above) a policy can be found that will have no consequences for the public except beneficial ones, obvious at a glance without any inquiry into their distribution. Sometimes, one will be able to determine the distribution of effects by considering the conse- quences of a policy for various classes and interest groups, whose respective sizes are known.[7]

At the stabilized end of the spectrum, therefore, "the public interest" means something which public policies, however pop- ular and however democratically arrived at, may actually con- travene. Just as a man may be so imprudent as to choose to do things which are against his own interest, so the people may choose imprudently, whether for themselves, taken all together, or against the interest of the public concerned in any given ques- tion. Yet those students of policy who hold that any policy which has been adopted by normal procedures in a democratic

---

7 Cf. Anthony Downs, *An Economic Theory of Democracy* (1957), p. 71. Using interest groups in this way to short-cut census calculations gives some basis to the contention, expressed by Pendleton Herring among others, that the public interest always consists of the interests of special groups other than the one under attack. See Schubert, " 'The Public Interest' in Administrative Decision-Making," p. 361. But this notion does not fit all cases, unless one makes it fit by stipulating that "the public" shall always count as an (un- organized) interest group itself, varying in composition from case to case. People have an interest in the continuance of government and the satisfaction of their vital needs, regardless of what organized interest groups they may happen to belong to; and, on occasion, some members of the public may be- long to none.

system may be held to be in the public interest [8] are not entirely unjustified, even as regards the deflated pattern. For they may be conceived to be thinking of the other end of the spectrum, where subjects of remedy are being added to the recognized list. There, too, popular policies may be mistaken. However popular, they may be ineffective; or worse, they may aggravate the difficulties which they were intended to remedy. Nevertheless, mistaken or not, they indicate what subjects of remedy people are beginning to be ready to have treated under the heading of "the public interest."

As we move across the spectrum, toward the unstabilized, growing end, reference, if not to popular choice, at least to popular assent, becomes more and more significant. Whether or not some new subject is to be added to the recognized list of needs depends upon whether the people—the people, not the public of any particular occasion, but the reservoir of "publics," the electorate—are willing to have it made part of the business of government; this is what recognition in this connection means. If the people cared nothing about recreation, or did not care to have the government protect and promote opportunities for it, then recreation would not now be a subject in which the public interest is involved. Or perhaps, since its position would be liable to change, one might better say, it would be a subject in which the public interest was as yet only tenuously involved. The most that could be said for a claim that the public interest was endangered by allowing people to do things which diminish opportunities for the public to obtain recreation would be to predict that after a certain series of choices and experiences, the electorate would come around to regarding recreation as a subject altering the public interest.

The assent of the people on such matters (as on any other) is not expressed in one election, or in one survey, or in one legislative session. It is settled public opinion that counts, something that becomes visible only as the cumulative results of secular change—results, which after a while cease to be seriously chal-

---

[8] For citations, see Leys and Perry, *Philosophy and the Public Interest,* especially pp. 25-38.

lenged, of the whole complex process of popular government. Microprocesses as well as macroprocesses operate; what happens in the courts must be taken into account as well as what happens in the administration and the legislature, in the competition of parties, and in the activities of interest groups. Nothing less is involved than a shift in the conception of the purposes of government, with an accompanying change in the language of politics.

This being so, it should be doubly clear that even at this end of the spectrum, the judgment that something should not be allowed, because it is against the public interest, is far from signifying the mere subjective preferences of a legislator or administrator. What the people will assent to is a fact, which may very well not accord with what an administrator prefers; and if it is a subject on which assent will become visible only in the future, if at all, it may not even be easy to predict that it will appear, so depending on it approaches being merely wishful.[9]

Of course, when the evidence of what the people are ready to assent to is obscure and ambiguous, policy makers have some freedom to make their own guesses about popular assent. Likewise, when despite all attempts at redesigning and compensation, there is a cross-conflict on policy between different vital needs, this again, though it is ultimately subject to popular choice, is a situation in which an administrator's or a legislator's personal assessment of the weight and trend of public opinion may play an important part. Whenever so much scope opens up for personal judgment, subjective preferences may determine what is identified as popular assent; but this does not remove the distinction between what the assent truly covers or will cover and what it may be pretended to cover.

---

[9] Herring's opinion that "the public interest" is a "subjective conception," the value of which is "psychological and does not extend beyond the significance that each responsible civil servant must find in the phrase for himself" (cited by Schubert in " 'The Public Interest' in Administrative Decision-Making") thus seems to me wholly mistaken, given the existence of the deflated pattern. "The public interest" has, like any other concept, generally acknowledged criteria which circumscribe its applications; and among these criteria, it happens to have some that discredit any attempt to use it as an expression merely of personal preference.

Since the recognized list of vital needs is perpetually unfinished, we may say that the deflated pattern is liable to expand indefinitely. Even so, it will not expand to the extent of making the public interest the supreme consideration, or a comprehensive consideration, in public policy. So long as the outline of the pattern continues the same—however far its boundaries are shifted in position—one may suppose that the requirement of being able to array "the public" against a special group or firm or person will be kept up. In some of the cases in which this can be done, other considerations, like justice or obligation or humanity, will continue to displace and supersede the public interest. Finally, the public interest will not function as a relevant consideration when the total dissolution of the government is in question. On this point—which I suspect holds for the inflated pattern as well—it has limitations which do not exist in the case of the greatest happiness principle or the notion (in welfare economics) of a Paretian optimum—or in the concept of the vital needs of the whole population. In some circumstances, the way to reach a Paretian optimum or to promote the greatest happiness of the people may be to dissolve the present government; but I do not think that we could ever say without absurdity, "Let us, in the public interest, dissolve the government."

THE CURRENT CRISIS OF EXPANSION

Representing the deflated pattern as a spectrum of subordinate considerations, which steadily grow in range and number, may exaggerate the smoothness, ease, and continuity with which the meaning of "the public interest" changes and expands. In fact, the concept of the public interest, like other familiar standards of social policy, is currently beset by a peculiar and unprecedented crisis, which may be an important cause of the uneasiness that many people have recently felt about its meaning. It is as though the concept had been pegged out stretch by stretch over the firm ground of a plateau, but was now being hurried over the edge of unsuspected precipices.

This feeling, that in talking about "the public interest" we are somehow wildly kicking about for a footing in mid-air, is one incident of the coming, which John Kenneth Galbraith has led us all in recognizing, of the Affluent Society. The emergence of surplus resources on a large scale threatens familiar standards with a crisis of redundancy, and the alarm has been so general that President Eisenhower was excited into appointing a commission to look for national goals. It is, to be sure, not the worst crisis that we face. It is certainly overshadowed by the cold war and the world population problem. There is even something ludicrous about it, like a millionaire complaining that he doesn't know where to go for his vacation.

One cannot even say, with an entirely good conscience, that the crisis has fully arrived. For there are puddles of misery remaining at home—seas of poverty abroad—and though, in a sense these could be mopped up painlessly, there are reasons for not being especially sanguine about the chances that they will be. Our political system serves a variety of interest groups, but it does not function well in serving groups that are not visibly useful to politicians seeking majorities. The neglect of some groups (the aged, for example) may be only transitory; but in other cases (migrant laborers, the Indians) it has persisted for generations, and seems likely to persist indefinitely.

Yet a crisis about social values is opening before us. The United States and a number of other countries have developed political and economic techniques which make it possible to assure every citizen of a decent livelihood (and more liberty on and off the job than any previous system has afforded). It is a scandal that the techniques have not been fully exploited; but few people any longer think that our institutions have to be totally demolished to remove the scandal. Hence socialism, in Western countries, has become a rhetoric without a movement. Moreover, the possibilities of our techniques are now so widely known—would it require more than a public investment of $500 million to take care of the Indians and the migrant laborers?— and so many people enjoy real benefits from the techniques that it requires a specially conscientious effort to keep the mopping-up problem in mind. This would suffice to account for widespread apathy; it also accounts for a good deal of perplexity about domestic politics. The apathy perhaps does not deserve to be excused (so far as it really exists); but the perplexity demands treatment, for it would survive any solution to the mopping-up problem. It would, in fact, spread farther.

One way of describing the crisis, of which the crisis which besets the expansion of "the public interest" is one feature, is to say that we have run out of the social goals that we—and the language of politics—have been used to: liberty, equality, material welfare, and the rest; and now, with the President's commission, we must cast about quickly for some new ones. A much better, because philosophically more illuminating, way of describing it is to say that we have for the first time in history passed into a situation in which it is really possible to choose social goals if we wish—Marx's kingdom of freedom; and it turns out that we are neither conceptually nor politically prepared for doing any such thing.

Liberty, equality, and material welfare are not very happily conceived of as goals; no more is the public interest. The goal metaphor of course fits in some respects. We choose policies with the aim of extending liberty, reducing inequality, serving the public interest; effort ensues, often effort directed at tentative goals; and the effort may be more or less successful in making headway. There, however, the analogy stops—just short of the points which it is currently most important for us to understand. The tentative goals that men have striven for in the name of liberty, equality, or the public interest are not liberty, equality, or the public interest themselves. It is not goals that (in the last analysis) we have been busy with, but remedies, and we have had social goals only when reaching them were ways of supplying remedies.

Goals literally conceived have the logical property that their location, and other characteristics as well, can be described independently of describing the condition of anyone traveling toward them. It would be absurd to hold that the only way of telling whether a runner was near or far from his goal was to consider whether he was tired, or limping, or had stopped moving; far from implying that he has arrived, or got any nearer, such facts are perfectly consistent with his having gone off in quite the wrong direction, and come to a halt in another country. The contrast with liberty and equality and the public interest could hardly be sharper. The only way that we have of telling whether the public interest has been served is by observing the condition of society, or of the public (whichever is to be the runner), to see whether remedies and precautions have been successfully taken against various distresses and dangers— dangers to institutions, distresses in respect to recognized vital needs.

It might be thought that the ideal in serving the public interest would be to make sure that public institutions were maintained whenever endangered and the members of the public supplied with goods and services sufficient to meet their recognized needs. Could not this be considered a goal—if not a goal of society, at any rate a possible goal for some person acting on behalf of society—and could it not be attained? Perhaps it could be said to be a goal, in the minimum sense (already metaphorical) of being a limit to directed activity; but then it cannot be identified with "the public interest." For goals can be attained; but we do not speak of "attaining" the public interest (or of "achieving" it or "fulfilling" it). Interests, public or private, are not the sort of thing that can be attained; they can only be protected —or advanced. Moreover, as we have seen, there is no end to the ways in which the public interest may be advanced. Even the deflated pattern is always expanding. The list of needs, and the institutions to serve them, are constantly changing.

If we say this, however, we may seem to invite the goal metaphor again, this time allied, as it often is, with another metaphor, that of maximizing a variable. The absurdities of supposing that people should adopt goals of maximizing liberty or maximizing equality are well known; they are caricatured in the notions of "license" and "uniformity." Equally staggering absurdities may be associated with maximizing the public interest. There is no scale for measuring the public interest,[10] and hence the public interest cannot be increased on such a scale, either indefinitely

---

[10] I do not remark the absence of scales and measurements with rejoicing. If a "welfare index" were invented and popularized, which would tell people at a glance something about the condition of fruit-pickers and Navahos, this might help a good deal in debates about the mopping-up problem.

or to an absolute maximum. More important, the concept of the public interest does not fix a unique optimum. Not only is there no agreement on what unique combination of social arrangements and income distribution it is beyond which one need not go on any occasion in maximizing the public interest, the alternative possibilities with which this combination, or rules for finding it, might be identified have not been formulated. Suppose that people can be satiated in respect to any finite list of needs; yet suppose that they must continue to suffer *some* deprivations, or else they will not put forward the effort necessary to maintain their standard of satiation. Does it follow that the public interest (whenever relevant) is served by reducing the amount of necessary effort, so that even stimulating deprivations vanish before the progress of satiation?

Finally, if the goal metaphor is to be applied to social choices on the same terms as to personal ones, it is important to recognize that we do not ordinarily talk like psychologists generalizing from rats running mazes (rats that run toward tangible goals); we do not conceive of people normally spending their energy in the pursuit of goals. The normal condition envisaged in ordinary language, on the contrary, is a condition in which men are either too much preoccupied with the struggle for existence, or the day-to-day routine which has been superimposed on that struggle, to have goals; or, supposing that they do have some time and energy to dispose of as they like, too passive about their opportunities. Only in very unusual circumstances would we speak of people having goals in taking a job or getting married. Having goals (admission to the school of electrical engineering; becoming a district manager before the age of thirty) is a sign of extraordinary ambition. Having them when they are not subordinate to the inescapable business of life—the business of earning a livelihood, establishing a home—is more extraordinary still.

The paradigmatic moment for choosing such autonomous goals comes when a person has mastered the business of coping with his environment, when he has developed such an efficient routine for handling his ordinary affairs that he has time and energy to spare. The goals that he then adopts, if he adopts any, may be noble or ignoble—freeing the slaves, or, for vengeance's sake, ruining an old rival. They may be neither. He may not choose to adopt goals at all; for he may prefer to spend his spare time making whoopee—or quietly cultivating his garden.

This point seems to me especially illuminating in the present connection. A nation, too, may perfectly well live and flourish without having any goals; this is part of the joke about the President's commission.[11] In any case, the change in a nation's prospects which occurs when surplus resources—the analogue in social terms of surplus personal time and energy—emerge on a large scale and the electorate can (if it chooses) adopt autonomous goals is of such enormous significance that it might well be marked, as it is in the case of persons, by denying the title of goals to previous considerations of policy. Whether we choose to describe the resulting crisis in this way or not, however— as one of having to choose goals for the first time (beyond the limits of the old values), or as one of having to choose new goals (the old ones having been reached)—it is easy to understand how the growing end even of the deflated concept of public interest happens to be surrounded at the moment by an unusual amount of perplexity, producing a special crisis of expansion. For what new subjects of remedy are going to be listed under the heading of the public interest will depend in part on what new activities are suggested for the government and other forms of social organization; and what these will be may depend in part on what goals (if any) the nation chooses. Such goals would make a difference to the direction of cultural development, and hence to the development of new personal needs and tastes, some of which would claim places as subjects of remedy on the recognized list.

Have we then arrived at the moment which Nietzsche foresaw, premature as his scorn for socialism may have been, the

---

11 A joke that, in view of the substantial accomplishments of the commission, should not be pressed too far. The commission's report—*Goals for Americans* (1960)—does nothing to clarify the concept of goals; but the liberties that the commission's report (like the commission's assignment) takes with the term are largely compensated for by the many valuable and interesting remedial recommendations contained in the report.

moment of transvaluation? The position of our society has changed so abruptly from supplying desperately insufficient remedies to casting about for supererogatory goals that it may seem our old system for remodeling political concepts, of depending on the slow shifts of secular change in ways of thinking, is obsolete. In the case of "the public interest," instead of waiting through myriad tentative introductions of new values, candidates for the recognized list of vital needs, and the gradual progress of some to general acceptance and an established position, must we not call together our preferences, and make up our minds now what goals we wish to seek? Otherwise, will not politics cease to be interesting (or intelligible) for want of orientation? Certainly we must know what the goals are before we can know how the concept of the public interest will expand to escort our journeys toward them.

If everything is to depend on preferences, however, and these, whether for having goals at all or for which ones to have, are to be expressed all at once, rather than in the course of gradually modifying traditional values, one must take seriously the difficulties about aggregating preferences that have been made manifest by recent studies in welfare economics and the theory of voting. Arrow and Black and other authors have laid out in exact and consternating detail some of the *formal* complications that may attend any attempt to pass from individual preferences —for example, as to the adoption of social goals—to a social ordering of alternatives.[12] They are complications that are especially likely to occur when unfamiliar subjects are approached without shared values, and individual preferences are therefore liable to vary every which way. When they do occur—when, for example, there is no policy that would gain a majority over each of the other ones proposed, or when (a connected case) the chances of a policy's being adopted depend on whether it is proposed earlier or later in the debate—we are prevented from identifying social choice with the results of voting in any rationally satisfactory way.

---

12 See Kenneth J. Arrow, *Social Choice and Individual Values* (1951); and Duncan Black, *The Theory of Committees and Elections* (1958).

Moreover, the complications raise doubts about the informal processes by which political choices are commonly narrowed down to choices between two alternatives. Arrow's proof that no system of aggregating preferences satisfies his apparently reasonable conditions does not apply to choices between two alternatives. But how coherent and intelligible, considered as ways of aggregating pure preferences, are the usual preliminary narrowing-down processes? The tactical confusion that prevails during many parliamentary debates—even with a well-informed electorate (say in faculty meetings)—does not encourage complacency on this subject.

In fact, we are very ill prepared, in concepts and social techniques, for choosing autonomous social goals; and we are not by this means going to find in a hurry new things to be remedied in the name of the public interest.

MICROPROCESSES OF EXPANSION
AND CHANGES OF TASTE

Let us not succumb to despair, however. It may be that an increased sense of purposelessness in politics is one of the inevitable drawbacks of prosperity; and we can just put up with it (or console ourselves with the cold war and the population problem). Moreover, if we are due to run out of social problems, must we vex ourselves about social goals? The revolution in our rhetorical habits will be considerable—how shall men talk about politics if they can no longer view with alarm, or exhort their fellows to organized efforts, if they cannot point to social goals, at least intermediate ones? Joseph Alsop would have to retire, and *The New Statesman* would have to be published without a front page. But, as we have seen, a society can prosper without goals; and perhaps, to remain prosperous, we need henceforth only repeat organized efforts that were initiated in the past.

At any rate, the crisis of social values, especially as it affects the concept of the public interest, is greatly aggravated by taking a macroscopic view of it. It is not the case that secular change in concepts of value has suddenly stopped; there is no need to tumble off the plateau—indeed, if we stop to look, we shall see that the plateau is still being extended in the old way, by man-made platforms; and the deflated pattern can be tied down to these. Grandiose choices wholly outside received concepts of social value can be avoided, fortunately; for microscopic processes of change are going on all the time inside our concepts, including the concept of the public interest.

It is best to take an example—indeed, we can hardly perform microscopic observation unless we do; and we are looking for shifts in conception that might appear in the details of any one of myriad cases. Consider how the disputes about public interest may arise from automobile traffic in cities. Whether or not this is the most puzzling of our surviving problems,[13] it is a substantial one and it is (as we shall see) intricate and novel in the ways that we need to investigate. It opens up, of course, into very general issues, which tend to escape the bounds of the deflated pattern—for instance, it may raise questions about the role of the automobile industry in the national economy, or about the waste incurred by fashions of obsolescence. Again,

---

[13] (March 1962.) The most puzzling perhaps—and very alarming, though not the most alarming—is the problem, revived lately by Paul Goodman's disturbing book *Growing Up Absurd* (1960), of finding meaningful work for our whole population. It seems absurd (as it has seemed all along, at each stage of the Industrial Revolution) to refuse the material abundance offered by machines—yet has not our technology disqualified a lot of people from having genuine parts in productive work? And will not the spread of automation disqualify even more? If social critics like Goodman are right, both the fact and feeling of being superfluous already pervade masses of our people. In connection with the present work, I might say four things about the problem: (1) It is obviously a problem that has something to do with finding autonomous goals—specifically, it is a problem about making social provisions to encourage the formation and pursuit of autonomous personal goals so far as these are demanded for psychic health and human dignity. (They may not be universally demanded; there are other ways of making work agreeable and meaningful.) (2) Considered as a problem about making or extending social provisions, it is a problem that presents itself in the old form of a demand for remedial actions and policies. But (3) it is a new subject of remedy and (4) it is likely to be a subject of shattering consequence, since the remedy needed may involve radical changes in our economic institutions—as might be gathered from the historic attention to the problem in socialist theory—most acutely, in Marx's early doctrine regarding the alienation of labor. If anything in my treatment of "the public interest" suggests complacency about our present society and its material prosperity, I hope this footnote will serve to cancel the suggestion.

however, the temptation to pass from trying to understand "the public interest" to trying to solve all our problems at once can be resisted.

Let us imagine a specific proposal, which has been put forward with the intention of relieving congestion in a certain city and envisages building new roads, closing several central streets, limiting others to one-way traffic, and moving the busiest shops out of the city center. Now assume that a number of offices and shops in the center put in motion schemes of expanding there. If these private schemes are realized, then more people and more cars will be attracted to the city center; and the plan of relief will be jeopardized, if not defeated entirely. The question thus arises, is it against the public interest to allow the offices and shops in the center to expand?

Part of the argument that doing so is against the public interest can be mustered on the basis of the recognized list of vital needs, as it stands. For one may hold that the traffic problem affects the safety of the public, and safety may be regarded as part of the recognized list. However, it is not clear that this is a very strong part of the argument, for slow-moving, congested traffic in the city may not be particularly dangerous to life and limb; fast traffic on crowded roads in the country is quite a different matter. At any rate, safety is not likely to be the whole of the argument.

Perhaps a more promising line—and one that reveals typical microprocesses of conceptual change—would be to try modifying existing subjects on the recognized list. A connection with the subject of health, for example, might be made by citing facts about smog and lung cancer and arguing that the fumes of congested traffic endanger the health of the public. This amounts to associating the given subject of health—the place of which on the recognized list, however formulated, is sure—with newly discovered medical hazards. Alternatively, one might try to stretch the received concept of health as a subject of public concern. It may be argued that the mental suffering and frustration felt by people who are continually trapped in traffic jams and crowded together on congested streets deserve as much attention as physical disease.

These two closely related, reciprocal techniques of stretch and assimilation show how the recognized list of needs—and hence the concept of the public interest—is constantly expanding at the microscopic level, quite independently of any grand questions about autonomous social goals. People are not ready straight-away, the first time the suggestion comes up, to treat mental health as a subject of public concern on an equal footing with physical health—as we can see from the fact that no notion of mental sanitation, which would help the present argument, has been developed. They are perhaps even skeptical of the first suggestions of a connection between automobile exhausts and smog and lung cancer. After a while, however, if suggestions of one or the other kind recur and multiply, a settled conviction spreads among the participants in politics. A given list of needs may stand all the while, but the content of these categories will have been enlarged, and so the concept of the public interest will have expanded.

It is a much trickier business trying to add a new category, which means trying to argue not so much that a recognized subject of public concern should be interpreted more liberally as that a certain new subject deserves as much attention as sub-jects already on the list. The possibility of giving alternative formulations, perhaps quite novel ones, of the recognized list of needs opens up an opportunity for doing this; but whether the opportunity can be successfully seized will depend on the validity with which one can claim that the electorate is ready to assent to having the public protected on the new subject, when it arises.

In the present case, one might argue that it is against the public interest to allow any undertakings that impair the ameni-ties of city life. This line of argument, again, may partly coincide with an attempt to modify and extend a received subject, that of recreation. Yet impressive as are the attractions of quietness—or if there must be noise, of eliminating the oppressive blur of traf-fic noises—and the pleasures of easy strolling and unobstructed views in uncluttered streets, there may be some awkwardness in connecting them with recreation as hitherto understood. Setting aside some land for parks is one thing; transforming the heart and business of a city in the name of recreation is something much more radical.

Moreover, one must not assume that the taste for these pleasures is universally shared; and this is what makes adding the subject of amenities tricky. Of the many people who like the noise and bustle of cities, some may actually feel that they suffer very little from delays and obstructions in traffic compared with the glorious pleasures of hearing it roar around them. Even those people who, on balance, dislike congestion and sincerely deplore it are not necessarily to be counted on the side of a plan to reduce traffic. For they may prefer being able to initiate and terminate journeys in their own vehicles, however much they are slowed up by congestion, to having to depend on scheduled buses and trains. As for the amenities of city life, they may value an air-conditioned car above any of them.

The existence of people with such tastes among the electorate, if they exist in substantial numbers, weakens the case for holding that it is against the public interest to allow further expansion in the city center and in the public interest to adopt the plan of relief. If these people are actually in a majority, the grounds for invoking the concept of the public interest are weakened to the point of collapse. For then it is an irreducible fact that the electorate is not ready to concede that the public, as constituted for this or any other similar question, needs to be protected on the subject of civic amenities.

Yet I think some footing can always be found for the reference to the public interest. First, it may be contended that though a substantial number, even a majority, of the electorate now feel hostile to the plan of relief, because they prefer other objects of policy and are indifferent to the subject of amenities, this feeling will change as the congestion grows worse and the benefits of such plans become more widely realized. This does not give as much foundation for invoking the public interest as the present preferences of the electorate would—but it is some foundation, and since we are dealing with the growing end of the concept, where the recognized list is expanding, future preferences have a natural claim to be considered.

Of course, this proleptic or predictive use of "the public interest" may be quite mistaken in the circumstances; it may, in fact, not be true that (so far as we can see) the preferences of the electorate are going to change in the way alleged so that assent to the subject of amenities will be obtained. Yet the reference to the public interest, though weakened still further, may still be saved. For, second, it may be argued that (though the present trend of events does not make it likely), still, if the electorate were subjected—or, by a series of choices, subjected itself—to a certain series of experiences, then the recognized list of needs would change along with popular assent so that the public interest was on the side of the traffic plan, because accepted objects of policy had changed, rather than on that of the schemes of expansion that would obstruct it.

This future hypothetical claim, the claim of last resort in the deflated pattern, may amount to very little. Probably one could always work out at least one series of choices and experiences that would lead to the required distribution of sentiments in the electorate; it might, on occasion, be a very long series, but nothing has been said to exclude that. But all sorts of alternative series, leading to quite different sentiments regarding the amenities of city life might be specified; and the result of each of these would have an equally good title to display the assent of the electorate. Choosing between these series, and thus between results that will affect the meaning of the public interest differently, looks suspiciously like a grandiose choice between social goals.

When I say "very little," however, I do not mean to suggest that the hypothetical future claim amounts to nothing. It would be quite proper to insist that each of the choices involved in any series would fall within the bounds of the procedures for expressing popular choice; and so the claim means at least that the community can arrive by democratic procedures at a position where the public interest is categorically on the side of closing the city center to traffic, for the sake of amenities alone. The more chance there is of initiating this series and arriving at this result, the more substantial the claim; and making the claim is at least a step toward initiating it, an exhortatory preliminary.

The hypothetical future claim may be taken to imply further that none of the choices in the series would be against the public interest in the sense of endangering present public institutions (apart from desirable reforms) or in the sense of producing sufferings in respect to the subjects already included in the recognized list of vital needs. So the claim amounts to predicting that a revolution in tastes can be brought about within the moving limits of the deflated pattern, and without offending against any of the subjects of public concern established at the closed end of the spectrum. This does not seem to me to be a negligible claim, though it is not likely to determine on which route we should travel—this or another equally qualified—or toward what goal.

12

A LAWMAN'S VIEW
OF THE PUBLIC INTEREST

JULIUS COHEN

Since what David Braybrooke has to say about the future of "the public interest" stems primarily from an analysis of the semantics of the concept, it might be helpful to check his basic assumptions against the use of the term by those who, perhaps more than any other group, employ the concept "public interest" as an integral part of their professional vocabulary. I refer, of course, to the lawmen. When vagueness and ambiguity beset constitutional and statutory language, thus depriving lawmen of positive legal anchorage for the support of a policy position before a court, they are apt to employ the concept of public interest in argument. The same is true of arguments before legislative committees, where technical legal language is stripped to a bare minimum and considerations of public interest are nakedly out in the open.

What does this term mean to judicial and legislative lawmakers who take the concept seriously, and not merely as a cheap rhetorical device to soften the impact of decisions reached on narrower grounds? Aside from its use as a phrase of art, such as in the Federal Communications Act, or in the oft-used concept "business affected with a public interest," it is, I submit, used in a dual sense: first, in a logical sense—i.e., to explicate the *meaning* of the established basic values of the community. Thus, it would be in the public interest to pursue a certain goal because it would be consistent with the *meaning* of a basic community value. Second, it is used in an instrumental sense—i.e., that a policy would be in the public interest if its consequences would implement one or more of the established basic values of the community. Implicit in the expression "established" is the fact that it would *not* be in the public interest to destroy them—thus the conservative role of the concept. But, the question might be asked: What community? If the community is the font of the values, it is the values which, at the same time, define the scope and membership—i.e., the outer bounds, as well as the internal configurations, of the community. In the eyes of the legal profession, the outer bounds are usually drawn on politico-geographic lines, ranging in size and importance from nation to state to town. Where there is a conflict in the values of the different communities, they are the values of the community considered to be on the highest rung of the hierarchical ladder that prevail. Implicit in this concept of community is a system of basic values which bind together and weld diverse human forces and relationships into an ordered way of life. The material that binds need not be of unpliable steel or cement; tough elastic capable of absorbing permutation and change can still sustain and outline an ordered structure. Nor are these values held by some impersonal mystic entity called "community." They are values held by humans; they concern the relational aspects of man in his social capacity; they are shared by humans, and in this sense take on the aspect of common or community values. The basic values may relate to substance as well as to the rules of the game—e.g., to ideals of human well-being, to fundamental methods for achieving them, and to basic procedures for resolving disputes when disagreement and conflict concerning means as well as ends arise. They ultimately determine what satisfactions are to be sought, who are to be satisfied, and at whose expense. The basic values need not have originated from all or most of the members of the community; indeed, as is more likely, they spring from the more articulate and influential within it. What makes them community values is acquiescence in them by its members, either overtly, implicitly, reluctantly, or by default.

When it is urged that it would be in the public interest to grant a right to remain silent before congressional committees, what is suggested is that it would be consistent with the meaning of the Bill of Rights. This is the logical use of the concept. When it is urged that it would be in the public interest to outlaw deceptive television commercials, what is meant is that it would, among other things, protect the consumer without destroying the system of private enterprise. In this sense, the concept is used instrumentally. Granted this view of the concept, it would make little sense to limit it to those cases in which "a person, or firm, or relatively small group of people with special interests is arrayed against 'the public' "—if by this is meant only those cases in which the interest of the public at large is sought to be protected against the unscrupulous few. For it would deny application of the concept in those instances in which the public might be arrayed against a small scrupulous group of people in a manner not in keeping with the basic values of the community. To suggest, for example, that the public interest would not be involved if the Jehovah's Witnesses were denied freedom of expression by a statute supported by a majority of the population would fly seriously in the face of experience. For our community values include not only concern for the majority but, under certain circumstances, for the minority as well. Our values have a qualitative as well as a quantitative dimension. To put it another way, there is a public interest in the private rights of those who elect not to follow the crowd, because it is consistent with one of our basic community values. Accordingly, it is difficult to comprehend the basis for permitting only certain conflict situations the privilege of this conceptual garb. *All* conflict situations which call for government action—no matter what the specific nature of the configurations—invite a consideration of community values, and hence of the public interest. They *may* involve situations in which so-called "special" interests are arrayed against the quantitative bulk of the community. But to limit the concept to this conflict pattern alone would, in my judgment, place an unwarranted crimp upon its usage. If, however, Braybrooke means to include in this limitation cases in which *any* group, no matter what size, is arrayed against another, then the limitation serves no operational function as a "limitation"—for it would encompass virtually *all* areas of legal control.

In his resolve further to narrow the concept of the public interest and to implement what he has chosen to call the "Deflated Pattern," Braybrooke suggests that it be limited to issues of domestic and internal concern, and to those issues with respect to which "responsibility for action and inaction lies exclusively with the government." The first proposed limitation is in keeping with legal usage. The second, however, provides no workable standard at all, for potentially the responsibility for *all* areas of *in*action may be considered within the exclusive domain of government.

A further suggested limitation would differentiate "the public interest" from such considerations as "humanity, justice, and freedom." But the difference between "the public interest" and these other concepts is not in substantive content but rather in function. They are not *competing* concepts, as is suggested; they are concepts that complement each other. "Humanity, justice, and freedom," whatever the specific meaning of this cluster of terms, constitute part of the community's scheme of basic values which it is in the public interest to implement. The cluster is an abstract expression of ends; "public interest" is either a conclusion concerning the efficacy of means, or a shorthand expression to the effect that the chosen ends are consistent with the established basic values of the community.

Accordingly, if the concept "the public interest" is not a *comprehensive* consideration to lawmen, it is not so because of *all* the reasons advanced by Braybrooke. It is so primarily because its scope is limited by politico-geographic considerations which govern the demarcation of "community." And if it is not a *supreme and insuperable* consideration, it is not because it is "displaced and superseded" by other considerations, such as "humanity, justice, and freedom." For, although they are on a very high level of abstraction, they are expressions of values which it is in the public interest to implement.

In putting substantive flesh on the bare bones of his deflated pattern concept, Braybrooke has chosen to employ the inductive case method so familiar to the legal profession. In so doing, however, it is not clear whether he is reporting what he has found concerning current usage or whether he is advocating a special application of the term by hypothetical example. If the former, it is subject to challenge; if the latter, the purpose of the advocacy is not disclosed. If it is to promote clarity and precision of analysis, it is, I regret to say, quite wanting—at least to lawmen. Let us look at his examples. According to Braybrooke, "Whenever a danger arises, we shall leap to the defense," is an expression of policy that would fit his definition of public interest. But danger to what? And what is meant by "leap" and "defense"? *Any* policy in which someone's freedom to do as one wishes is curtailed by government must be based on some danger to others. Otherwise why regulate it to begin with? If the "others" succeed in incorporating their policy into law, is this an example of "leaping" and "defense"?

A second example: It is alleged to be in the public interest to permit normal legal procedures—e.g., confrontation of witnesses and cross-examination—unless the "safety of the state" is involved. But what is "the state" and the conditions of its "safety?" Are the basic procedures which assure human rights part of the apparatus called "the state"? Is "the state" endangered when a part of its basic apparatus is threatened? A third example: It is *not* in the public interest, according to Braybrooke, to permit exorbitant drug profits at the expense of those who need medical care, if the profits are not reasonably related to incentives for research; it is in the public interest if it is so reasonably related. This is a bit more incisive in its attempt to detail a basic community value, but it suffers from a lack of operational clarity. Must it, for example, be related to incentives for discovery and invention in the drug area, or to incentive generally? Incentive now; or in the future? Would the same norm be applicable to profit making through speculation with drug stocks on the stock market? A final example: It would be in the public interest, it is asserted, not to strike where the deleterious effect upon the public would be beyond a "tolerable level" or would be "disastrous" to the public. Without some notion of what is "tolerable" or "disastrous," the meaning of "public interest," in Braybrooke's sense of the term, remains somewhat in limbo.

I must confess a bit of discomfiture at finding myself in a state of doubt and uncertainty in the face of unhesitating assertions by Braybrooke that the solutions to these problems, which face up to the substantive implementation of "the public interest," are "quite clear" or "quite straightforward."

Nor does the spectrum theory which is advanced provide any special illumination for the lawman. What it does is merely formalize what the lawman has always assumed: that at one end of the spectrum are community values that are established with relative firmness; at the other end there are inarticulate value gropings which await crystallization. The lawman's conservative penchant for seeking anchorage in the given, and his inventiveness in adapting the new to the old, testify to his long awareness of the value spectrum.

Now, what about the future of "public interest"? Braybrooke foresees a "crisis" in that we have reached a stage of goallessness. "We," meaning the public, do not know just where we wish to go, hence we do not know where we want the government to go; our society is suffering from that dread sociological disease called anomie; since we are fast becoming a public without an interest, it is feared that the concept of the public interest, like the whooping crane, is facing extinction. But I do not share Braybrooke's despair. For the lawmen have a vested interest in "the public interest" as an operational concept: They would be tongue-tied without it. Accordingly, as long as there are lawmen, the concept will flourish. Being so hardy and indispensable a lot, it can be said with reliance that the concept of the public interest which to them is a vocabulary must will have a bright and secure future. Although the interest of the public might be jaded or directionless at the moment, trust the lawmen to argue that it still would be in the public interest to retain what the public already has until it has discovered what it is that might be better. And, until more exact methods are devised and utilized for recording changes in values, and for translating what is, at bottom, individual and incommensurate into something called "community values," the concept of public interest will still function to embellish public goals forged by our more traditional tools and techniques.

13

IS THERE A PUBLIC INTEREST THEORY?

GLENDON SCHUBERT

My investigation has been concerned primarily with the usages of the public interest concept to be found in the writings of political scientists during the last three decades. Although I recognize that members of our profession have no copyright on the term, and that, indeed, the uses of the concept by nonpolitical scientists are doubtless of vastly greater significance—at least if one is to measure importance in terms of what goes on in the world—than its appropriation and exemplification in our professional literature, nevertheless, I believe that there is a justification (other than that of convenience) to support the sample that I have chosen to examine. Without any intention of denigrating our professional reputation as a group of, shall we say, independent thinkers, I think it is fair to assume that a broad sampling of political science writings of the past generation is likely to reflect with reasonable faithfulness the larger universe of meanings attributed to the public interest concept in the behavior of American society—and I mean by this to include specifically, of course, American *political* society, which is the relevant body of data with which one must be concerned if he is interested in the contemporary theory of the public interest in the United States.

In a brief paper, it is manifestly impossible for me to discuss the data upon which my findings and conclusions are based.[1] I shall therefore direct my remaining remarks to a brief summary of my own classification of public interest theorists, and to an even briefer summary of the research of other critics of public interest theory.

I

In the larger study from which these conclusions are drawn, I have employed two principal bases for classifying the data, which consist of theoretical statements about the public interest in various kinds of decision-making situations.

First, I have identified five types of roles relating to decision making by the national government; I have limited the analysis to the national level of government for the purpose of simplicity. The first of these, which I call the "constituency" factor, involves political decision making by persons who are not public officials: the public, political parties, and interest groups. Congress, the Presidency, administrators (including regulatory commissioners), and the judiciary comprise the other four factors; obviously, these are all *official* decision makers.

The other major basis for classifying the data borrows from a conceptual scheme suggested by Wayne A. R. Leys, in an article in which he took issue with the orthodox theory of administrative discretion that had dominated thinking in the field of administrative law for the preceding half-century—and that, indeed, continues to hold sway in the writings of lawyers and political scientists alike. The godfather of orthodoxy was Ernst Freund, formerly Professor of Law at the University of Chicago, who taught that the solution to the problem of the official endowed with discretionary powers was to increase the *definiteness* of legal standards ("legal," in this context, meaning primarily statutes and administrative rules). The essence of Leys' critique is that Freund had oversimplified the problem by dealing with only one aspect of it. Leys himself would distinguish three classes

---

[1] The data are presented and discussed at length in my book, *The Public Interest: A Critique of the Theory of a Political Concept* (1961).

of discretionary powers: (1) technical discretion, which is freedom in prescribing the rule but not the criterion or end of action, (2) discretion in prescribing the rule of action *and also* in clarifying a *vague* criterion—this is the authorization of social planning, and (3) discretion in prescribing the rule of action where the criterion of action is *ambiguous* because it is in dispute—this amounts to an instruction to the official to use his ingenuity in political mediation.[2]

I have adapted Leys' basic system of classification in the following way. I shall divide contemporary theorists of the public interest in governmental decision making into three groups: rationalists, idealists, and realists. The rationalists, who correspond to Leys' first category, envisage a political system in which the norms are all given, in so far as public officials are concerned, and the function of political and bureaucratic officials alike is to translate the given norms into specific rules of governmental action. The idealists, who correspond to Leys' second category, conceive of the decision-making situation as requiring the exercise of authority in order to engage in social planning by clarifying a vague criterion. The realists are the counterpart of Leys' third category; these theorists state that the function of public officials (both political and bureaucratic) is to engage in the political mediation of disputes; the goals of public policy are specific but in conflict. Both the rationalists and the realists are opposed to the idealists, in the sense that both groups are positivists; but there are important differences in their respective theories of the public interest, and retaining Leys' classification system is of considerable help in discriminating among the differences.

II

The rationalists are a propublic, proparty, and anti-interest group. They postulate a common good, which reflects the presumed existence of various common—frequently majoritarian—interests. The common good (or commonweal, to use the

---

2 Wayne A. R. Leys, "Ethics and Administrative Discretion," *Public Administration Review,* 3 (1943), 18.

older term) finds expression in a popular will (public will, will of the people); the common obligation of all public officials is faithfully to execute the popular will. To this extent, there is consensus among rationalists. Differences of opinion are many, however, as to the appropriate channels for authentic interpretation of the public will. Basically, there are two factions: party rationalists and popular rationalists. Party rationalists defend a stronger two-party system as the chosen instrument for expressing the public will; popular rationalists would do away with political brokers and consult public opinion directly in order to discover the will of the people. Party rationalists tend to be Anglophiles with regard to the political party system, the relationship between legislators and political parties, the relationship between the executive and the legislative departments. (Incidentally, the model of British political processes envisaged by the Anglophiles bears no necessarily close correspondence to contemporary reality.) The party rationalists urge, therefore, that congressmen ought to be the disciplined members of a majority or a minority party, with the two parties dividing over issues of public policy. Popular rationalists think that congressmen ought to carry out the wishes of their constituents.

The Anglophiles believe that the Presidency should be weakened and subjected to the control and policy direction of Congress, which they have already defined as the legitimate expositor of the public will. Other party rationalists, however, would link presidential leadership to a stronger two-party system, thus strengthening the Presidency. Popular rationalists would accomplish the same result by casting the president in the role of instrumental leader of direct popular majorities. At this point, the distinction between party and popular rationalists disappears, because all rationalists agree that the proper function of the bureaucracy is to carry out the policy norms supplied by hierarchical superiors (Congress and the president). Administrative rationalists would use scientific management to rationalize the behavior of administrators; legal rationalists would accomplish the same result among judges according to the prescriptions of analytical jurisprudence. In both instances, administrators and judges are supposed to exercise technical discretion to carry out norms which they do not make, but which are supplied to them in the form of constitutional provisions, statutes, and executive orders—made, of course, by the representatives of the people, who implement the public will. There is a schism among rationalists regarding how best to rationalize the independent regulatory commissions; administrative rationalists want to place the commissions within the ambit of presidential control, and legal rationalists want the commissions to be subject to the administrative direction of the judiciary. Either way, it is variously argued, the commissions would become subservient to the will of the people, and the common good would be assured.

The idealists are propublic, antiparty, and anti-interest group. By "propublic," I mean, of course, that idealists support the true interests of the public, which do not necessarily coincide with the interests of the public as perceived by the public itself. Idealists believe that the public interest reposes not in the positive law made by men, but in the higher law, in natural law. They describe the public interest as a thing of substance, independent of the decisional process and absolute in its terms. They advise the public official to excogitate the true essence of the public interest by means of a mental act of extrasensory perception. This does not necessarily imply communion with the public will, because no will may yet have been formulated regarding the relevant issues; in any event, there is no assurance that the public will will be right. The public interest becomes whatever the still, small voice of conscience reveals to each official.

Such an approach renders superfluous, if not downright dangerous, such orthodox appurtenances of democratic politics as political parties and interest groups. These latter are perceived as disturbing interferences with official excogitation of truth, virtue, and justice. According to idealist thought, congressmen are responsible neither to political parties nor to their constituencies; they have a higher obligation to God and to their own consciences. Those who advocate converting the Presidency into a plebiscitary dictatorship emphasize the evils of party influence; proponents of the stewardship theory of the Presidency wish to surmount the pernicious demands of selfish special interest groups. In either case, the president is urged to rise above the mundane level of democratic political processes and to become the Father of his Country, the patron of all of the people, a leader of crusades both at home and abroad who should receive love and adulation—not criticism—from his subjects.

The same images recur in idealist discussion of administrative decision making. Administrative engineers advise administrators to be creative manipulators and to resist the seductions of interest groups. Guild idealists warn—almost in the words of Madison—of the danger of party politics, and demand that administrators be given elbowroom for the exercise of craft and conscience. Substituting judges for administrators, equivalent prescriptions are offered by the spokesmen for sociological jurisprudence and scientific idealism, respectively. Thus, the themes which permeate idealist public interest theory are the invocation of natural-law ideals; hostility to the instrumentalities of democratic politics—i.e., political parties and interest groups; elitist notions of superior intelligence and wisdom; and the abetment of public officials, from the president on down, to become aggressive evangelists who will strive mightily—and ruthlessly, if necessary—in behalf of the public interest. The public interest, of course, is what the elite thinks is good for the masses. Idealist dogma, as dogma, is basically antithetical to democratic theories of governance.

The realists are a prointerest group. It is not accurate to say that they are antiparty or antipublic. However, they define "party" and "public" in such a way that these terms lose the identity that we have ascribed to them in discussing rationalist and idealist thought, to say nothing of their usual, everyday meaning in American speech. Political parties become merely a special kind of interest group, and "public" becomes segmented as "publics," in which form it, too, merges in the concept of "interest group." The realists, in other words, do not oppose the public and political parties; they devour them.

There are three major strands of realist theory, and as befits a pattern of thought so colored with pluralism, the three major strands are each primarily oriented to one or more of the other social sciences. Bentleyan realism draws predominantly upon the outmoded sociology of the turn of the century; the source of inspiration for psychological realism is self-evident; and law and economics are the wellsprings for due process-equilibrium realism.

The Bentleyans direct attention to the competition among multifarious interest groups and assert that this is the reality of political behavior at all levels of governmental (as well as non-governmental) decision making. The official responds to these pressures; his decisions register the thrust of the balance of power for the time being. It makes no difference whether the decision maker is a congressman, the president, an administrator, or a judge; his role is essentially the same, although the patterns of access and the particular constellations of groups that enter the lists will vary according to the institutional context in which the official decision maker functions. To the Bentleyans, the public interest has significance only as the slogan which symbolizes the compromise resulting from a particular accommodation or adjustment of group interaction.

Psychological realists go beyond the essentially mechanical formulations of the Bentleyans, and focus attention upon the conflict of interests within the mind of the decision maker. The rather fuzzy Bentleyan notion of unorganized groups is redefined by the psychological realists in terms of Dewey's concept of a self-conscious search for the consequences of choice. Thus, the role of official mediation described by the psychological realists adds a significant factor to the formulations of the Bentleyans: the personal value system of the decision maker. He is limited, of course, to the values that he understands and recognizes, but he is not necessarily limited to the values with which he personally agrees. His acceptance of such broad components of the democratic ethic as the concepts of "freedom, equality, and opportunity" may lead him to take into consideration interests other than those actively pressing in behalf of specific alternatives of choice in a particular decision.

At this point, the line between psychological realism and social engineering may seem to be pretty shadowy, but the distinction is nonetheless viable. The social engineers write on a blank slate: creative manipulation leads to the fabrication of any interest group pattern needed to support the predetermined goals established by the decision maker. Official mediation looks to the interstices of a framework provided by the interaction of activated groups and asks what the effect would be, upon this pattern, if certain other interests were weighed in the final decision. In this sense, the official mediator functions as a catalyst; but since the critical conflict is internal to the decision maker rather than in the external environment, psychological realism's search for consequences is a more operational concept than Bentley's mystical notion of the leadership of unorganized groups. Nevertheless, both are different ways of thinking about the same processes.

As we have seen, psychological realists apply the concept of official mediation to congressmen, the president, administrators, and judges alike. There is a close functional relationship, however, among politicization, constituency size, and the limits of official horizon. In Harlan Cleveland's image, the president stands a little higher on the mountain than anyone else, and consequently can see further; district court justices and subordinate administrators, presumably, have much more limited horizons. But what of the Supreme Court? Are the justices on a separate alp? I do not think a meaningful answer to this question is possible at the present stage of underdevelopment in the measurement of power by the political science profession; but the question raises doubts, in any event, about the application of Cleveland's hierarchical image, rather than about psychological realism's concept of official mediation.

The next logical step beyond psychological realism is to prestructure the environment of decision making and to condition the mental processes of the decision maker. It is to these matters that the due process realists call attention. Although all realists premise their theories of the public interest upon a philosophy of ethical relativism, rather than the absolutism characteristic of rationalists and idealists, the due process-equilibrium realists lean most heavily upon what is, at least crudely, a mathematical probability theory. According to the theory, people accept democratic decision-making processes because these provide the maximum opportunity for diverse interests to seek to influence governmental decisions at all levels. A plurality of decision-making points afford access to a plurality of interests, which can seek to change or to provoke particular decisions. The job of official decision makers—irrespective of whether we speak of congressmen, the president, administrators, or judges—is to maximize continuity and stability in public policy, or, in other words, to minimize disruption in existing patterns of accommodation among affected interests. The extent to which agitation continues, before the same or other decision makers, provides a rough measure of the extent to which adjustment has, in terms of the equilibrium standard, been successful or "satisfactory."

Now this kind of thinking is quite conservative in its general overtones. It underscores the adjectives in advocating gradual, peaceful, evolutionary, orderly change. It does not tilt, it slants, the scales of judgment in favor of the status quo. The votaries of liberalism preach a brand of ethics in which most Americans feel they ought to believe; but it is not a way of life, nor is it the basis for our system of government. It is the Constitution, not the Declaration of Independence, that provides the model for the American political system. The general model leaves largely unspecified, however, the structure and functioning of decision-making processes in Congress, the Presidency, administrative agencies, and the courts. It is particularly upon administrative decision-making processes that the due process-equilibrium realists have focused their attention.

Instead of leaving the "representativeness" of the administrator's personal value system, or the particular configuration of interests in a specific type of decision, up to chance, due process theory would so structure both of these factors in the decision-making process as to maximize the probability that the resulting decision has been made, in fact, after consideration of all relevant interests and perspectives. Due process theorists do not claim that any particular substantive result will automatically be the "right" decision; they do not guarantee that every decision arrived at after such full consideration will be "in the public interest." This is the point that seems so difficult for absolutists, who live in a world of dichotomies, to comprehend. What the due process theorists do claim is that decisions reached as a result of such full consideration are more likely to meet the test of equilibrium theory—i.e., "satisfaction," acceptance, and the like—

and to do so most of the time, than are decisions arrived at as the necessary consequence, at least in a statistical sense, of processes that assure less than full consideration. *Decisions that are the product of a process of full consideration are most likely to be decisions in the public interest.*

There has been some, but very limited, application of the concept of "administrative due process" to congressional, presidential, and judicial decision making. Although some critics have decried placing "the organization man in the Presidency," the fact remains that the applicability of the model of "administrative due process" to these other decision makers is a function of bureaucratization of congressional, presidential, and judicial decision-making processes. Certainly, there is considerable evidence to support the proposition that the trend in each of these areas is towards greater bureaucratization. To this extent, the potential extension of the public interest theory of the due process-equilibrium realists is correspondingly enhanced.

III

Two decades elapsed after Beard's historical studies of the national interest as a concept, before any systematic analyses of the public interest concept appeared in the literature of political science. Beginning in 1955, however, several political scientists and philosophers have ventured independent (from each other, and from my own work) exploratory critical essays on the subject of public interest theory. A survey of the findings of these critics suggests, however, that they have little to add to the results of my own investigation of public interest theory. Some of them (e.g., Banfield, Sorauf, Leys and Perry) suggest differing perspectives from which the literature may be viewed and appraised. Such alternative formulations do not appear to lead to insights or to comprehension of public interest theory significantly different from that produced by the conceptual schema that I have employed, however. Any systematic typology may have utility for analytical purposes, but no matter how the literature is classified and the data are compared, no systematic body of "public interest theory" appears extant. American writers in the field of political science have evolved neither a unified nor a consistent theory to describe how the public interest is defined in governmental decision making; they have not constructed theoretical models with the degree of precision and specificity necessary if such models are to be used as description of, or as a guide to, the actual behavior of real people. A theory of the public interest in governmental decision making ought to describe a relationship between concepts of the public interest and official behavior in such terms that it might be possible to attempt to validate empirically hypotheses concerning the relationship. If extant theory does not lend itself to such uses, it is difficult to comprehend the justification for teaching students of political science that subservience to the public interest is a relevant norm of official responsibility.

Moreover, critical investigation has failed to reveal a statement of public interest theory that offers much promise as a guide either to public officials who are supposed to make decisions in the public interest or to research scholars who might wish to investigate the extent to which governmental decisions are empirically made in the public interest. For either of the latter purposes, it would be necessary to have operational definitions of the public interest concept; and neither my analysis nor that of other contemporary critics suggests that the public interest theory prevalent in America today either is or is readily capable of being made operational.

IV

Rationalist theory has limited relevance to the empirical world, since it speaks primarily of faithful execution of decisions that somebody other than the actor has made; it offers little guidance to the decision maker who is expected to make policy in the face of the conflicting demands of an articulate and organized clientele. In fact, the more important the decision—and as a usual consequence, the more complex the decision-making milieu—the less guidance has rationalist theory to offer. It might, for instance, indicate what would be responsible presidential behavior in signing commissions for the promotional lists of the

armed forces; it most certainly will not be very helpful to the
president in deciding whether and how to get a man to the
moon. To get back down to earth, it will not even tell him when,
and in terms of what criteria, he should exercise his veto power,
since the Constitution clearly did not presume that the president
would take his orders from Congress (or vice versa) in exercising
his power to grant or to withhold his approval of enrolled bills
—even if we assume, with the rationalists, that constitutional
intent is the fundamental consideration in such circumstances.
The theoretical apparatus of the rationalists, however elegant it
otherwise may be, is limited precisely by their insistence that a
science of political behavior cannot be concerned with political
choice. The model constructed by the rationalists is a sausage
machine: the public will is poured into one end and out of the
other end drop neat little segments of the public interest, each
wrapped in its own natural casing.

Idealist theory, to the contrary, speaks precisely to the macroscopic type of decision with which the rationalists cannot be
concerned. But what does idealism have to offer, other than
moralistic exhortations to do good? It leaves the decision maker
to rely upon his own best lights whether these are conceived of
as a Platonic soul, a Calvinistic conscience, or as Catholic natural
law. It may be that any of these provides the best standards
available for guiding some decision makers in some situations;
but labeling as "the public interest" either such a process or the
result that it produces adds nothing to what we would have—
except from the point of view of the engineering of consent—if
there were no such phrase as the public interest. With or without
the label, we must rely upon the prior political socialization
and the ethical preconditioning of the individual decision maker
for whatever kind or degree of responsibility that ensues in such
circumstances.

Moreover, the concept of the public interest logically is irrelevant to decision making in accordance with idealist theory,
in which ultimate obligations and responsibility are nonpolitical.
It is neither to the public nor to hierarchical superiors nor to
the affected clientele that the decision maker looks for guidance;
his responsibility lies in faithfulness to his personal perception

of other abstractions, such as "justice," that are at least equally
as devoid of a predictable content as "the public interest." Unless
the idealists are prepared to advocate the "brainwashing" of
candidates for public employment to assure the establishment of
a single party line among government officials, the practical
utility of their theory would seem to be quite limited unless, in
the alternative, they can explain how men with differing value
orientations are to commune with the infinite and come up with
common answers. Idealist theory really implies an officialdom of
supermen, which in turn evokes all the difficulties to be encountered in breeding a race of official heroes—or, if it makes a
difference, of heroic officials. None of the idealist writers in recent
years seem to have improved very much upon Plato's discussion
of this subject, nor do they appear to have resolved the age-old
dilemma: how to keep the tyrants benevolent.

Realists advise the decision maker that his job is to resolve
the conflicting claims of competing interest groups, and to keep
the boat from rocking so far as possible. Except on the merely
mechanical and purportedly descriptive level of naive Bentleyan-
ism, he should do this with as much consideration as he is capable
of giving, or as he can be made capable of giving—by the structur-
ing of the decision-making situation—to the probable consequences of his choice. The principal difficulty with the theory,
even in its most sophisticated form, lies in its generality, for the
due process-equilibrium realists describe wondrous engines (including the human mind) into which are poured all sorts of
miscellaneous ingredients which, after a decent period of agitation, are spewed forth from time to time, each bearing a union
label reading: "Made in the Public Interest in the U.S.A." But
their hero is neither the Charlie Chaplin of modern times nor
Prometheus unbound; he is the counterpart of the politician
described by Herring in *The Politics of Democracy*.

The problem facing realist theorists is to demonstrate how it
is possible to bridge the hiatus between the ideal they posit and
the empirical world. It is true that the statements of at least the
administrative-due process realists do suggest the possibility of
constructing more detailed models of specific decisional processes
in particular agencies with identifiable functions to perform.

Such models, whether as descriptions of existing agencies or as blueprints for reorganized or new agencies, might lend themselves, at least in principle, to empirical verification. Assuming, for the sake of argument, that the paperwork can be done, it would still be necessary to construct and implement, upon an experimental basis, at least one model prefabricated political decision-making process; budget estimating might be a good place to begin. Assuming that this also could be done, ahead lie questions of continuous reorganization to cope with predictable problems of obsolescence, the development of more genuinely interchangeable human cogs, and—not least—the impatience of the American public after it becomes known to the world that the Russians have perfected a successfully functioning (and much bigger) organization of the same type several months before the American protomodel is announced. And that announcement, we might as well anticipate, will come at the same time that the American team of responsible budget analysts is about to produce its first underbalanced budget—which will be made, needless to say, in the public interest.

V

It may be somewhat difficult for some persons to accept the conclusion that there is no public-interest theory worthy of the name and that the concept itself is significant primarily as a datum of politics. As such, it may at times fulfill a "hair shirt" function, to borrow Sorauf's felicitous phrase; it may also be nothing more than a label attached indiscriminately to a miscellany of particular compromise of the moment. In either case, "the public interest" neither adds to nor detracts from the theory and methods otherwise presently available for analyzing political behavior.

I recognize also that there may be some who will consider this paper incomplete, since I have criticized the public interest theories of other persons without making any attempt to "do something positive" by suggesting a public interest concept of my own. The expectation that the iconoclast ought to pick up the pieces and build a new and better temple on the ruins of the old runs like a steel thread through the moral fiber of most Americans, including academicians. I would dispute the premise. I would also argue, in any event, that if the public interest concept makes no operational sense, notwithstanding the efforts of a generation of capable scholars, then political scientists might better spend their time nurturing concepts that offer greater promise of becoming useful tools in the scientific study of political responsibility.

THE ONE AND THE MANY:
A NOTE ON THE CONCEPT

J. ROLAND PENNOCK

In this chapter I wish to deal briefly with two of the many issues clustering around the concept of "the public interest": (1) is it a valid concept? and if it is (2) is the public interest different from the sum of private interests? Many students have been led to question the usefulness and even, in some sense, the validity of the term because of its vagueness. Others seem to feel that it must have a single, precise meaning waiting to be found out and that if only we could discover it administrators, legislators, and others who are called on to act in the public interest would be aided in the performance of their duties. It appears to me that both are mistaken.

That the term is vague cannot be denied. For certain purposes this indeterminacy may deprive it of usefulness. But this is by no means to say that it is not a valid concept in the sense of one that conveys meaning. Our language and ability to communicate would be impoverished indeed if we were to outlaw all words and phrases that are inherently vague. Take the word "beauty." The dictionary definition confirms our intuitive recognition of its vagueness: "the quality attributed to whatever pleases or satisfies in certain ways, as by line, color, form, texture, proportion, rhythmic motion, tone, etc." Students of esthetics are in notorious disagreement as to what constitutes beauty. Yet when it is a matter of applying the concept to a particular kind of thing, or in a particular context, there is frequently wide agreement as to the appropriate standards. To take an example about which every man is his own expert, and yet on which there is a considerable measure of agreement at least within a given culture, consider the term "a beautiful woman." We may agree or disagree with the verdict of the judges of a beauty contest, but no one would dream of *defining* "a beautiful woman" proce- durally (or "operationally"), that is, as "one who wins a beauty contest"! Nor would one deny that there is such a thing as a beautiful woman. As a matter of fact, while even acknowledged experts may disagree as to which one of a bevy of beauties should be judged "Miss America" the measure of agreement far exceeds the range of conceivable dispute. We can be sure that the winner will not be one whose curves have turned to bulges, that her teeth will be regular and gleaming, her complexion clear, her nose straight, and so on and so forth.

And so it is with "the public interest": much of its vagueness disappears when it is placed in a specific context. Take the con- cept of a "business affected with a public interest." For many years this was a term of legal art, to which the courts gave a fairly clear and definite meaning. During most of the time between *Munn* v. *Illinois* (1877) and *Nebbia* v. *New York* (1934) it was only the marginal cases that provoked disagreement as to the meaning of public interest in this context. It was to be sure a somewhat artificial usage. Even in the heyday of the "businesses affected with a public interest" doctrine it would have made sense to argue (and it would have been admitted) that there was a public interest in some regulation (but not price fixing) of businesses not "affected with a public interest." But even for this extended usage there were acknowledged limits. Something of the nature of those limits during the period when a laissez-faire philosophy predominated in this country is suggested by the case of *Loan Association* v. *Topeka* (1874, 20 Wall. 655). Taxpayers could not be levied upon to provide a subsidy to bring a manu- facturer of iron bridges to Topeka because this was not for a "public purpose." "Private interest" was contrasted with "public use"; and the tests applied were similar to those used in the "business affected with a public interest" cases. It was recognized that in an indirect and remote way the location of a manufacturing concern in Topeka might serve a public purpose, but this was not enough. The concept, as it was then understood, called for a more direct and recognized service to the public to justify handing over taxpayers' money to what was, at least immediately, a private interest.

It is extremely unlikely that, if the same case were to be tried today, *de novo,* the same result would obtain. The ideological context has undergone radical change. Laissez-faire views have given way to a more positive concept of appropriate state activities, and the interest that was then felt to be too remote to be considered would in all likelihood now be felt sufficient to support a public purpose.[1]

The Federal Communications Commission, and many other licensing agencies, are directed to pursue the public interest in part by granting permits to conduct certain types of business when they find that "public convenience and necessity so require." The terms "convenience" and "necessity," thus paired, in themselves are hardly more specific than "interest." And it is true that such phrases do leave, and are intended to leave, the administering agencies wide discretion. Nonetheless the contexts of the regulatory purpose involved, of the governing statutes, and of administrative interpretations give more specific meaning. Thus at any given time the way in which a regulatory commission is to pursue the public interest, while open to dispute, is far more clearly defined than is the phrase "the public interest," considered *in vacuo.*

Sometimes we contrast the public interest with private rights. It is then the residuum after private rights are exhausted that part of the general welfare is not included in acknowledged private claims. What is it that is thus contrasted with the private?

---

1 However, as recently as 1936, the unreconstructed Supreme Court invalidated a food processing tax because the payment of subsidies to farmers for which it was earmarked was held not to be for "the general welfare." [U.S. v. Butler (1936) 297 U.S. 1.]

Something different? or only private interests that have not crystallized as "rights" or that might otherwise be overlooked? In other words, is the public interest more than the sum of private interests? About this question there seems to be much misunderstanding. I should like to hazard four propositions with which, on reflection, I believe there will be general agreement; and to suggest that they largely, if not wholly, eliminate the problem. First, the public interest is not confined to interests that are recognized by those whose interests they are. We frequently recognize that a person has interests (often calling them "real" interests) of which he is not aware or which he even denies. Even speed laws are partly in the interest of the very people whose activities they curb. Second, the public interest includes the interests of persons who are not yet born. How far the present generation should save for the benefit of its successors is always a difficult question. But nearly all parents have, and feel, an interest in providing for the future of their own children (living or prospective) at some expense to themselves. When society makes this choice, the problem is not essentially different. Both public interest and private interest, in other words, include future interests.

The last point suggests that private interests may be conceived narrowly or broadly and that when the public interest is said to include more than the sum of private interests it may be at least partly because private interests are at that moment being conceived rather narrowly. My third proposition grows out of this same fact. It is that private interests must be conceived as including the individual enjoyments, satisfactions, fulfillments, and so on that come only in and through society. When one thinks what a life of solitude would be like it is apparent that most of our interests are dependent upon society. And if we think of the pleasures of each other's company and of conjoint activity we see that many of our interests are directly social. Society, and its supporting structure, government, become the sources of satisfaction of so many of our interests that we even come to value them, as we say, for their own sakes. That is to say, we acquire an interest in the preservation and further development of society and government as essential means to the satisfaction of many different and more specific interests. As is frequently the case with such generic means to valued ends, we come to think of society and even of the state as valuable in themselves. Anything that injures the society or the state injures us. Yet of course the society, and specifically its government, may injure our personal interest in a way that makes us contrast the two.

Finally, however, I would say that anything that is part of the public interest must be capable of recognition by individuals as an interest that they share in the sense that they wish to see it furthered or think it ought to be furthered. Nor do I believe that this limitation rules out anything that those who protest against identifying the public interest with the sum of individual interests would think ought to be included.[2]

In summary, when anyone, whether judge, administrator, legislator, or private citizen, seeks to make a decision in accordance with the public interest, he must weigh a number of factors. He must consider the claims of private rights. These claims may appear as limitations upon the public interest, as when one tries to balance national security needs against the right of the individual to be able to cross-examine opposing witnesses; or they may appear as part of the public interest, as when the individual in the case just cited contends that it is in the public interest that the right to privacy or the right to fair trial be protected. When it is a matter of interpreting the law, he must consider the apparent purpose of the law and the lawmakers, the interests which the legislation appears to have been designed to protect or advance, the current notions of the "public interest" as applied to the matter at hand, and also his own ideas of the real interest of the public. Judges and others will differ as to the relative weights that ought to attach to these sometimes conflicting claims. Frankfurter will stress the conscience of the com-

---

2 Cf., for instance, Gerhard Colm, "In Defense of the Public Interest," *Social Research*, 27 (1960), 295-307. Actually, as appears at various points in his argument, what Colm is concerned about is the identification of "public interest" with the sum of individual "self-interests." But there is no reason for identifying "interest," with "self-interest." For an excellent discussion of this subject, emphasizing the inevitably normative quality of the term "interest," see S. I. Benn, "Interests in Politics," *Proceedings of the Aristotelian Society*, 60 N.S. (1959-1960), 123-140.

munity and Hand the conscience of the judge, while others will feel bound by the intention of the lawmakers, at least where that can be determined with any assurance. But few will deny all relevance to any one of these elements. Fewer still will claim that the weighing process is necessarily completely arbitrary, although the verdict may always be surrounded by a penumbra of doubt.

What then is the "public interest"? In general, it is a spur to conscience and to deliberation. It is a reminder that private rights are not exhaustive of the public interest and that private interests include much more than self-interests. A term that plays this role, even though it lacks precision, is as valuable as it is inescapable. Moreover, in many particular applications, the context of the situation gives the phrase greater definition. For such uses it has the special virtue that it serves as a receptacle for accumulating standards. A legislature that delegates to an administrative agency the power to regulate in accordance with the public interest is not merely "passing the buck"; it is providing the means for applying a dynamic and increasingly precise policy based on experience, continuing contact with special interests, and freedom to pursue the general welfare as they come to see it.

15

THE CONCEPTUAL MUDDLE

FRANK J. SORAUF

The vocabulary of politics very likely has more than its share of words and phrases whose definition lies obscured in a half-light of confusion and disagreement. Tag words such as "liberal" and "conservative" have achieved a notoriety of imprecision. Not only have they acquired a cumbersome baggage of special historical usages, but today their meaning often runs no deeper than political invective. But we are widely reassured that politics (and its study) is an art rather than a science, and that a certain genteel fuzziness—often masquerading as literary elegance —would not be out of place. As a consequence of their impressionistic study of politics and their desire to avoid recondite jargons, academic political scientists have adopted for their use much of this vocabulary of political debate and public affairs. Concepts such as that of the "public interest," therefore, reverberate both in legislative chambers and academic halls.

The propensity of political scientists to draw upon the vocabulary and concepts of everyday politics has, of course, spared their discipline an abstruse and grating jargon. Aside from the work of the "behaviorists," most of their writings are remarkably free of the polysyllabic conglomerates and esoteric usages that clog the literature of the rest of the social sciences, except history.

But readability and accessibility of language has often been bought at the price of failure to develop precise and operational concepts for scholarly analysis. Generalizations, theories, and even accurate description can be no stronger and no more valid than the concepts and definitions in which they are expressed. As David Easton has written:

> A science, it is often said, is as strong as its concepts; and if this is true, the vague, ill-defined concepts unfortunately so typical of research in political science reduce the discipline to a low position on a scale of maturity in the social sciences. It is the rule rather than the exception to find difficulty in referring political concepts back to the things to which presumably they refer.[1]

In its distaste for a specialized terminology, academic political science has probably underestimated its acceptability as well as its importance. Poets and literati, after all, write without embarrassment of spondees, trochees, dactyls, and iambs.

Easton's strictures apply to few concepts in political science as aptly as they do to the "public interest." Even in scholarly usage it has assumed an astounding variety of definitional hues and shades.[2] Generally it has come to mean some criterion or desideratum by which public policy may be measured, some goal which policy ought ideally to pursue and attain. But just *whose* standard it is to be remains the problem. It may variously be an ethical imperative (such as the natural law), some superior standard of rational and "right" political wisdom, or the goals or consensus of a large portion of the electorate. Or it may be some amalgam, some almost mystical balance of narrower interests in which the final product appears to be considerably greater than the sum of its "selfish" parts.

Moreover, the meaning of public interest has extended beyond the idea of a guiding goal for policy making. A number of writers

---

[1] *The Political System* (1953), p. 44.

[2] For a closer examination of the various meanings clinging to the public interest see Frank J. Sorauf, "The Public Interest Reconsidered," *Journal of Politics, XIX* (November 1957) 616-639, and Wayne A. R. Leys and Charner M. Perry, *Philosophy and the Public Interest* (1959), a discussion document prepared for The Committee to Advance Original Work in Philosophy. For a more general analysis of concepts of the public interest, see Glendon Schubert, *The Public Interest* (1960).

have identified it with the democratic political process of compromise and accommodation. Their public interest resides in the complex procedures of political adjustment and compromise which the democratic polity employs to represent and accommodate the demands made upon its policy-making instruments. Here the public interest as means and procedure replaces the public interest as end and goal, and one is left with an understanding of the public interest which has little to do with the wisdom or morality of public policy itself. Presumably, any policy evolved without violence or offense to the system is in the public interest; at the least, considerations of the public interest are irrelevant to it. Similarly, others have defined the public interest as a system of functional prerequisites for the operation of these accommodative processes; it here becomes a series of "the necessary conditions for the pursuit and enjoyment of interests, of the different institutional arrangements that are actually conditions for the pursuit of interests. . . ." [3]

In yet other hands the public interest assumes an elusive and ineffable content. In this regard Horace M. Gray has remarked:

> The concept of the "public interest," like the equally vague and undefinable common law "rule of reason," has validity and usefulness as a fictional device for the ordering of human affairs though we never quite succeed in defining it with scientific precision. [4]

This, then, is the public interest as a potent political myth, and as with any myth, its value rests in *not* defining it, in not drawing it out from the shrouds of mystery. By semantic shorthand the public interest also often reflects a congeries of unspecified ethical and rational interests which might be lost or disregarded in the policy-making process.

Clearly, no scholarly consensus exists on the public interest, nor does agreement appear to be in the offing. Not only do scholars disagree on the defining of the public interest, they disagree as well about what they are trying to define: a goal, a process, or a myth. Effective communication and cumulative scholarly work suffers inevitably. Add to this confusion the even greater

---

[3] *Philosophy and the Public Interest,* p. 24.
[4] Quoted in *Philosophy and the Public Interest,* p. 27.

imprecisions of the political arena—where public interest too often means, with or without elegant rationalizations, merely *my* interest—and the result is semantic chaos. Although semantic confusion may serve someone's short-run needs in political debate, scholarly discussion and analysis need better tools than this.

Undoubtedly one of the public interest's more fundamental infirmities—its confusion of the normative and the real—contributes to this definitional tangle. In much of contemporary usage public interest means an interest possessed by (and, presumably, at least dimly perceived by) "the public" or some segment of it; in this sense it is a real, empirically identifiable interest. And at the same time it refers to a goal in the interest (i.e., "best interests" or "enlightened self-interest") of the public, whether or not that public is or is not sufficiently enlightened to grasp it. So, the "is" and the "ought" are inextricably knotted together in this single phrase, the public interest.[5] The questions of the distribution, organization, strength, and tactics of interests consequently merge with questions which arise out of the rational and ethical evaluations of public policy objectives.

Granted that we will never achieve a completely "value-free" study of politics, there is a powerful argument to be made for determined attempts to achieve a maximum degree of separation of the two. Theories and generalizations about the political process must be built with terms and concepts as nearly free as possible of normative overtones and implications. By the same token, it seems to me, the normative issues of political choice will never be illuminated by little rubrics which establish without evidence certain postulates about the existential world. Concepts such as those of the public interest, which embrace both problems, do not bridge the gulf between the two. They merely confuse the valid distinction between them.

Involved, too, in this combination of the "is" and the "ought" is the matter of the democratic ethic. If one assumes in a democratic political system that what is desirable and ethical is also a "real" organized political interest, he judges unfavorably any

---

5 For an excellent discussion of this problem, see C. W. Cassinelli, "Some Reflections on the Concept of the Public Interest," *Ethics*, LXIX (October 1958), 48-61.

activities on behalf of competing interests. So to judge the competing interests in democratic politics denies the axioms that
each man is his own best judge of what he wants and that the
workings of the free political system will determine the final
priority of interests which will be enacted into policy. As soon
as one presumes to assess the ethical value of competing political
interests, he reduces democratic political choice to the choice
between public "right" and self-centered "wrong."

Beyond the confusion resulting from this alliance of "is" and
"ought," the public interest fosters more analytic confusion by
attempting to reconcile in an elusive catchword a series of very
troublesome conceptual issues. At its level of generality it em-
braces and smothers a number of questions touching political
interests, representation, and policy formation. It makes assumptions—all at once—about the nature and organization of political
interests, about the responsibility of elected representatives, and
about the making and administration of public policy. These are
all, needless to say, problems which have troubled the practitioners and theoreticians of politics since the first recorded stir-
rings of representative democracy. Just the single question of
whether the elected representative is to cater to the wishes and
mandates of his constituents, yield to the leadership of a party,
or assert his own vision of the goals of the good society remains
a troublesome one. It has been and ought to be continually
thought about and reflected on—but on its own terms and merits
rather than on the posited concept of representation underlying
someone's definition of the public interest.

These, then, are among the chief weaknesses the "public interest" has as a tool of scholarly inquiry. It has, however, been
argued that even though the term has restricted value to the
cloistered academician, it still maintains considerable usefulness
in the hurly-burly of the political arena. The world of politics
is widely thought to have its own standards of clarity and its
own rules of debate. Yet I am not at all sure why it should feel
any lesser need than the scholarly world for unambiguous concepts and precisely framed questions. Public interest confuses
general political debate to the same extent—and often for the
same reasons—that it confuses academic inquiry.

At its most primitive level in political debate public interest serves as little more than rationalization for some particular group's interest. The process of rationalization may be the very human and unconscious one of erecting one's personal goals and preferences into universals. Or it may involve the calculated design of propagandizing one's interests in the most pleasing possible light and in the most prestigious semantics. There is, indeed, a proper place for universals and ethical norms in political debate, but one may doubt that such a discourse is served by trading catchwords and assertions of virtue. To argue that one's interest ought to prevail because it is "in the public interest" only steers the argument into an unprofitably circular course.

No single criterion or standard, such as the public interest, can subsume or encompass all that is good and desirable for society—regardless of the system of values one prefers or propounds. The matter of the goals of a contemporary industrial society consists in reality of a series of specific, policy-centered questions which involve the entire range of our concern, from a realistic approach to the emerging nationalism of Africa, through care for the ill among the aged, to the resolution of domestic racial conflict and tension. The answers to these policy questions will be hammered out painfully and pragmatically, and they will certainly be expressed in alternatives and wisdom considerably more specific and vastly less grandiose than the all-encompassing guise of a "public interest." If one argues that a public interest exists in all these problem areas, and if he can go the next step and identify it, all well and good. But why then resort to a concept of the public interest?

There is also a school of thought which argues that the public interest can be defined on a level of abstraction high and broad enough to touch the universal goals of man—liberty, security, food, and shelter, for instance.[6] But these abstractions have little to do with problems of public policy, little to do with the issues of American politics. The question at the moment is not "security," but whether social security coverage ought to be extended, and if so, to whom and under what conditions. "Liberty" as

---

6 See *Philosophy and the Public Interest,* p. 23.

such is not at issue; we confront instead questions such as the jailing of individuals for refusing to answer the questions of legislative committees. If the public interest frames the political dialectic in terms of generally agreed upon symbols, the "binders" of political debate,[7] it keeps it at least one level of abstraction above the reality of actual political conflict and practical political alternatives.

The public interest promotes another oversimplification. It is no secret that Americans have long been uneasy over social and political conflict in American life. The institutions through which we wage our political conflict—parties, interest groups, "politicians"—bear a heavy burden of popular resentment for their imagined disruption and disregard of the unities of American life. As a symbol of unity and community in our politics, and as a warning to contending interests, public interest overrides the complex proliferation of interests in our political system and "solves" in one glib phrase the dilemmas of a political pluralism. Although no society gains from the exaggeration of conflict and disagreement, neither does it in the long run gain from myths which ignore legitimate differences of interest and imply that these interests are divisive and faintly antisocial. Certainly it does not profit from concepts which promote and encourage political cynicism.

Substantially these paragraphs have argued that the "public interest" works toward moralization and simplification in our political debates, even though the policy issues of concern to our democratic discussion are, to take Oscar Wilde from context, rarely pure and never simple. To reduce them to simple alternatives and black-white moralities does them the greatest violence. Nor is political maturity or the democratic ethic served by myths which ignore and deny the validity of opposing political aspirations. The practitioners of politics, just as the academic political scientists, need phrases and concepts which will clarify competing interests, separate the "is" from the "ought," shield the debate from undue moralism, and frame practicable and specific policy alternatives. Above all, they need intellectual tools

---

[7] Walter Lippmann, *Public Opinion* (1946), p. 163.

for discussing the morality and wisdom of political policy, not in vague moralizations and rationalizations, but in terms of identifiable results and consequences and in terms related to policy itself. The record of the public interest has been one of lifting political debate out of the realities of our political process and away from the complicated equities of its choices.

That the "public interest" has meaning for some public officials and interest groups is an incontestable fact. That it may in these terms affect the shaping and administration of public policy is equally incontestable. Observation of American politics will also afford instances of its effective use as a unifying symbol and a social myth. Even should scholars reject the public interest for their own analysis, they must observe and record its prevalence and influence in the political system. But it is only as political datum that the public interest has a definable relevance to the study of politics and public policy.[8]

The tools of the scholarly craft are words, concepts, and hypotheses, and what the craft produces can be no better than the tools with which the scholar works. Whereas imprecision, vagueness, and mythology may serve some strategic purpose in the world of affairs, they contribute nothing to the formulation of valuable generalizations and theories about politics and the evolution of public policy. And to draw distinctions between the semantic needs of scholars and practitioners—to argue that what is not good enough for the scholar should suit the politician—does little to further the effective political dialogue which our democratic politics presumes. Perhaps the academicians ought to take the lead in drawing up a list of ambiguous words and phrases "which never would be missed." For such a list I would have several candidates, but it should suffice here to nominate the "public interest."

---

8 Some particularly acute reader of the literature on the public interest, or of Schubert's analysis of it, may note that my position here is somewhat stronger and more negative than the one I took four years ago in the *Journal of Politics*. What appears to be an inconsistency is none in reality; I have simply changed my mind on a few issues touching the public interest in the intervening years.

16

THE USE AND ABUSE OF "THE PUBLIC INTEREST"

BRIAN M. BARRY

"What is the public interest?" Instead of being mesmerized by the contemplation of this pseudo-question let us observe the words "public" and "interest" in use in everyday discourse and then see if we cannot make some sense of "the public interest" by assuming that the constituent words have exactly the same sense when put together as they have when used separately in other contexts.

INTEREST

To say that x is in A's interests is to say that he would want it if he were rational and not altruistic or principled in a certain way to be made precise later. By "rational" I mean (1) "perfectly knowledgeable," (2) "having perfect capacity to compute," and (3) "perfectly in control of himself so that the achievement of long-run ends are not sabotaged by momentary impulses"; in other words "calculating" in the widest sense of the word. This is the way "rationality" is used by Hume and also in most economic analysis.

We can approach a more precise characterization of what it

is about an action or policy that makes it in someone's interests in two stages. As a first approximation let us say that an action or policy is in a man's interests if it increases his opportunities to do what he wants. Health, freedom, leisure, money, and power are obvious examples and we find these just the sorts of things an increase in which is said to be (still at a first approximation) in a man's interests.

Thus John Locke wrote: "Civil interests I call life, liberty, health and indolency of body; and the possession of outward things such as money, lands, houses, furniture and the like." [1] And Talcott Parsons gave more limited criteria but criteria based on the same idea:

> Other things being equal, it would always be irrational not to maximize wealth and power [because they] are potential means to any ultimate ends. . . . It is primarily these generalized means to any ultimate ends, or generalized immediate ends of rational action, to which Pareto gives the name "interests." [2]

We can best introduce the necessary qualifications to our first approximation by considering, first, that wealth and power are assets. Within limits they can be saved (i.e., held ready for future committal) or committed. If committed, they can be either invested (i.e., tied up in a way not desired intrinsically in hopes of having *more* to commit in the future), transferred to the use of another to do with as he thinks fit, or consumed. If consumed, they may be used to satisfy one's own wants or someone else's wants.

I mentioned that even a rational person would not necessarily want his interests advanced if he were altruistic or principled in a certain way. This can now be explained. If he believes that opportunities should be distributed in a certain way as of right, then he will not wish his own interests to be advanced if this

---

1 *The Second Treatise of Civil Government* and *A Letter Concerning Toleration*, ed. J. W. Gough (1948), p. 126.
2 *The Structure of Social Action* (1937), p. 262. "Maximize" is here unfortunate in that it implies that it would always be rational to *make an effort* to secure more wealth and power. But it would be senseless to work every waking hour and leave no time to enjoy the money thus accumulated. Parsons should have said "welcome an increase in."

can be done only at the price of ruling out a move toward what he would regard as a more desirable distribution.

By saying only "in a certain way" I cover myself against the case where someone wishes to use his own opportunities in the way another would like. In *this* case he would be quite rational to want a policy in his interests since this gives him more chance to get the total situation that he wants. This is a rather fine point, however. The main thing is that Parsons is wrong in identifying self-interest and rationality, even with the hedge of "other things being equal." Rationality, as Hume pointed out, is neutral between egoism and altruism. Subject to the qualification made earlier in this paragraph, a rational egoist is the only man who will *always* welcome policies in his own interest.

Now let us drop the first approximation and ask under what circumstances a rational egoist would agree that an increase in his opportunities would not be in his own interest. The answer is: where he knows he is likely to be irrational and where he takes precautions. A man who knows he is carried away by the gambling spirit will avoid going to the races with more money in his pocket than he can afford to lose; a homicidal maniac in his lucid moments, a somnambulist in his waking hours, and an alcoholic or drug addict when able to think clearly may all welcome restraint.[3] And if a man isn't himself able to make the rational calculation, others can try to think their way into his value system, or impute what seem reasonable values to him (based largely on the value systems of more rational people) and act "in his interests"—i.e., prevent him from doing things he would regret later and make him do things he will be pleased later to have done.[4]

---

[3] *McCall's* (November 1961): ". . . a time-lock cigarette case for problem smokers . . . can be set to open only at fixed intervals during the day!"

[4] Note that this applies to any committal of opportunities, whether investment, transfer, or consumption—not only to consumption. I am indebted to the philosophy department at Princeton for a discussion in which this point came out. Note also that the distinction between increasing a man's opportunities and preventing him from committing them disastrously is often marked by a distinction between "acting in his interests" and "acting in his *best* interests." Here is an example of the latter use almost literally drawn from random: ". . . there is a wide streak of irrationality, an obvious and

We are now in a position to see some of the reasons why a man may want to make appraisals of actions or policies in terms of someone's interests (including, in "someone," himself).

1. He may want to advance his own interests and make the appraisal as a preliminary to deciding what to do.

2. He may want to issue prescriptions of a prudential nature—advice, warning, recommendation—to others, and appraise things in terms of the recipients' interests as a preliminary.

3. He may want to guess what someone will do. If he thinks the man will pursue his self-interest, he can then construct the syllogism "A man in the position of Mr. *N* who acted in a self-interested way would do *x*. Mr. *N* will act in a self-interested way. Therefore Mr. *N* will do *x*."

4. Instead of using the appraisal as a straightforward prediction of Mr. *N's* actions he may use it as the starting point for a prediction (or explanation) working out what Mr. *N would* do if he were self-interested and, using this as a bench mark, seeing how far he is likely to deviate (or has deviated) from it, and why.

5. Finally, he may be a trustee for *N*, or at least feel himself responsible for *N's* well-being; and he may boil this down to "looking after *N's* interests."

There is just one more point about "interest" to be cleared up. It is this: A person may be affected in a number of different ways by a certain policy, as he is impinged on by it in different roles or capacities. As a motorist, tighter enforcement of the speed limit is not in his interests, as a pedestrian it is; as an importer of some raw materials it is not in his interests to have higher tariffs all round, as a seller who has to compete with foreign rivals, it is; and so on. I shall therefore distinguish between a man's interests *in some particular capacity,* and his *net interest* in a policy (that is, how he is affected over-all, striking a balance between the pluses and minuses incurred in his various capacities).

---

constant inability of many . . . convicts to think and act in a manner consistent with their own best interests" [*Reader's Digest* (November 1961), p. 103].

PUBLIC

One hundred and thirty years ago, Sir George Cornewall Lewis offered a general definition of "public" which is impossible to improve upon:

> Public, as opposed to *private*, is that which has no immediate relation to any specified person or persons, but may directly concern any member or members of the community, without distinction. Thus the acts of a magistrate, or a member of a legislative assembly, done by them in those capacities, are called public; the acts done by the same persons towards their family or friends, or in their dealings with strangers for their own peculiar purposes, are called private. So a theatre, or a place of amusement, is said to be public, not because it is actually visited by every member of the community, but because it is open to all indifferently; and any person may, if he desires, enter it. The same remark applies to public houses, public inns, public meetings, &c. The publication of a book is the exposing of it to sale in such a manner that it may be procured by any person who desires to purchase it: it would be equally published, if not a single copy was sold. In the language of our law, public appear to be distinguished from private acts of parliament, on the ground that the one class directly affects the whole community, the other some definite person or persons.[5]

Jeremy Bentham's discussion in *Principles of the Penal Code* has some extra points highly relevant for my purposes, while resting on the same general distinction as does Lewis' definition:

> 1st. *Private Offences.* Those which are injurious to such or such assignable individuals [footnote: An *assignable* individual is such or such an individual in particular, to the exclusion of every other; as Peter, Paul, or William], other than the delinquent himself.
> 2nd. *Reflective Offences, or Offences against One's Self.* . . .
> 3rd. *Semi-public Offences.* Those which affect a portion of the community, a district, a particular corporation, a religious sect, a commercial company, or any association of individuals united by some

---

5 *Remarks on the Use and Abuse of Some Political Terms* (1832), pp. 233-234. And here is an additional example, from the many which might be given. "Pious and charitable" bequests tend to be distinguished by their "public purpose" and we find, not surprisingly, the same criterion. "A charity, in the legal sense, may be . . . defined as a gift . . . for the benefit of an indefinite number of persons. . . ." [Supreme Court of Massachusetts, in Jackson v. Phillips (1867) 14 All. 539.]

common interest, but forming a circle inferior in extent to that of the community.

It is never a present evil nor a past evil that constitutes a semi-public offence. If the evil were present or past, the individuals who suffer, or who have suffered, would be assignable. It would then be an offence of the first class, a private offence. In semi-public offences the point if a future evil,—a danger which threatens, but which as yet attacks no particular individual.

4th. *Public Offences.* Those which produce some common danger to all the members of the state, or to an indefinite number of non-assignable individuals, although it does not appear that any one in particular is more likely to suffer than any other.[6]

PUBLIC INTEREST

The only really satisfactory way of approaching "the public interest" would be to take a great number of examples of actual uses—from court cases, newspapers, books, speeches and conversations—and see what could be made of them. This I intend to do elsewhere. Here I must skip this and suggest some groups of examples, leaving it to the reader's intuitive judgment to decide how adequately they cover the range of actual uses. I shall divide them into two sets: those concerned with positive action by a government and those concerned with negative action, the former being action designed to secure a benefit to "the public," the latter being action designed to prevent a harm to "the public." [7]

The so-called "police power" is generally said to be directed to negative actions "in the public interest" and I shall offer Ernst Freund's list of the "primary interests" of the public enumerated in this connection:

(1) *Safety, morals and order.*
   (a) All legislation for the prevention of crime and maintenance of peace. . . .
   (b) All legislation for the prevention of accidents and disease. . . .
   (c) All legislation concerning intoxicating liquors, gambling and vice.

---

6 *Theory of Legislation* (1867, 1931), p. 240.

7 For a sensible statement of the distinction and its significance see Allison Dunham, "City Planning: An Analysis of the Content of the Master Plan," *Journal of Law and Economics,* I (October 1958), 170-286, especially 180-182.

(d) Regulations for the maintenance of order in public places and for the enforcement of peace and quiet.

(2) *Economic.*

. . . trade regulations for the prevention of fraud; the control of combinations, trusts, and corporations; certain phases of labor legislation; regulation of the business of railroads, banking, insurance and other classes of business affected with a public interest. . . .[8]

Positive action is simply the provision of goods and services by a public authority to a nonspecific group. The good or service may be one where it is impossible or difficult to limit the benefit to those who pay without letting "free riders" share as well; but it need not. And where it is not it may or may not be charged for. It will thus cover, for example, public provision of medical care, roads, street lighting, "defense," education, news, access to cultural opportunities, and consumer goods. Whether the provision of any of these by a public authority will be said to be "in the public interest" in a particular case will depend on what the alternative is.

Ideas of the prerogative power, reason of state, and the *arcana imperii* all lie behind "the public interest" but its meaning has now extended beyond "the interest of the state" [9] as the above examples show.

COMMON INTEREST

In the rest of this chapter I shall suggest one reason for the important position which the public interest plays in arguments for or against actions and policies, laws, and institutions in modern states. First I shall explore the idea of "common interests," showing that once the notion is properly understood,

---

8 In Rexford Guy Tugwell, *The Economic Basis of the Public Interest* (1922), pp. 8-9. The Freund article is there cited as "Police Power," *Cyclopaedia of American Government* (n.d.), pp. 706ff.

9 As an example of the survival of the *'arcana imperii'* concept Charles A. Beard points out [*The Idea of National Interest* (1945), p. 15 footnote] that "the public interest" is the usual expression used when the executive refuses to disclose information. "Joint resolutions of the American Congress calling on the executive for information and reports upon foreign policies, invariably include the phrase 'if compatible with the public interest.'"

there clearly are "common interests" shared by all the members of any society. Second, I shall consider the scope for common interests in some particular action; third, I shall extend the inquiry to common interests in a rule or policy which specifies that actions of a certain kind are to be taken whenever certain conditions are satisfied (e.g., whenever someone commits a murder). Finally, I shall suggest that it may under certain circumstances be in everyone's interest to agree to a higher-order rule under which certain policies which harm some and benefit others are adopted, because everyone has good reasons for hoping that he will gain more on the swings than he loses on the roundabouts.

My first point, that there are net interests common to all the members of a society, has been questioned by some thinkers [10] on the ground that any proposal which becomes practical politics is opposed by some group. But this is a superficial analysis because it ignores the question: Why are some logically possible proposals never advocated by anyone at all? Why for example is nobody in the United States in favor of having the Strategic Air Command take off and drop all its bombs on the United States? Obviously because nobody at all believes this would be in his interests. To point out as if it were a great discovery that all proposals *which are actually put forward* meet opposition is as naive as expressing surprise at the fact that in all cases which reach the Supreme Court there is something to be said on each side. (If there isn't, someone has been wasting an awful lot of money.)

Once we remember that "being in A's interest" is at least a triadic relationship (between A and at least two policies) we can easily see how empty it is to talk in general about common and divergent interests. For any given proposal there is nearly always at least one that compared to it is in someone's interests and at least one that compared to it is contrary to someone's interests. To say that two or more people have a common interest is to

---

[10] For example, Arthur F. Bentley, *The Process of Government* (1949), p. 122: ". . . we shall never find a group interest of the society as a whole." David B. Truman, *The Governmental Process: Political Interest and Public Opinion* (1951), p. 51: ". . . we do not need to account for a totally inclusive interest, because one does not exist."

say that there are two policies *x* and *y* such that both persons (or all) of them prefer *x* to *y* from the point of view of their own interests. On this definition it is safe to say that *any* two people have a common interest as between *some* two policies and *any* two people have a divergent interest as between *some* two policies; and the same is a fortiori true of groups.

Common interests exist even among enemies,[11] as do divergent interests among allies.[12] Instead of speaking in blanket terms about people or groups with common or opposed interests, we should speak of people or groups whose interests coincide or conflict with respect to the adoption of *x* rather than *y*. If once we do this it becomes plain that there are considerable possibilities for "common interests" so interpreted, among all the citizens of a country as well as among wider groups.

Nevertheless, common interests in a single action among all the members of a society are not very frequent. This is particularly true where the benefit redounds to assignable persons, that is, where each person can say precisely what he has gained. The second step, therefore, is to recognize that there are causes where some hazard is averted which might indifferently have struck any member of the community but would probably not have struck all. For example, suppose high seas will cause flood-

---

11 See Thomas C. Schelling, *The Strategy of Conflict* (1960), pp. 4-5, 11; and also Schelling, "Reciprocal Measures for Arms Stabilization," *Arms Control, Disarmament and National Security,* ed. Donald G. Brennan (1961), p. 169: "It is not true that in the modern world a gain for the Russians is necessarily a loss for us, and vice versa. We can both suffer losses, and this fact provides scope for cooperation. We both have—unless the Russians have already determined to launch an attack and are preparing for it—a common interest in reducing the advantage of striking first, simply because that very advantage, even if common to both sides, increases the likelihood of war. If at the expense of some capability for launching surprise attack one can deny that capability to the other, it may be a good bargain."

12 E. E. Schattschneider, *Politics, Pressures and the Tariff* (1935), p. 224: "The very nature of tariff legislation, since it involves a vast number of independent conflicts of interest, is such as to bring out the fissures in almost any group, however homogeneous it may seem in other relations. Indeed, in tariff legislation it is often the interests which lie nearest to each other in the families of industries which have contradictory needs. Add to this the fact that trade associations may be formed on many bases, most of which bear no reference to the tariff, and it may be seen that interests within single groups are often complex."

ing costing £100 per head to half the population unless the dykes are strengthened at a cost of £10 per head to the whole population. The action of strengthening the dykes would be in everyone's interest *provided* nobody knew in advance whether or not he would be among the half who would be flooded. If some knew they would be safe anyway, the levy would represent to them a £10 loss rather than a bargain-rate insurance with an expected value of $.5 \times £100 = £50$.

Third, we should notice that as well as averting an evil which *might* indifferently have struck anyone, a government may have a set policy of compensating the specific individuals who suffer from some particular misfortune. If this set policy is considered prospectively, it will also give rise to benefits to nonassignable individuals. This can be seen easily if we think about an insurance policy. Looking at it retrospectively each person can work out whether he has gained or lost from having his house insured against fire; but prospectively he is simply forced to work out whether, given the premium and the risk of fire, it is worth having insurance. He knows that at the end of the year he will either be glad or sorry that he insured his house. But that is no help to him in making up his mind because he has no way of telling now whether he will be glad or sorry.

Many government programs—medical care, unemployment relief, and so forth—are of this kind. Though the benefits and costs are always specific, nobody can know whether over the course of his life he will gain from them or not, so it may be in everyone's interest to support such programs and save worry. This is the sort of thing I refer to as a *policy;* it consists not simply of a decision to give *A* ten dollars a week but to give everyone in such-and-such conditions ten dollars a week. Most laws are "policies" in this sense; indeed laws which specify individuals to be punished are distinguished as "acts of attainder" (and prohibited under the United States Constitution).

Very often where there is no common interest in a specific act there will be a common interest in a policy under which acts of this type will be carried out. For example there may be no single road in the United States to whose building cost it would be in everyone's interest to contribute; but it may still be in everyone's interest to contribute to the costs of a policy under which roads will be built all over the country wherever some criterion of "need" is satisfied. This is of course the basis of the "package deal" and logrolling.

Rousseau's use of the distinction between what he calls "laws" and "decrees" is precisely the same as that which I have been making between "policies" and "particular acts." Since in supporting a policy you are in effect writing a blank check which events may in the future write your name on, it behooves you to be careful. Before voting to make the penalty for murder severe, remember you may some day be in the dock. Before voting to make it lenient remember you may some day be the victim.[13] In voting on particular actions, however, the people are not making a "general" judgment, because (in Bentham's term) the gainers and losers are assignable. This is a job of deciding between interests and should be left to executive or judicial agencies, according to Rousseau.

The mental block against accepting this point of view which some people appear to have may arise from confusing it with a crude "harmony of interests" theory of the kind Pareto dissected as follows:

> [Some] writers, such as Pufendorf, Hobbes, Spinoza, and Locke, think that there is a sanction for natural laws in the fact that the individual who violates them does harm to Society and hence to himself as a member of society.
>
> The fallacy lies (1): In disregarding the amounts of gain or loss, on the assumption that *all* individuals are to act in one way or *all* in another, and in not considering the case where some individuals are to act in one way and some in another. (2) In going to extremes along the line of the above and considering gains only, or losses only. In fact, let us adopt the premise that if *all* individuals refrained from doing *A* every individual as a member of the community would derive a certain advantage. But if all individuals *less one* continue refraining from doing *A,* the community loss is very slight, whereas the one individual doing *A* makes a personal gain far greater than the loss he incurs as a member of the community.[14]

---

13 See, for an extended development of this idea, John Rawls, "Justice as Fairness," *The Philosophical Review*, LXVII, 2 (April 1958), 164-194.

14 Vilfredo Pareto, *The Mind and Society* (*Trattato di sociologia generale*) ed. Arthur Livingston (1935), pp. 945-946.

Pareto's strictures do not, however, apply to Rousseau (or, I suspect, to the authors mentioned by him). Rousseau does not deny that it may be in your interest to *break* a law which benefits you qua member of the community; all he says is that it is certainly in your interest to *vote* for it, and that if you have voted in favor of a certain punishment for a certain crime you have no business to complain if your wish for a certain general policy is applied to you in a particular case. Exactly the same point may be made about contracts: it is in your interests to enter into some contracts even though it would be even better for you if you could avoid performing your part of the agreement.

Clearly, even when we look at policies rather than actions, the principle that the state should advance common interests is still of limited scope. There are many questions where any action will clearly benefit some section of the population and hurt another section, or benefit one far more than another. Must the idea of "common interest" stop here? Not necessarily, and it is this possibility which I shall explore in this final part. Under favorable conditions it may be that everyone can reasonably expect to gain if a higher-order policy is adopted which specifies some criteria and says that *any* action or policy which satisfies these criteria is to be put into effect.

These criteria could of course be of any kind but I shall mention two possible ones here. The first is that any action or policy which is favored by a majority of some electorate should be enacted. If the electorate consists of all the adults in the community this may not be an unreasonable higher-order policy for everyone to assent to. If all those in the electorate are self-interested, the main dangers, which may make some wish they had not agreed to the system, are:

1. irrationality by a majority;
2. a certain fixed minority, noticeable by their religion, "race," language, etc., being "ganged up on" by the rest;
3. "intense" minorities being voted down by majorities who have little at stake in a matter. If this happens often, *everyone* may be worse off in the long run.

These difficulties can be mitigated to a large extent, in theory, by having instead the rule that actions or policies which will maximize the total utility of the whole community should always be put into effect. (How to ensure that the government will actually do this is of course another question.)

The classical economists, from Bentham to Edgeworth, often adopted this line of justification for utilitarian recommendations,[15] and in spite of Lord Keynes' dictum that "in the long run we're all dead" J. R. Hicks revived the idea in the 1940's: [16]

> If the economic activities of a community were organized on the principle of making no alterations in the organization of production which were not improvements in this sense [17] and making all alterations which were improvements that it could possibly find, then, although we could not say that all the inhabitants of that community would be necessarily better off than they would have been if the community had been organized on some different principle, nevertheless there would be a strong probability that almost all of them would be better off after the lapse of a sufficient length of time.

The limitations on this approach are fairly easy to see: Some decisions have such large effects on distribution that it would be idle to expect them to be more than cancelled out by small changes. This reduces the policy to too much of a lottery if applied inflexibly. Nevertheless, where decisions have fairly small effects on distribution and do appear to be justified on general utilitarian grounds, public authorities often carry them out with general approval, and it is plausible to think that underlying this approval is a general assumption that in the long run everyone will gain if public authorities always act on this basis.

It is important to recognize that where this higher-level policy is in operation, it is that which is "in the public interest" and not the particular policies and actions which are carried out because they satisfy it; e.g., that it is the "majority principle" or the "principle of utility" which is "in the public interest," rather than this or that application.

In just the same way, where some particular policy is in every-

---

15 See Gunnar Myrdal, *The Political Element in the Development of Economic Theory*, tr. Paul Streeten (1953), pp. 211-212.

16 "The Rehabilitation of Consumers' Surplus," *Review of Economic Studies*, VIII, 2 (February 1941), 111.

17 That is, changes where the gainer *could* compensate the losers and still be better off.

one's interest in its own right, it is incorrect to say that the specific actions carried out under it are in everyone's interest. For example, even if it is in everyone's interest to hang murderers it is obviously not in any specific instance in the murderer's interests to be hanged. The hanging may indeed be described as being "in the public interest" but only in one of two limited senses. Firstly, there is the sense in which people's interests in some particular capacity are contrasted with their net interests. In this sense, the hanging is in everybody's interest qua citizen (since all citizens have an interest in deterring murder), though of course in the case of the murderer himself this is considerably outweighed by his private interest in staying alive.

And secondly, there is an important sense of public interest parasitic upon this one in which it means not the interest of everyone qua member of "the public" but the *net* interest of any large and nonassignable group. In this sense, of course, "public" comes to refer to an actual group of people, and this group is often contrasted with an opposing "special interest" group. Using the expression in this way one would contrast the (net) interest of the murderer with the (net) interest of the nonassignable group of "all citizens except the murderer."

17

PROLEGOMENA TO
A THEORY OF
THE PUBLIC INTEREST

EDGAR BODENHEIMER

Any endeavor to lay down a theory of the public interest claiming to be entitled to general recognition is obviously a very hazardous undertaking. Specific policy objectives designed to promote the public interest are not only extremely multifarious and diversified but must also necessarily be adapted to the varying needs of different societies and social systems. The discussion of the question whether it is possible and worthwhile under these circumstances to make an attempt to develop a generalized doctrine of the public interest is the main object of this paper. This discussion will require an analysis and appraisal of certain views with respect to the nature of the public interest which enjoy a rather wide currency in political and social theory today, and the first half of this essay will be devoted to a description and criticism of these views. The author's own suggestions for a possible avenue of approach to the problem which may lead to a practicable and desirable goal will form the theme of the second half.

I

It has been assumed by a number of writers that a workable conception of the public interest can be gained by simply adding up and totaling the individual interests existing in a community in a more or less mechanical fashion. It was particularly Jeremy Bentham who believed in the possibility of such a quantitative determination of the public good. To him, the interest of the community was identical with "the sum of the interests of the several members who compose it." [1]

It is submitted that this view is predicated upon the unrealistic assumption that an individual can have no interests antagonistic to the interests of the political community as a whole. Inasmuch as Bentham conceived of the individual as an essentially selfish being, as Bertrand Russell has observed,[2] the Benthamite doctrine could be accepted only on the supposition that the sum total of selfish individual actions could be equated with the maximum happiness of the community. Although this view was once widely held, it has become disconfirmed by the experience of the last hundred years. An individual may have an interest in the minimization of his tax load, whereas the fulfillment of certain indispensable community or state functions (for example, in the field of economic policy, education, or national security) may render some tax increases necessary. An individual may have an interest in making an easy gain by putting upon the market a product of shoddy quality, but the community is interested in maintaining a level of production which protects at least the safety and health of the members of the public. An individual may wish to withdraw his children

---

1 Jeremy Bentham, *An Introduction to the Principles of Morals and Legislation* (1823), Ch. I, iv. More recently, a similar view was voiced by C. W. Cassinelli who maintains that "the idea of opposition between public interest and individual interest is not consistent with a democratic ethic" and that such opposition stems from "a decision to adopt standards of value which make the highest ethical goal or policy relationships incompatible with individual initiative." See Cassinelli, "Some Reflections on the Concept of the Public Interest," *Ethics,* LXIX (1958), 49, 58, and above.

2 Bertrand Russell, "Freedom and Government," in *Freedom: Its Meaning,* ed. R. N. Anshen (1940), p. 261.

from school at the age of thirteen in order to make them help support the family in gainful employment, but the community may consider an extension of the period of compulsory education beyond this age necessary for the training of informed and competent citizens. An individual may have an interest in paying substandard wages to his employees, but the community interest in economic health may call for a strengthening of the purchasing power of the population. Two manufacturing firms may have strong desire to get together and fix the prices of their products, but the public interest may call for a maintenance of competition for the benefit of large masses of consumers. Although Bentham was concerned with the aggregate of individual interests rather than with particular instances of private interests, these examples would nevertheless tend to demonstrate that without a qualitative evaluation of individual interests a proper determination of the public good might encounter serious difficulties.

The identification of the public interest with the arithmetical sum total of private interests overlooks, among other things, certain perplexing and contradictory elements in the human psychological structure. We can interpret our interests from a lone wolf, isolated point of view which responds exclusively to the self-assertive sides of our natures. We are also able to evaluate our interests as responsible members of a social group whose personal well-beings cannot be wholly dissociated from the well-being of the community to which we belong. For example, a man living in a city having an inadequate police force may express total disconcern with this problem on the ground that he possesses a good gun and an effective protection against burglars; but his position would undoubtedly be a different one if he were sensitive to considerations of civic responsibility. The strength of the self-regarding and other-regarding impulses in human nature varies, of course, with particular individuals. But even in the psychological makeup of one individual the balance of these conflicting tendencies is rarely stable and unalterably fixed. A conception of our interest dictated by short-range considerations may be corrected by explanations or arguments which bring home to us certain by-products and consequences of our

actions which we had failed to take into account. It happens
not infrequently that a person holding a certain view changes
or abandons it upon hearing a persuasive speech which explores
the deficiencies and weaknesses of this view. Accordingly, a legislator confronted with a definite reaction of a constituent to a
proposed piece of legislation need not in all cases assume that
this individual would necessarily adhere to his standpoint if he
were in possession of all the information which is accessible to
the legislator himself.

The difficulties facing a quantitative determination of the
public interest do not only stem from the shifting, uncertain,
and tentative character of the individual's own appraisal of his
interests. Even if every individual had a definite, final, and
unalterable conception of his best interests with respect to any
matter calling for community action, there still remains the
serious problem of ascertaining these interests in order to compute their sum total and thus to solve the public interest equation. A vote for a legislator on the basis of a party program
published prior to election in many cases will not serve as an
infallible guide to the political choices made by members of
the electorate. Furthermore, if there should be wide divergences
among the individual interests capable of being identified,
should the numerical weight be the sole factor in deciding
which of them should be given preference or at least priority?
Should the desires voiced by a majority be entitled to greater
consideration than those of a minority? How can we make sure
in a situation calling for immediate action that the legislative
will is in fact a faithful reflection of "the sum of the interests
of the several members" who compose the community?

Perhaps the chief thought that Bentham meant to convey by
his statement was that a legislator considering what is in the
public interest should always have in mind the interests of all
whom he represents. If understood in this broadest and most
general sense, the thought expresses an important truth. But
when we condescend upon particulars in determining as to how
the public interest can be properly ascertained in a given situation, the formula raises more questions than it is able to answer.

II

Although the public interest cannot be determined by a mechanical counting of private interests, it is likewise impermissible to identify it with the policy decisions of the public authorities. In other words, it cannot be conceded that the public interest consists in whatever the public authorities by their fiat declare it to be. If the organs of government were always and necessarily endowed with the will to accomplish as well as the capacity to discern the best interests of the community unfailingly and without deviation, then perhaps there would be room for an identification of the public interest with governmental decision making. Every informed person is aware of the fact that, under the conditions of the actual world, this identification is without a rational basis. Government officials may misconceive the community interest, make serious and unquestionable mistakes in framing and executing public policies, and may lead the ship of state to ruin and disaster. They may also be motivated by selfish desires in exercising their responsibilities and interpret their public functions purely in terms of personal advancement or aggrandizement of power. These facts are so well understood that no elaborate documentation or historical verification would appear to be necessary.

It is likewise inadmissible to equate the common good with the interest of a mystical collective organism, hypostatized into an independent entity. Since such an entity can only act through human beings, such a conception of the public interest meets the same objections which must be leveled at the position discussed in the preceding paragraph. The large majority of thinking individuals will unquestionably reject the view that the command of the ruling authorities should be regarded as an automatic reflection of the public good.

The view has sometimes been propounded that the public interest should be equated with the cumulative content of statutory enactments emanating from the actions of the elected representatives of the people. Such a view can be found, for example, in a decision of the Supreme Court of Pennsylvania, in which the following language appears: "Before any commission can decide whether a contract is contrary to public interest, it is necessary to find what is or what is not in the public interest. The power to make such determination rests with the legislature and without such declaration the commission would be without a standard or criterion." [3] If all the Court seeks to suggest in this passage is that the primary power to specify the public interest resides in the legislature rather than in the executive organs of the government, it would be difficult to take issue with the statement. The Court adds the observation, however, that the phrase "public interest" as used in this connection is "a concept without an ascertainable criterion." If this means that the only way to impart an intelligible meaning to the notion is by way of a positive legislative concretization to be accepted as a final judgment as to what is in the public interest, one may find grounds for quarreling with this approach. It might perhaps be acceptable if Rousseau's conviction that the general will cannot be wrong would offer any clues to the solution of the problem. But for Rousseau, the general will was not the will expressed by a representative legislative body, but the will of the whole community conceived ideally and rationally in terms of its best interests.[4] Rousseau would have denied that the administration of the public interest would necessarily be safe in the hands of an elective body of legislators. Since his time we have become more acutely conscious of the fact that the elected representatives of the people may not only make erroneous judgments as to what is necessary or desirable for the community, but may in some instances be motivated by considerations quite unrelated to the maximum promotion of the common good.

Finally, the observation should be made that there exists no compelling need to confine the public interest to the range of governmental objectives.[5] It is entirely possible that nongovern-

---

[3] Bell Telephone Co. v. Driscoll (1941) 21 A.2d 912, at 916.

[4] See Carl J. Friedrich, *The Philosophy of Law in Historical Perspective* (1958), p. 124.

[5] It is pointed out by W. A. R. Leys and C. M. Perry, *Philosophy and the Public Interest* (1959), p. 47, that some authors have entertained this restricted view of the public interest.

mental agencies or even individuals may perform acts which are conducive to the public interest, and that these acts are not merely done in compliance with a governmental mandate. Thus, when the Rockefeller Foundation engages upon an ambitious project for the improvement of the agricultural system in an underdeveloped country, when a church devotes itself to the alleviation of human misery and poverty by the institution of a large-scale relief and charity program, or when a private university uses its financial and intellectual resources effectively for the education of young citizens, few will deny that such activities are undertaken in pursuit of the public interest.

III

The discussion up to this point has moved within a negative frame of reference designed to eliminate certain pitfalls which stand in the way of an acceptable solution of our problem. We have attempted to expose two fallacies in the approach to a theory of the public interest, viz., the fallacy of quantitative determination and the fallacy of determination by governmental fiat; we have concluded that resort to either of them leaves us stranded in a blind alley. We must now proceed to determine whether there exist any positive and nonsubjective standards which will render possible or at least facilitate the task of giving meaning to the concept of the public interest.

At the start of this discussion, a fundamental assumption will be made which cannot easily be validated by direct and detailed proof but which might be considered as falling within the category of John Stuart Mill's first principles of knowledge verified by reason.[6] This is the assumption that the public interest must be understood as the genuine interest of the whole community and not as the camouflaged interest of an elite or minority actuated by totally self-serving goals.[7] The fact that the over-

---

[6] Mill, *Utilitarianism,* ed. O. Piest (1957), pp. 7, 44.

[7] Cf. Carl J. Friedrich, *Constitutional Government and Democracy,* rev. ed. (1950), p. 462: "A true and ideal 'American' representation would . . . consider the interests to be most important which all Americans have in common and which are therefore most 'general.' "

whelming majority of men and women would reject the second
alternative if exposed to the historical evidence of its consequences would not in itself disprove the tenability of this view.
The further consideration of rational judgment must be added
that no plausible ground can be found why the world should
be considered the playground of a few for whom the large majority of men and women are mere objects rather than human
beings entitled to be treated as ends in themselves. For those
who reject this assumption as arbitrary and irrational, the ensu-
ing discussion will be meaningless and unconvincing.

If we identify the public interest with the good of all, or most,
we must first reach agreement on a standard by which the good
of all, or most, can be measured. We have already rejected the
view according to which it can be determined by simply adding
up individual expressions of private desires and preferences, because we know that people sometimes take a short-range view of
their interests and are capable of doing acts hurtful to the common weal. Although the opinions of private citizens as to the
best ways of promoting the public interest are entitled to the
most serious consideration, it may sometimes be necessary to
revise or even disregard private conceptions of the public interest which on balance are found to be unacceptable or impractical.

It is submitted that what all citizens want if they look at the
problem intelligently and conscientiously, without in any way
sacrificing their personal needs and wants, is a well-ordered and
productive community in which everybody has an opportunity
to develop his capabilities to the fullest. People need food and
love, the chance to found a family; they have to be clothed and
sheltered. They also wish to contribute to the good of the community by work and effort, although the character of this contribution permits of infinite variety. Furthermore, men require
opportunities for recreation and the satisfaction of their non-
material, spiritual needs. Human happiness thus rests on the
fulfillment of multiple demands varying in intensity and strength
in different human beings. According to the testimony of the
teachers of wisdom, the greatest happiness is derived, not from
mere satisfaction of animal instincts, but from making contribu-

tions (large or small) to human civilization in the material, mental, ethical, religious, or aesthetic spheres of life.[8]

A social structure which affords the widest possible opportunities for the activation of all human energies and talents can hardly draw censure from reasonable men, and there seems to be a growing convergence among the peoples of the world toward a general acceptance of this view. Wherever unrest stirs on the globe today, it is because of manifestations of an urge to create wider fields for productive work under decent conditions of life for all men and women in the manifold domains of human endeavor. All measures which promote, serve, and benefit the human desire for affirmative and constructive participation in the enterprise of civilization must be deemed to be in the public interest because they increase the good of all as intelligently conceived.

A notion of the common good similar to that advanced in this essay was propounded by the Austrian jurist Alfred Verdross. He maintained that the *bonum commune* aims neither at the maximum satisfaction of individual desires nor at the promotion of collective utility or expediency, but at the establishment of social conditions under which individual persons are able to build, through industry and productive work, a life which is in consonance with the dignity of the human being.[9] This approach is predicated upon the assumption that it is impossible to exclude the normative or ideal element from any determination of the public interest. Verdross' definition, for example, implies that indolence, laziness, and destructiveness are qualities which,

---

[8] For a modern view see Erich Fromm, *The Sane Society* (1955), p. 72, who comes to the following conclusion: "A healthy society furthers man's capacity to love his fellow men, to work creatively, to develop his reason and objectivity, to have a sense of self which is based on the experience of his own productive powers."

[9] Alfred Verdross, *Abendländische Rechtsphilosophie* (1958), p. 245. Cf. also Jean Dabin, "General Theory of Law" in *The Legal Philosophies of Lask, Radbruch and Dabin,* tr. K. Wilk (1950), p. 355: "What the public requires as its own good, what is specifically the good of all without distinction, is a sum total of general conditions under the protection of which the legitimate activities of everyone within the public may be exercised and developed comfortably."

although they are possessed by some individuals, can find no place and recognition in any philosophy of the common good. His formula also suggests that policies designed to advance the common good must aim at the furtherance of human dignity rather than at the promotion of human degradation. Few people would be inclined to disagree with him on these two basic postulates.

In the field of actual government administration dealing with concrete public policies, the choices to be made by the trustees of the public interest between conflicting social goals or value patterns are often not nearly as clear-cut or self-evident. Choices must, however, be made inasmuch as no society recognizes all interests as being entitled to equal weight. In determining the public interest of the United States in our own day, for example, we do not recognize the interests of the race haters as entitled to parity with those of the advocates of racial tolerance; religious freedom is looked upon as a value entitled to protection, while religious intolerance is denied such protection; we do not put the actions of loyal citizens on the same plane with those of the protagonists of revolutionary violence. It would probably be impossible to find a society in which the prevailing notion of the public interest views all human desires, demands, and claims as being equally entitled to satisfaction. In the light of this fact, the validity of the belief of William James that "the essence of good is simply to satisfy demand" may be seriously questioned by the sociologist as well as by the ethical philosopher.[10]

We conclude this part of the essay with the observation that a general theory of the public interest which takes into consideration the normative aspects of the problem cannot, of course, provide us with an elaborate catalogue of nostrums and panaceas designed to cure specific evils that may befall the body politic and social. The solutions of concrete problems will necessarily vary with the seriousness and scope of the challenge, the temper of the people, and the degree of technological and intellectual advancement. Thus, a theory of the *specific objectives* of ac-

---

10 William James, *Essays on Faith and Morals,* ed. R. B. Perry (1943), p. 201.

tivities which serve the public good must in many respects be contingent and responsive to particular needs, conditions, and exigencies.

IV

This broad determination of the character of the public interest leaves open a question which can only be treated cursorily in this essay because its full exploration would require prolonged and detailed research and study. This is the question of the relationship between the promotion of the public interest and the protection of the individual rights of the citizens.

In a social system which cares for the individual and wishes to preserve his rights there will, in all likelihood, exist a certain amount of dialectical tension between individual freedom and public necessity. In theory this dialectical tension could be eliminated in two radically different ways. First, it could be neutralized by making the protection of individual liberties the sole object of governmental action and reducing the scope of the public interest to this exclusive function. But the entire history of constitutional adjudication in the United States furnishes ample proof for the proposition that constitutionally sanctioned individual rights may come into conflict, so that a choice may have to be made between two interests which, as a matter of general principle, appear to be both entitled to constitutional protection. Thus, the interest of the press in free comment and criticism of judicial action may in some cases be at odds with the right to a fair trial; [11] the rights of private property owners may become pitted against the legitimate interests of agricultural or industrial groups; [12] the rights of employees and workers to organize effectively cannot always be reconciled easily with the rights of other employees and workers to stay free of union affiliation.[13] In such instances, choices between inconsistent consti-

---

[11] See Craig v. Harney (1947) 331 U.S. 367.

[12] See Miller v. Schoene (1928) 276 U.S. 272; Head v. Amoskeag Mfg. Co. (1885) 113 U.S. 9.

[13] See Lincoln Federal Labor Union v. Northwestern Iron & Metal Co. (1949) 335 U.S. 525; Railway Employees Department v. Hanson (1956) 351 U.S. 225.

tutional values must be made by the courts, and justified expectations of private individuals or groups may have to be disappointed. A view of the public interest conceived independently
of the rationale of vested rights protection will sometimes furnish the only criterion apt to be helpful in a satisfactory solution
of the problem.

The other theoretical alternative for the elimination of conflicts between vested rights and public authority would be the
complete subordination of individual liberties to public policy
determinations. Under this alternative, the decision to grant,
withhold, broaden, or restrict individual rights would be governed exclusively by considerations of the public interest. Without doubt, this solution would introduce a factor of great uncertainty and risk into the protection of individual rights and
would commit this area entirely to discretionary treatment by
the lawmaking authorities. As the Norwegian legal philosopher
Frede Castberg has shown, this solution is predicated on the
assumption that individual rights are not rooted in respect for
the personality of the human being, but solely in utilitarian
considerations of state policy.[14] Inasmuch as this assumption is
widely rejected in this country, no elaborate criticism of its
validity will be attempted in this essay.

If we admit that no complete congruity can be shown to exist
in all cases between individual freedoms and the public interest,
it devolves as a major task upon legislative bodies and administrative agencies to find a proper accommodation and adjustment between these two values of the social order. This is an
arduous and difficult assignment which calls for much wisdom
and restraint in those upon whom the burden has been imposed.
In our own society, we consider the execution of this task so
fraught with danger to the well-being of individuals, groups, and
especially minorities that we entrust an independent and de-
tached judiciary with the ultimate decision in arbitrating between the claims of private right and the requirements of public
administration. The essential problems of establishing justice in
the relations of men among themselves and with their govern-

---

14 Frede Castberg, *Freedom of Speech in the West* (1960), p. 424.

ment are posed in the context of this adjustment of private demands with the needs of all.

Philosophically, the problem can be viewed as an attempt to solve an antinomy which exists not only on the societal level but also within the psychological constitution of each individual human being. Just as in society tensions often arise between private claims and community benefit, thus in the depth of the individual personality, self-assertive and competitive tendencies often struggle with social and co-operative impulses. The public interest approach looks primarily to the social constituent in human beings and attempts to interpret their interests in the light of the standards that would guide a rational and conscientious man aware of the fact that he does not live in this world alone but must adapt his conduct to the interests of others and the good of the whole.[15] The individual rights approach views the same range of problems from the vantage point of man as an individual who desires to project his personality into the world and to further his personal aims and ambitions. Both of these approaches are humanistic in character inasmuch as they are actuated by considerations of the well-being of all men rather than by an intention to enhance the power and advantage of one group of men at the expense of other groups. The two approaches can be brought together if it is realized that the individual and the social interest are not always homogeneous or congruous, but that in a "good society" they may be made to coincide widely and effectively, so as to produce a state of affairs where each individual can develop his particular capabilities in a way which inures to the benefit of all.

---

15 See in this connection Walter Lippmann, *Essays in the Public Philosophy* (1955), p. 42: "The public interest may be presumed to be what men in the end would choose if they saw clearly, thought rationally, acted disinterestedly and benevolently."

18

PUBLIC INTEREST
IN THE IDEOLOGIES
OF NATIONAL DEVELOPMENT

JOHN D. MONTGOMERY

I

The concept of public interest had its origins in Western law and philosophy. It is closely related to the emergence of individual economic and other legal rights, and to the Western view of the state's role as an ultimate guardian of the individual right to moral self-fulfillment. In this form, its relevance to other societies is therefore problematical, especially if it is to be used as an ethical guide in deciding the public issues involved in economic and political development. Its very existence in the underdeveloped world may be challenged. Yet in spite of the difficulty of arriving at an adequate definition of public interest in universal terms, the concept itself is of overwhelming importance. It offers, to the Western mind at least, the ultimate ethical justification for demanding the sacrifices which the individual may be called upon to make in the interests of the state, and it prescribes certain of the ultimate goals of organized society. In the underdeveloped world it may afford an ethical basis for choosing among technically feasible alternative courses of action leading to the desired development. In the absence of some concept of public interest as a moral injunction upon the exercise of sovereignty, the ways of Mao Tse-tung and Nehru would have to be distinguished in terms of their technical achievements alone.

The concept of public interest is also important to elements of the Western world engaged in assisting technical and economic growth abroad, both for the positive guidance it can offer in suggesting and developing individual country aid programs, and for the restraint of other Western diplomatic and political activities that are not in the interests of the receiving country. The demands of practical politics confronting the requirements of economic growth therefore compel men of action to enter, however hesitantly, into this preserve of moral philosophy.

One useful definition of public interest as a basis of determining public policy is the economic model described elsewhere in this volume by Richard Musgrave. Applying a Benthamite measuring device to public policy, Musgrave shows how a precise formula of public interest may be derived by adding together private interests and subtracting from the total any legitimate private interests that are in conflict. The residue, harmonized mysteriously into a community value, comprises those interests which introduce benefits without injuring anyone. Additional economic activities beyond the satisfaction of private wants are rationalized not under the Bentham model but in terms of "welfare economics." [1]

The economic formula just described implies the existence of a "marketplace" or of some other device for taking a census of individual needs and demands and for offering a choice among alternative economic commitments; it requires a "government" or other authority to register and co-ordinate private needs and public requirements; and it assumes the existence of a coherent and demanding "public." There are difficulties in using this concept of public interest to justify many expenditures in the

---

[1] P. A. Samuelson, *Economics, An Introductory Analysis* (1958), pp. 616-623.

public sector even in affluent twentieth-century America; but its use in a subsistence economy poses problems of an altogether different order. For one of the principal characteristics of transitional societies is that their private interests and demands have been essentially satisfied by family, clan, tribal, or community units that embrace economic, social, cultural, and political functions in the same undifferentiated institutions.[2] In the economic sense there is no adequate "marketplace" at which demands are registered and fulfilled or no "government" equipped to regulate them. Even the "public" may not be identifiable in underdeveloped societies. Neither the larger community of the nation nor a specific consensus on purposes and values may have emerged or found the means of expression. Public interest defined in these terms could not constitute a useful resource for political judgment.

The economist's approach to the political and ethical problems of development is nevertheless indispensable in another context. It provides an operational assumption which is easily accepted by the leadership of the underdeveloped world [3] and by practitioners of foreign aid: that "growth," in its economic sense, is desirable and therefore in the "public interest," however it may additionally be defined. For while not all economists accept the schematic definitions of staged growth proposed by Max Millikan and Walt Rostow,[4] there is a widespread (though by no means universal) acceptance of the hypotheses that economic growth can be studied in a systematic fashion, can be predicted, and can be influenced by improved planning and the application of external aid resources.

---

[2] See Bert F. Hoselitz, "Tradition and Economic Growth," in *Tradition, Values, and Socio-Economic Development,* eds. R. Braibanti and J. J. Spengler (1961), pp. 83-113.

[3] Wilbert E. Moore, "The Social Framework of Economic Development," in *Tradition, Values, and Socio-Economic Development,* especially pp. 61-62.

[4] See Center for International Studies, Massachusetts Institute of Technology, *U.S. Foreign Policy, Economic, Social and Political Change in the Underdeveloped Countries and its Implication for United States Policy,* Study No. 12, Committee on Foreign Relations, U.S. Senate (1960), pp. 2-3, 13-58, 66-68, 90-96; Max F. Millikan and W. W. Rostow, *A Proposal, Key to an Effective Foreign Policy* (1957), pp. 43-54; and Rostow, *Stages of Economic Growth* (1960).

Acceptance of these hypotheses by the leaders and planners of developing societies can provide some technical substitutes for the missing elements of "public," "government," and "market-place." The occupants of the geographic "nation"—however haphazard its historical origin—can be considered in effect the public, even if their ethnic or cultural traditions are heterogeneous or separatist, because it is in this context that development will take place. In the interests of economic development alone, any leadership that effectively asserts control or "government" over the territory of the new nation and its occupants can find its own justification. Finally, individual demand for consumer items in the traditional "markets" can be ignored and even suppressed in the interests of speeding the growth processes whenever the free market might reduce the capacity of the economy to make capital investments, provided political stability is not threatened by such action. Thus economic theory offers some operational guidance to the mechanics of development by positive growth as an overriding purpose of the state.

If the probability and desirability of material development may be assumed, economic theory may produce means both of clarifying the requirements of development and of contrasting them with the "opportunity costs" of satisfying consumer demands. Economic theory may also be used to justify the allocation of resources on a national basis, and to support the degree of national planning necessary to accomplish this conceptual task. The final decisions in each of these cases still have to be made by the political leadership on the basis of factors that lie entirely outside the range of this technical knowledge, however. They require a consideration of noneconomic values which, however irrelevant to the acknowledged needs of a developing state, may yet represent ultimate purposes and therefore command the unspoken loyalties of the individual subject-citizens.

II

Public interest has also been defined in practical terms by statutes and courts of law in the Western world. When the nation-state developed an administrative bureaucracy working under law rather than for a king or a noble class, a view emerged of the *public* interest as one which transcended that of the ruling segment of society. Both statutes and tradition began to require civil servants to execute laws in the public interest, convenience, or necessity, and courts enforced such requirements without specifying any further standards except those of conscience and judgment.[5] The defining of public interest in the absence of general standards has occurred on a case-by-case basis, without the achievement of a universal definition.[6] Courts have also applied the criterion of public interest in resolving litigations between two adversary parties. The higher good which has been invoked in the name of public interest has gradually created an encumbrance upon private enterprise and restrained activities thought to be injurious to the community.[7] The "public interest" has pragmatically emerged as something affecting certain industries whose operations have concerned more than their owners, competitors, employees, and immediate customers.

No general definition of public interest has emerged from either set of decisions. Courts have pragmatically used the concept as a basis for making and justifying choices in the name of the state and thus contributed to a general awareness of public interest as among the ethical components of statehood. This ethic-consciousness may be the most significant contribution of jurisprudence to Western apprehension of contemporary political behavior. In each of these uses new concepts of the "public" have emerged. The civil servant may regard the "public" as the

---

[5] NBC v. U.S., 63 S. Ct. 997, 1009; American Sumatra Tob. Corp. v. SEC, 110 Fed (2), 117.

[6] See Davis v. American Meter Co., 36 Erie 109; Bowden v. Carter, 65 So(2) 871,873. When courts have sought to apply specific criteria to public interest, they have sometimes resorted to an economic measure. "Public interest means . . . something in which the public, the community at large, has some pecuniary interest, or some interest by which their legal rights or liabilities are affected." State v. Crochett, 206 Pac 816,817.

[7] Wolf Packing Co. v. Ct. of Ind. Rels., Kansas, 262 U.S. 522; 43 S. Ct. 630. Tyson & Bro. v. Bantor, 273 U.S. 418; 47 S. Ct. 426. People v. UMW, 201 Pac 54, 56; L. & C. Mayers Co. v. FTC, 97 Fed (2), 36 S. "Property becomes clothed with a public interest when used in a manner to make it of public consequence, and affect the community at large. It then becomes subject to control by the public for the common good." Munn v. People of State of Ill., 94 U.S. 113, 126.

citizens who present a consensus of agreement to accept the will of the majority, and who possess the power or right to participate in political decisions; for the courts it may speak with a collective moral force tantamount to Holmes's "brooding omnipresence."

The juristic conceptions of public interest are even less appropriate to present conditions in the developing world than are those of the economic model of the harmony of interests in a system of free enterprise. There may be in many non-Western societies neither civil servants conscious of a duty to the public welfare nor a tradition in which public officials and private entrepreneurs look toward the welfare of those who pay taxes and obey regulations. Even the concept of private adversary interests does not exist in many underdeveloped societies. Most large-scale enterprise is a public or private monopoly above judicial restraint, while in the conduct of small business transitional societies seldom differentiate among the interests of individuals as such. In fact, the family or kinship group often plays the dominant role in resolving the kinds of conflicts regarded in the West as a product of individualism; it affords its own set of community values, in which a larger public interest may be unimportant. In many parts of the underdeveloped world, private rights must come into being before litigation can be used to introduce ethical restraints, and institutional means must be found for reconciling their conflicts under a rule of law.

Both the economic and the juristic views in the Western national context represent public interest as possessing an element of restraint upon the exercise of private rights, but capable of emerging only because such rights already exist. Public interest in the West thus becomes a means for advancing individualism as a creative force calling for efforts beyond those required for immediate personal ends.

III

The problems of statecraft posed to the leadership of the developing countries include three that have an institutional significance for public interest: identifying or creating a "public" coextensive with national boundaries and citizenship in countries dominated by ethnic, tribal, or irredentist divisions; developing political institutions providing an opportunity for peacefully and justly choosing among alternative courses of action; and coherently identifying individual demands through the operations of the marketplace even in a subsistence or barter economy. The complications of the first problem are posed by the model of the Congo in crisis, wherein a prestate society failed in its effort to act in the public interest because there was no public and none of the responsibility and leadership needed to identify it. The second problem is illustrated by the shifts in basic policy choices that have occurred with each change of government in Guinea, Cuba, or even Burma. The third problem is that encountered in the states of Indo-China when an American aid program seeks to advance the economic welfare of a country by importing goods for sale on the private market, relying upon projected public demands as a basis of selecting the import items, and risking the wasteful choices made by frivolous demands of impoverished people who suddenly encounter a new supply of consumer items. For the purposes of this discussion these problematic elements may be identified as those of "nation," "government," and "market." Their immediate technical importance has given them priority over the ideological questions posed by the emergence of a concept of public interest.

One hallmark of a well-developed society is that in it these three technical questions are already resolved. A readily identifiable and inclusive "public" supplies the basis for the limitations upon the free market that are required for protective and developmental purposes; a stable "government" provides the means for allocating resources in a consistent fashion, over relatively long periods of time, and irrespective of incidental changes in leadership; and simple monetary processes provide a measure of public demand and produce responses in the form of a supply, only minor amendments in these economic relationships being necessary to accommodate public interests not revealed in the "marketplace." [8]

---

[8] See Chapter 9 in this book, p. 113, where Musgrave discusses the justification for control of the drug traffic. Note, however, that these minor amendments account for a very large share of the gross national product allocated to such public interest expenditures in the United States.

Concurrently with the development of these institutions in the West, the concept of public interest arose as a moral consensus of group action based upon individual human rights. Although no one formulation of these may be considered universally acceptable, one such recent and comprehensive statement has achieved international recognition in the Charter of Human Rights, summarized elsewhere in this volume.[9] Such statements represent aspirations which have been gradually embodied in Western law and given constitutional sanction even though they may not yet be adequately or generally applied. They focus on the individual as the source and center of political values, particularly as he seeks moral self-fulfillment. The institutional safeguards to his legitimate aspirations can even be regarded as an index to the acceptance of public interest as a governing consideration An ultimate function of the state in Western theory is the protection of human rights as they inhere in the individual citizen.[10] In this sense public interest lies somewhere in the direction of an ennobling of individual wants.

For reasons already suggested, the individual-optimizing conception of public interest is not often found in the underdeveloped world. The desire to achieve nationhood has been less espoused in the colonial areas as a means of enriching individual life than as a desire to see the last of the privileged strangers in their midst; the wish for better government and economic development has found popular expression largely in appetites for conveniences and comforts rather than in the search for self-fulfillment; and the sense of human rights has found its principal manifestation in racist or nationalist utterances and in the highly vocalized desire to be left alone. The first impulse of underdeveloped nationhood is toward power, not conscience.

The imperfect conception of public interest in the under-

---

[9] See Chapter 5 in this book, p. 58ff.

[10] Cf. W. Y. Elliott, "The Co-Organic Concept of Community Applied to Legal Analysis: Constitutional and Totalitarian Systems Compared," in C. J. Friedrich, ed., *Community* (1959), pp. 50-64. R. M. MacIver asserts that the highest value in "community" is "socialization," which he equates with "individualization"; *Community* (1917), p. 169.

developed world thus poses a formidable task to Western leaders, to whom the issues are urgent because they may influence the directions in which the new countries will develop: How can Western support of efforts to establish approximations of "nation," "government," and a responsive "market" in underdeveloped societies contribute to the prospects for freedom in the world? Even the techniques required to introduce these institutions are difficult enough. But if no approach to the responsibilities of the state for protecting individual human rights is taken, the efforts to encourage economic and technical improvement may actually delay the emergence of public interest in this form. Technique conferred upon power is more likely to yield totalitarianism than democracy unless the element of conscience or countervailing power is added.

Creating a nation where only villages, nomadic tribal areas, or city-states have existed, where the very geographical boundaries are the ruins of colonial ambitions, and where traditions and tribes cry out only to be left undisturbed, is a task inviting Hobbesian speculation about the physical bases of government and the use of force in order to gain peace. Gentler rationales of collective action—Rousseau's moral general will, Bentham's calculation of a public interest, and Adam Smith's definition of the major issues of morality and technique—cannot be readily applied in most of the underdeveloped world.

The problem of building a national consensus of purpose and loyalties has been approached in most of the underdeveloped world along other lines. Institutions for the protection of traditional values and the recognition of individual freedoms have not often developed out of precolonial history because the one was not internally threatened and the other did not exist except as a by-product of Westernization. Decisions to build toward a modern statehood have been taken by the leaders of the new nations out of their own experience, judgment, and insight. And the fact that these decisions have generally ignored the individual values that supplied the basis of public interest in the West is a matter of grave concern in the ideological cold war.

Many theories of statecraft that have appeared in the underdeveloped world have tended to emphasize national will or purpose rather than public interest in the Western sense.[11] In his theories of "guided democracy" President Sukarno expresses contempt for all forms of liberalism, which he even describes as "maleficent."[12] All decisions made in public bodies require unanimity of support, he argues, and hence should take place without benefit of parties, majority-minority relationships, or even debates followed by voting in parliament.[13] For Sukarno democracy "is guided by the inner wisdom in the unanimity arising out of deliberation amongst representatives, meanwhile creating a condition of social justice for the whole of the People of Indonesia *(Pantja Sila)*."[14] The terms "democracy" and "social justice" refer to national independence and the regeneration of Indonesian traditional institutions,[15] rather than to their West-

---

[11] Important exceptions to this statement and the analysis that follows are found in India and elsewhere. Cf. James S. Coleman, "Conclusion: The Political Systems of the Developing Areas," in *The Politics of the Developing Areas,* eds. Gabriel Almond and James Coleman (1960), pp. 548-556, and 566-576 for an examination of specific ideologies in underdeveloped nations. Cf. also Thomas Hodgkin, "A Note on the Language of African Nationalism," in *St. Antony's Papers, No. 10, African Affairs, No. 1,* ed. Kenneth Kirkwood (1961), pp. 22-40.

[12] *Speech delivered by President Soekarno [sic] on June 25, at the Installation of the Gotong Rojong Parliament* (Republic of Indonesia, n.d.), p. 2; *President Sukarno's Address on the Fifteenth Anniversary of the Republic of Indonesia,* August 17, 1960 (Republic of Indonesia, 1960), pp. 2, 37.

[13] Sukarno, *Speech* (June 25), p. 4; *Address* (August 17, 1960), p. 18.

[14] From the 1945 constitution and the *Political Manifesto, Republic of Indonesia,* of August 17, 1959 (Republic of Indonesia, 1959), p. 9. *Pantja Sila* is a frequently used term in Indonesian political rituals referring to the five "pillars of the state," Belief in God, Nationalism, Internationalism, Democracy, and Social Justice. Democracy "contains three essential elements": *Mufakat* or unanimity, *Perwakilan* or representation, and *Musjawarah* or "deliberation between [sic] representatives." *To Build the World Anew, President Sukarno's Address Before the Fifteenth General Assembly of the United Nations, 30 Sept. 1960* (Republic of Indonesia, 1960), pp. 29-31. Social Justice in the *Pantja Sila* refers to rejection of colonialism and imperialism: p. 33.

[15] Village institutions are especially venerated as a source of inspiration for those engaged in building the new state. *Address by His Excellency President Sukarno of the Republic of Indonesia to the Colombo Plan Conference on Nov. 11, 1959* (Republic of Indonesia, 1959), pp. 7-8, 11.

ern meanings. Even the term "public interest" is used in a special corporate sense.[16]

A more specific effort to introduce an amalgam of Western and traditional values into the political life of an underdeveloped country was President Ngo-dinh-Diem's sponsorship of *Nhan-vi* ("personalism") in Viet Nam. Elements of Roman Catholic social philosophy, Confucian public ethics, and traditional Vietnamese attitudes were fused in his intensive effort to develop an active political morality among this predominantly Buddhist population. The purpose of *Nhan-vi* was the "reconciling of the demands of collective discipline and social justice with those of individual liberty"; [17] the propagation of its code of ethics took place through compulsory month-long courses for civil servants [18] and through governmental channels. Its content in the hands of President Ngo himself attained a dignity and clarity of expression in spite of its shifting character as new crises emerged, and despite its vagueness when confronted with problems of specific human rights in besieged Viet Nam.[19] Other spokesmen for personalism invoked it for a variety of cynical purposes. The President's brother Nhu, his chief political spokesman, used it as a rationale for attacks on private capitalism; his influential sister-in-law used it in her sponsorship of the controversial monogamous 1958 Family Law prohibiting divorce in a society that has previously encouraged polygamy; and government commissions used it for campaigns against corruption and vice, especially if it profited political enemies.[20] None of the recent agitation for civil rights and government reform made reference to

---

[16] "Every individual has the obligation of serving the public interest, serving society, serving the nation, serving the State." Sukarno, *Political Manifesto* (August 17, 1959), p. 56. Moral responsibilities of the state toward the individual have gone unremarked.

[17] *Major Policy Speeches by President Ngo Dinh Diem* (Saigon, Press Office of Presidency, Republic of Viet Nam, 1956), p. 26.

[18] These courses were offered at a special academy at Vinh-Long, whose instructors were Roman Catholic priests.

[19] See John C. Donnell, "National Renovation Campaigns in Viet Nam," *Pacific Affairs,* XXXII (March 1959), 73-88.

[20] Ngo-Dinh Nhu developed this theme in an unpublished talk called "Why We Must Defend the Existing Regime" (November 15, 1957). See also "National Renovation Campaigns in Viet Nam," pp. 76, 80.

personalism, and the evidences are that the intellectual and civic leaders of the country regard it as a synthetic device created for the convenience of the President rather than as an instrument of self-fulfillment.

A strong moral tone often pervades the theories of statecraft emerging in the underdeveloped world, usually, however, without reference to human rights. The religious element in U Nu's approach to the welfare state (*Pyidawtha*) in Burma represents a morality that has characterized Burmese attitudes toward the state since the independence movement began. In practice this morality has resulted in sacrificial diplomatic gestures (such as requesting the United States to withdraw its aid in 1953, primarily because of an unwillingness to receive favors from a nation whose policies it was criticizing in the United Nations) and in elaborate efforts to accommodate the requirements of efficient economic (especially industrial) development even at the cost of immediate advantages (especially in agricultural improvements).[21] There is a moral basis for requiring individual sacrifice for the public benefit in Buddhist *Pyidawtha,* and in the British-derived parliamentary traditions political freedom is an important fact of public life; but even in Burma the concept of the individual's optimum moral self-fulfillment is not a foundation of public policy.

Moral aspirations have also underlain the concepts known as "Pan-Africanism," "The African Personality," and *"Négritude"* among the intellectual and political leaders of West Africa. As in the case of the *Pyidawtha* movement, elements of its moral indignation derive from Marxism. While much of the momentum of these movements derives from anticolonialism, resentment at past evidences of racialism, and a feverish desire to gain the symbolic advantages of national independence, in practice there has been little incentive to stay the hand of progress simply

---

21 See Frank N. Trager, *Building a Welfare State in Burma 1948-1956* (1958), especially pp. 80-88, 101. For a discussion of the Marxist elements in Burma's politics, see John Seabury Thomson, "Marxism in Burma," in *Marxism in Southeast Asia,* ed. Trager (1959), especially pp. 50, 57. The irrational elements in Burmese politics are not based on myths of individualism, either. See Lucian W. Pye, "The Spirit of Burmese Politics" (1959).

out of concern for human rights.[22] Most of the documents created by these movements are suffused with moral indignation over the past or devoted to technical economic and political questions of planning and organization. The absence of a high priority for the creation of conditions relating to individual self-fulfillment in the public interest has been almost universal, except among spokesmen whose traditions are essentially Western.[23]

Some ideologies of the developing nations thus possess strong moral overtones, but these may have little relationship to Western concepts of individual rights or public interest. In the search for unifying concepts for the underdeveloped world the role of the West has been generally confined to suggesting techniques for achieving the goals of modernization, leaving the ideology and the symbols to evolve from the traditions and institutions undergoing change. But the equally important task of discovering individualistic values in these new systems is one to which the Western nations have hesitated to contribute. Except where their immediate security interests are involved, they have been

---

[22] This statement does not apply universally even in Africa. In Nigeria, for example, the federal judiciary is given the role of defending human rights against the three regional governments. Even this apparent parallel to the 14th Amendment and the Bill of Rights of the U. S. Constitution does not refute the point entirely, however, since the original concern and later citations were over the rights of ethnic (tribal) minorities in the three regions rather than individual rights as such.

[23] "Socialism" and "Democracy" are terms frequently invoked but seldom defined in relation to the concepts presented here. See David E. Apter and James S. Coleman, "Pan-Africanism or Nationalism in Africa" (New York: American Society of African Culture, Third Conference, 1960, mimeographed), especially pp. 21-27. Dr. Kwame Nkrumah's Speech on the Motion for Independence (July 10, 1953) contains no assertion or declaration of the rights of man except as they relate to freedom from colonial exploitation (reproduced in George Padmore, *Pan-Africanism or Communism, The Coming Struggle for Africa* (London) App. III. It is significant that in Ghana the traditions of "tribalism" have been repudiated as "an impediment to the building of the modern state" (see Samuel Allen, *Négritude: Agreement and Disagreement* (American Society of African Culture, Third Conference), but the substitution of "individualism" for "tribalism" has not been suggested. Nkrumah's *Autobiography* (London, 1957), pp. 141-142, refers only on passing to human rights. The Asian-African (Bandung) Conference of 1955 refers only to the evils of colonialism in its section on Human Rights and Self-Determina-

restrained by a sense of respect for the sovereign right of other nations to choose their own destiny, even if the choices may be dangerously wrong.

IV

Decisions relating to economic, social, and political modernization can no longer be made at leisure and in terms of domestic factors only. The requirements of change are posed not only by the deeply and universally sensed needs of a coherent community, but also partly in response to external forces. External political and economic forces play an urgent part in determining directions and implementing the dictates of change in the underdeveloped world. Political competition with Communist neighbors in forcing newly independent nations to decide upon extreme measures of self-defense, and to find means for promoting economic growth faster than internal demands or normal economic rivalry would require. This sense of competition is brought to bear partly by the threat of failure to out-

---

tion (Padmore, *Pan-Africanism or Communism*, pp. 446-447). But the early origins of Pan-Africanism among Negroes outside Africa, especially the works of its American founder, Dr. W. E. B. DuBois, include many references to individual rights. Cf. his resolution adopted by the Pan-African Congress of 1919, and Padmore, *Pan-Africanism or Communism*, pp. 124-125. Similarly, the Senegalese poet-statesman Leopold Sedar Senghor, strongly influenced by French and Catholic educational institutions, retains an interest in the abstractions of individual self-fulfillment as an end of the state. Cf. *African Socialism, A Report to the Constitutive Congress of the Party of African Federation* (American Society of African Culture, 1959), especially pp. 29, 30, 34. This recital does not, of course, display all the ideological currents moving through Africa. There are indications that Kenneth Kaunda, Tom Mboya, and especially Julius Nyerere ("Africa's Place in the World," *Symposium on Africa* (1960), especially pp. 150-152, but note also pp. 154-157) are concerned with the preservation of individual rights in the Western sense. Here again the origins and appeal of the ideology are not, strictly speaking, those of "Pan-Africanism," "The African Personality," or "*Négritude*." St. Clair Drake has concluded that "no elements were present in (West African) societies leading toward self-generated change in the direction of individualism and equalitarianism, as was the case in the capitalistic and rationalistic societies of Europe and Africa. African societies had to wait for the introduction of such elements from without." Drake, "Traditional Authority and Social Action in Former British West Africa," *Human Organization*, 19 (Fall 1960), 3, Special Issue, p. 151.

perform Communist-controlled states, and partly by the enormous symbolic importance of economic achievements in the international relations among the new states.

The desire for progress extends beyond the technical requirements of economic development and involves both sides of the Iron Curtain. Even an austerity-minded Marxist leadership has felt compelled to pay more attention to consumer demands than the revolutionary ideology would otherwise tolerate because of political pressures arising from the comparative disadvantages suffered by consumers in Communist countries. The requirements of international competition thus force the leadership in both Communist and non-Communist countries to develop means of assuring security and displaying symbols of progress that differ from the indigenous conception of appropriate national goals. Even neutral powers are impelled to introduce social and economic change in much the same fashion as those committed to either bloc.

The external pressures that interfere with the processes of nation building are not confined to the cold war factors. Regional relationships may bring about a faster or slower pace in the supplying of consumer and capital goods than internal conditions would dictate. Smuggling, uneven regional military requirements, and the presence of varying amounts of foreign aid in most of the underdeveloped countries may also affect the capacity for responding adequately to individual consumer demands or the needs of capital investment. The character of economic change is thus affected by economic and other concerns generated both inside and outside the national boundaries.

The internal and external forces that have compelled the leadership of the poor nations south of the Tropic of Cancer to seek aid from the industrialized world to the north are clear enough. But how is the public interest of the latter countries served by responding to appeals from without their borders? Relatively large annual sums are being redistributed by the Western powers among underprivileged elements of other nations. The allocation of such great national resources to the benefit of other countries has even been attacked as contrary to the public interest of the donor countries.[24] In response to this "realism," a substantial effort has been made to relate foreign aid to our own national security and to the needs of the American economy. Such justifications have not, however, fully explained the humanitarianism of United States aid operations as they have extended deeper into the underdeveloped world.

The explanation for the increasing involvement of the industrial nations in the underdeveloped world rests only partly on classical economic, military, and mercantilist factors such as the development and exploitation of sources of raw materials, markets, and labor. Indeed, even the traditional justifications for foreign aid, apart from purely military objectives, included humanitarian grounds. Following the traditional symbolic gesture of offering aid in natural emergencies overseas, the United States moved in, even among her former enemies, to deal with the chaos following war and revolution.[25] The extension of foreign aid to allies and neutrals followed, and recent declarations regarding the role of foreign aid in the developing world have suggested openly that the United States should seek to improve the prospects of individualism as an emergent value in the underdeveloped world.[26]

Western ideas have provided one source of inspiration for defining national purpose to the leaders of the new countries. These ideas are mixed with ethnic customs and traditional values into a nascent nationalism, often accompanied by an experimental socialism. Technicians engaged in drawing up foreign aid programs, on the other hand, have ostentatiously looked to economic standards of progress and to military and technical requirements in an effort to avoid the appearance of ideological intrusion. But the application of these technical standards in the ordering of the resources of the state has often been un-

---

[24] Cf. Elgin Groseclose, "Diplomacy or Altruism," in *Foreign Aid Reexamined,* eds. James W. Wiggins and Helmut Schoek (1958); and Eugene W. Castle, *The Great Giveaway* (1957).

[25] *U.S. Army and Navy Manual of Civil Affairs Military Government,* FM 27-5, OPNAV P22-1115, par. 5.

[26] See President Kennedy's "Message to Congress Concerning Foreign Aid," *New York Times* (March 23, 1961); *Department of State Bulletin,* XLIV (April 10, 1961), 1137.

consciously conditioned by considerations of the moral values of the Western community and by a desire to protect individuals against the possible violent change. In this way attention to human rights has gradually appeared in the West's perception of the public interest of the underdeveloped world in both the selection and the administration of aid projects. Neither the requests of the national leaders nor the Communist approaches to development have always displayed such solicitude.

Centuries of experimentation with the institutions of democratic goverment have given the Western nations some understanding of the ways in which human values may be preserved under conditions of stress. The indifference of Communist development diplomacy to these values provides the greatest contrast in the two systems. On this basis both Eastern and Western pipelines have made the mechanics of public administration and economic development available to the leadership of the underdeveloped countries; but it is in these areas, in spite of their technical nature, that the advice of East and West may be most readily distinguished.

The prospects for creating respect for human rights in tribal ideologies or in monolithic mass party states may not at once seem promising. To preach the right of individual free speech where decisions are taken by unanimous acclaim of councils of elders, to urge a free press where the only newspapers are produced by a ministry of information, or even to suggest rights of public trial and privilege of counsel in a society where law is the order of the stronger: these are clearly revolutionary acts that may appear both irrelevant and threatening to the political leadership. They seem to have little to do with the massive foreign aid activities necessary to promote economic development; the dams, roads, and power systems may indirectly yield the possibility of a better material life, but they can do little in the protection of individual dignity. The West's unique and most important potential contribution to the developing states is neither sought after by the recipients nor generally recognized by the donors of foreign aid as a mission of leadership.

The responsibility of the Western world for the moral and political consequences of its aid diplomacy is nevertheless increasingly apparent. It can no longer be doubted that American diplomacy, including foreign aid operations, powerfully influences domestic policies in many underdeveloped nations. New choices are made possible by American aid, involving not only international alignment but also internal growth, social change, distributive justice, and national purposes. The impact of the American presence, of American men, money, and materials, and of American points of view has a powerful negative as well as positive potential in terms of the public interest; [27] it is seldom neutral.

The means available for introducing and supporting these concepts, even those which would represent no infringement on sovereignty, have been deliberately neglected. While it would not be appropriate to discuss the techniques of foreign aid in detail here, this fact can be easily demonstrated. Aid to educational institutions in the underdeveloped world has usually been extended with a minimum of personnel and an emphasis on buildings and curricula; grants and scholarships have induced leaders and scholars to come to the United States more frequently for technical purposes than to explore the ideas and principles that made technical progress both possible and necessary in this society. Few programs have been devoted to the private antecedents of public interest, and American diplomats have avoided any commitment to the nexus between Western values and progress. If the West determined to inject the moral dimensions of public interest into its aid programs for the developing nations, it would follow that there would be greater emphasis on getting technicians and teachers overseas who were conscious of an American commitment to the concept of public interest; more attention to the content of educational planning so that language, literature, and even vocational studies could relate to life as well as livelihood; information programs developed to convey as much of human dignity as they do technical achievements and the possibilities of consumer abundance; project aid allotted as much for its moral impact on a people as for its political timeli-

---

27 John D. Montgomery, *The Politics of American Aid, An Analysis Based on American Experiences in Southeastern Asia* (forthcoming), Chs. I and VI.

ness. There would be more informality in diplomatic negotiations for cultural and technical exchanges, and less attentiveness to restrictive details imposed by bureaucratic caution; more regional efforts toward disarmament and less on overseas bases; more sympathy for nationalistic movements and less commitment to abstract and unreciprocated obligations to *colons*, settlers, the West, or capitalism; less "realism" on the surface of our overseas operations and more of the "idealism" that is equally responsible for their existence.

American aid and diplomacy can thus contribute to building the institutions that are implied by the related values of individualism and public interest. They can strengthen the economy in which a middle class can flourish; they can stimulate public discussion of political affairs and encourage the study of the political and social sciences at home and abroad. They can even support centers of advanced learning in which leading native scholars and writers can study their own national traditions and purposes. By teaching the ideologies of both freedom and responsible social action, the United States can indirectly contribute to the building of national mythologies in which these larger purposes of public interest can find expression.

Conveying a perception of the public interest in underdeveloped nations will require as much an invigoration of domestic perceptions of Western diplomacy as it will a reorientation of Western operations overseas. In the underdeveloped world the individual-oriented public interest requires identification as well as implementation, a task which presents a major challenge to the techniques and morality of the West.

19

THE RELEVANCE
AND GENERALITY OF
"THE PUBLIC INTEREST"

WAYNE A. R. LEYS

A survey of recent literature in 1958-59 revealed several distinct and general meanings that may be intended by "the public interest." After summarizing the results of that survey, I shall interpret the findings with the methods of emotivism, pragmatism, ordinary language philosophy, and existentialism. The issues developed by these rival interpretations were implicit in the 1960 discussions of our Society (ASPLP), and I hope that this chapter will identify the issues that are in need of further study.

The 1958-1959 survey was conducted by Charner M. Perry and me under the auspices of a committee of the American Philosophical Association. Our points of departure were two papers by political scientists, Frank J. Sorauf and Glendon Schubert, Jr.,[1] both of whom reported vagueness and confusion about "the public interest" in current usage. Mr. Perry and I first

---

[1] Sorauf, "The Public Interest Reconsidered," *Journal of Politics*, 19 (November 1957) 639, and Schubert, " 'The Public Interest' in Administrative Decision-Making," *American Political Science Review*, 51 (June 1957), 346-368.

examined recent literature and prepared a summary of our findings. The summary was submitted to more than one hundred
philosophers, lawyers, and local scientists, seventy-five of whom
responded with comments and criticisms.

Our conclusion was somewhat different from the conclusions
of Sorauf and Schubert. Interdisciplinary discussions of "the
public interest" did, indeed, seem to be unsatisfactory; but our
impression was that the difficulties were not due to vagueness or
to limitless variety of meanings. Contemporary authors and our
correspondents, for the most part, were attributing one of several general and definable meanings to "the public interest."
After much pondering of uncongenial vocabularies, we were
able to recognize one descriptive meaning and three normative
meanings. We reported these meanings, along with the philosophical issues as they then appeared to us, in a document entitled *Philosophy and the Public Interest*.[2] The identified meanings were as follows:

1. Formal meaning: whatever is the object of duly authorized, governmental action.
   A. Simple conception: the intention of king or parliament.
   B. Pluralistic conception: the objectives that are sanctioned by any
      legal or political process, it being assumed that, as a matter of
      fact, decisions are made in various ways and in various places.
2. Substantive meaning: the object that *should* be sought in governmental action (or in nongovernmental action that is a delegation of
   governmental power or accepted in lieu of governmental action).
   A. Utilitarian or aggregationist conception: the maximization of
      particular interests.
   B. The decision which results when proper procedures are used.
      (i) Simple conceptions: due process of law, majority rule, etc.

---

2 This 72-page document was published by the Committee to Advance
Original Work in Philosophy (Western Division of the American Philo-
sophical Association). The document contains extensive bibliographies perti-
nent to such questions as the following: Are Ideas about Public Interest
Clarified by Distinguishing Levels of Abstraction?; Should "Public Interest"
Be Defined?; Does Political Pluralism Give a New Meaning to "Public Inter-
est"?; Are the Theories of the Public Interest Explained by the Decision-
Making Process?; Can We Avoid Paradoxes Concerning Non-Governmental
Action in the Public Interest?; "The Public Interest" as a Justification for
Governmental Regulation; Self-Regulation in the Public Interest; The Public
Interest in Fiscal Policy, Taxation and Governmental Expenditures; The
Public Interest in the Common Defense and Foreign Policy.

      (ii) Pluralistic conceptions: observance of the procedural rules of whatever legal or political process happens to become the decision-maker for a given issue.

  C. A normative conception of public order (de Jouvenel, F. Knight, Lippmann, etc.). It is difficult to give a fair characterization of this conception that will make sense to those who do not share it.

A fourth normative or substantive meaning had been noted by one of our correspondents, although we did not list it separately in our summary because it was vaguer than the other three:

> Over and above such technical terms (legal uses of "the public interest") there seems to be a genuine semantic need for a *vague* context or inclusive frame of reference. Such a term is "commonwealth." Whenever the attempt is made to give it precise, technical meaning, some other vague term or phrase must be introduced which has the virtue of ambiguity. A useful analysis here would be to show why and where ambiguous terms are needed; I think that on the whole they serve to *identify* but not to *define* a context or situation within which "public" and its related terms operate. "Public interest" has been used as such a vague context word, but the courts and the theorists have been compelled to give it a more precise and limited meaning, hence, the groping for some vague term like "common welfare," etc. to serve where "public interest" used to serve.[3]

The four normative meanings tend to appear in literatures dealing with distinctive problems, but it would be a mistake to assume that they were confined within strict disciplinary boundaries.

"The public interest" as an aggregate or maximization of goods and services is what economists and philosophers often discuss. The essays of Richard Musgrave and David Braybrooke (in this volume) come under this heading.[4]

---

[3] The statement of Herbert W. Schneider in Leys and Perry, *Philosophy and the Public Interest,* p. 31. Compare the comment of Peter F. Drucker in the same place: " 'Public interest' is not a 'normative' term in the usual meaning of this word. It is what I would prefer to call an 'organizing' concept. By this I mean that it does not tell us what decision should be—it is not a concept of what ought to be. It tells us what is relevant to the discussion and to the decision."

[4] Braybrooke, of course, is trying to restrict the meaning to something less than the sum total of individual goods, but still his "deflated" meaning is an aggregate of shared or compatible interests.

"The public interest" as the outcome of a proper procedure is frequently the meaning of lawyers and political scientists. In the discussion of Musgrave's paper at the 1960 meeting, it was the political scientists who seemed to be having the most trouble with the economists' theories about efficiency in maximizing utilities. And in the discussion of Braybrooke's paper, it was the lawyers who did most of the quarreling with his formulation. The procedural conception of "the public interest" is sometimes expounded by calling attention to the difficulties of calculating and agreeing upon the aggregationist conception (greatest happiness, maximization of interest satisfactions, common good, and so forth).

The "public order" or "social tie" meaning of "the public interest," as expounded by de Jouvenel and Lippmann,[5] seems to rest upon an even stronger impression of the controversial and divisive tendencies of society. It seems to appeal to men who are not sure that "due process of law," "majority rule," and the like, can be counted on to function in our time.

CONTEMPORARY PHILOSOPHICAL SKEPTICISM

Except for Thomism and a few echoes of Plato, contemporary philosophy does not give much support to the findings which Perry and I reported. We suggested that interdisciplinary discussions of "the public interest" would be less difficult if a few general conceptions were defined. But most of the

---

[5] Bertrand de Jouvenel, *Sovereignty; An Inquiry into the Political Good* (1957), p. 111. Walter Lippmann, *The Public Philosophy* (1955), pp. 41-42. Running through such books is an awareness of political divisions and the uneconomic policies which are required to prevent civil war. This sort of political sophistication is not apparent in the old Socialist literature and the latter-day exposition of the public interest. See the simple approach to the needs of "the public sector" of the economy in John Kenneth Galbraith, *The Affluent Society* (1958), Ch. 18. Among self-styled "liberals" during the past three decades it is not unusual to find the first (aggregationist) conception of the public interest applied to business corporations and economic activities, whereas a procedural conception of the public interest is applied to sumptuary questions. I am referring here to the enthusiasms for the regulation of business and the rigid defense of the rights of speech, assembly, religions, etc.

recent philosophical writers have been very skeptical about the possibility of defining normative meanings *generally*. The emotivists and the existentialists have talked against the cognitive nature of such terms, but at the end of their discussions what is most often demolished is the *generality* of practical ideas. The generality of practical or moral ideas has also been attacked by pragmatists, intuitionists, and ordinary language philosophers.

Although philosophers do not usually go so far as to say that all action must or should be on a case-to-case basis (the disillusioned viewpoint of many practical politicians and administrators), they spend a great deal of time picking to pieces the two kinds of moral generalizations which, in the past, have gotten action off of a case-to-case basis: (1) abstract principles, such as the Greek philosophers sought to define, and (2) general strategies of history (*vide:* the Hebrew prophets, St. Augustine, Hegel, Marx, and so on).

EMOTIVIST INTERPRETATION

I shall now try to interpret current discussions of "the public interest" from the standpoint of emotivism, the philosophical theory by which some logical empiricists tried to understand persistent controversies in the domain of morals, politics, and religion. According to this theory, one component of the meaning or reference of many words is an emotion, attitude, or sentiment that, by historical accident, has been associated with the words in the experience of the person who uses the words. Such emotive meanings are different from the objective or factual meanings on which scientific agreement can be achieved by making predictions, specifying a method of verification, and making the verification.

The emotivist, finding that a meaning is emotive, either stops trying to reach an agreement on the meaning of the emotive term or endeavors to engineer agreement by some nonscientific process. If he is professionally engaged in scientific inquiry, he no longer looks for a scientific meaning for the term.

Sorauf and Schubert, the two political scientists previously mentioned, evidently were attracted to the emotivist interpreta-

tion of "the public interest," after assuring themselves that disagreements regarding the definitions were going to remain with
us for some time. Sorauf concluded his essay by saying:

> Yet, its practical services in American politics add nothing to the
> value of the public interest as an instrument for political analysis.
> The public interest must certainly be studied and recorded, but only
> as political data, only as a factor in the political decisions of many
> citizens and decision-makers. Political scientists must not, of course,
> ignore the importance of widely-used political yardsticks, but they need
> not adopt them for their own use.[6]

Schubert, commenting on Sorauf's essay and his own writings
on the subject, wrote:

> These three articles, which are the results of two independent in-
> vestigations, share a common conclusion: there is only one construct of
> public interest theory which promises to be useful either as a guide
> to responsible decision-making or behavioral research. This construct
> defines the public interest not as substance but rather in terms of the
> structuring of decision-making processes.[7]

Perry and I noted that Sorauf and Schubert had been much
concerned with the efforts of political scientists to achieve accurate descriptions of political and legal processes. They were
obviously hopeful that descriptive generalizations or models
could be improved to the point that they would have more
predictive value in explaining and anticipating the decisions
issuing from the interplay of interest groups or pressure groups.
A number of our correspondents thought there was some bias
or some mistake in this pressure-group theory. Perry and I were,
therefore, persuaded to make the following comment, which, I
believe, exposes an inference that many emotivists make:

> Theorists who are skeptical of the possibility of using the Utilitarian
> standard sometimes fall back upon the formal meaning of the public
> interest. The alternative to the Utilitarian or economic point of view
> thus seems to be an abandonment of any normative conception of the

---

[6] Sorauf, "The Public Interest Reconsidered."

[7] Schubert, "The Theory of the Public Interest," *PROD* (Political Research: Organization and Design), I (May 1958), 35.

public interest. The logical alternative to Utilitarianism, however, is #2-B, a specification of the rules or procedures for decision-making, or #2-C (the public interest as the social tie of public order).[8]

A purely descriptive or formal "public interest" is any object chosen by the government, presumably the outcome of a power struggle. This is not the same as the normative conception of "the public interest" as the object chosen by following a procedure; for, if the conception is normative, it prescribes the procedures. It is the result of *due* process or a *proper* or *legitimate* procedure, as opposed to any procedure whatsoever.

Insofar as emotivism leads to preoccupation with what, as a matter of fact, the *de facto* decision makers decide, it offers no general guide to the person who has not made up his own mind and who is trying to decide which policy is "in the public interest." A citizen or an official may address himself to a fact-finding and fact-predicting study, using the formal definition: "The public interest is the objective that can be made to stick." This same man may make an ethical decision, as follows: "I shall support whatever objective I believe can be made to stick." He may feel that he has escaped from the responsibility for evaluation and commitment, but his evaluation and commitment will, nevertheless, be controversial and emotive.

A health commissioner, for example, is delegated legislative power to decide what health hazards shall be met with quarantine. An epidemic of amoebic dysentery is detected in a city where a great fair is in progress. The health commissioner is expected to study the extent of the hazards and compare them with the benefits that accrue from the fair. If he should close the fair when one case of dysentery is reported, undoubtedly

---

8 Leys and Perry, *Philosophy and the Public Interest*, pp. 44-45. Another comment on the shift to and from factual or descriptive meaning was made by Arthur Murphy (p. 11): " 'Interest' can pass for a psychologically descriptive term. . . . However (the public interest) is descriptively identified, it is presumably one interest among others and the question why and within what limits it is entitled to precedence remains unanswered. The notion of common good, which is plainly normative, was an attempt to answer this kind of question. . . . 'Public Interest' is an attempt to give a descriptive meaning to this notion while still claiming for it a normative function."

his decision would not stick. If he waits until thousands of cases are reported, his tenure of office will undoubtedly be terminated. Somewhere, in between these extremes, is a disease prevalence which he could cite and with which he could make his decision stick.

Although the health commissioner may be guided by a hopefully scientific calculation or prediction of disease incidence that will bring support for a quarantine, he has not really avoided a normative definition of "the public interest." He has adopted one variant of the normative definitions, the one which he believes will be accepted by enough of the power-holders to permit him to act without committing political suicide. It is a variant which would be bitterly denounced by "nonpolitical" doctors and many others.

In the balance of this essay I shall restrict the discussion to the ethical or normative problems concerning "the public interest." Before concluding my remarks on emotivist interpretation of the phrase, let me distinguish, as sharply as possible, the scientific questions about "public interest," to which many of the emotivists turn their attention.

One of the questions as to fact is this: What does "the public interest" mean in the statutes, court decisions, and other official actions in which the words are used? Can we develop generalizations that accurately summarize the official usage? Does it extend beyond the maintenance of domestic peace, the protection of citizens against certain kinds of dangers, and the like? Does it include monetary stability? Does it include economic growth? This was one of the questions to which Braybrooke addressed himself (although he was also discussing the normative question). As anyone who reads law knows, generalizations of this sort are difficult, requiring many qualifications and exceptions. Such generalizations are a kind of factual study, though it is questionable whether they can become scientific (systematic).[9]

A second factual inquiry attempts to determine how strong are the motivations which we call "devotion to the public inter-

---

[9] Cf. H. L. A. Hart, "Positivism and the Separation of Law and Morals," *Harvard Law Review*, 71 (February 1958), 626.

est." As distinguished from personal or private interests, how important are public interests in explaining historical events? Does concern for "the public interest" have to be taken into account in order to make accurate predictions of future events? [10]

Some light is thrown on these factual questions by normative inquiries into what we can and ought to mean by "the public interest," but these factual problems call for hypotheses which are expected to be verified. In so far as the emotivist succeeds in limiting his investigation to the factual questions, he is avoiding the ethical question; but if he has to act, he will have to take an ethical position.

As one reads the emotivist interpretations of "the public interest," one suspects that some emotivists are justifying their avoidance of the ethical question by emphasizing the difficulties of the factual question. The insinuated argument seems to go this way: "There is very little agreement on this subject, and official documents and acts are not consistent in the meaning they attribute to 'the public interest'; therefore, we are well advised to waste no time trying to clarify the meaning of 'the public interest'; therefore, let us pay attention to the personal and group interests which constitute an important part of the verifiable facts of political life."

Perry poked a hole in this argument, when he pointed out that " 'interest' does not denote an observable fact and is not operationally definable." Hence, the reasoning that leads the skeptics to doubt the reality of a "public" interest may equally cast doubt on the imputation of a group interest to a group.

> We may [says Perry] conjecture, perhaps not prove, that in any group, from the largest to the smallest, there is a mixture of harmony and conflict of interests. . . . Nor do the difficulties arise merely from the reference to groups. They arise also because we are imputing a subjective cause or motive to an actor, and consequently they occur as well when we are concerned with individuals. If a salesman, irritated by a rude remark, offends an important customer, we may guess that

---

10 Although he is not writing to support an emotivist interpretation, Gerhard Colm is addressing himself to some of these factual questions in "In Defense of the Public Interest," *Social Research*, 27 (Autumn 1960), 295-307. It should be clear that I am not contending that all descriptive studies are made by emotivists.

he neglected his interest to indulge his temper or we may say that the satisfaction from expressing his irritation was more important to him than the prospect of making a sale.[11]

When I treat the conclusions of Schubert and Sorauf as "emotivist interpretations," I identify them with the emotivist theory which Carnap, Ayer, and Russell were advocating in the mid-thirties. Schubert and Sorauf do not seem to retain a curiosity about the partially rational processes of persuasion, as did Charles L. Stevenson when he adopted the phrase "emotive meaning." As Stevenson explained:

> . . . having decided to use the term, I was accordingly insistent, throughout *Ethics and Language,* upon the absurdity of condemning (persuasively) all persuasion, and upon the necessity of seeing that our beliefs and attitudes stand in an intimate and complicated relationship.[12]

My comment on the emotivist interpretation may be summarized as follows: It may be true that "the public interest" is usually infected with accidental emotional associations. It may be true that these associations increase the difficulties of analysis and communication. But these facts are hardly grounds for dismissing "the public interest" from theoretical vocabularies as "nothing more than a label attached indiscriminately to a miscellany of particular compromises of the moment." [13]

PRAGMATIC DETERMINATION OF RELEVANCE

When pragmatism was a leading point of view in the philosophical journals, it seemed to be as hostile to general normative ideas as emotivism has been in recent decades. John Dewey was dethroning abstract normative principles.

To one who is professionally preoccupied with philosophy there is much in its history which is profoundly depressing. He sees ideas which

---

11 Perry, Reviews of *The Public Interest* by Glendon Schubert and *Democracy and the Public Interest* by Howard R. Smith, *Ethics,* LXXII (October 1961), 64.

12 Stevenson, "Meaning: Descriptive and Emotive," *Philosophical Review,* LVII (March 1948), 136.

13 Schubert, *The Public Interest* (1960), p. 223.

were not only natural but useful in their native time and place, figuring in foreign contexts so as to formulate defects as virtues and to give rational sanction to brute facts, and to oppose alleged eternal truths to progress. He sees movements which might have passed away with change of circumstance as casually as they arose, acquire persistence and dignity because thought has taken cognizance of them and given them intellectual names. The witness of history is that to think in general and abstract terms is dangerous; it elevates ideas beyond the situations in which they were born and charges them with we know not what menace for the future. And in the past the danger has been the greater because philosophers so largely purported to be concerned not with contemporary problems of living, but with essential Truth and Reality viewed under the form of Eternity.[14]

This quotation and many others suggest that Dewey would avoid all pretense of *general* definitions of such a phrase as "the public interest." Pragmatism would seem to be the ultimate in case-to-case thinking. In *The Public and Its Problems* Dewey partially defined the public interest as the interest of bystanders, but he left the nature of the interest to be determined from case to case.

As the early polemics of pragmatism recede into the past, however, the animadversions against abstractions do not obscure for some of us an insight that is quite compatible with a high regard for abstract thinking—viz., the clarification of meanings by defining the problems to which words are relevant.[15]

Thus slightly reconstructed, a pragmatist might not reject out of hand the several *general* and normative definitions of "the public interest." The pragmatist could, indeed, eliminate some of the arbitrariness in the opposed definitions, by defining the *kinds* of problems to which each definition is relevant (the kinds of problems that each meaning of "the public interest" is likely to solve), thus:

---

14 Dewey, *German Philosophy and Politics* (1915), p. 12.

15 Elsewhere I have called attention to another of Dewey's prejudices, which is not necessarily connected with his insight into the nature of relevance. I refer to his distaste for political and legal methods that are not "scientific," influenced by predictions of consequences, etc. If one believes that thought and action should solve problems, there is no good reason for denying that a ritual may not solve some problems.

A. "The public interest" as a common good, an aggregate of interests, the maximization of interest-satisfactions, etc. This meaning is pertinent when the *procedures* of government are problematic or in dispute. Thus, in the Constitutional Convention of 1787, appeal was made (in the Preamble) to such goods or goals as insuring domestic tranquility, providing for the common defense, promoting the general welfare, etc. Thus, also in great struggles over procedures, as in the passage of the Taft-Hartley Act and in efforts to amend the Act, an "aggregate" kind of "public interest" is used as a guide. Thus, also, the debate over the one-party system in countries having high illiteracy rates.

B. Procedural conceptions of "the public interest." This meaning is relevant, when *goods* and *goals* are in conflict and apparently undebatable. Thus, in the awarding of a TV channel or other natural resources, goal-oriented discussion often becomes futile. The solution of the problem will be sought on the basis of accepted procedure. Officials who have been duly appointed hold hearings prescribed by law. If no one entitled to be heard is denied a hearing, if the commissioners are not caught accepting a bribe, if they are not detected in prohibited ex parte communications, etc., their decision will be accepted as in the public interest, even though the quarrel on "the merits" goes on.

C. "The public interest" as loyalty to a public order, the social tie, etc. This meaning of "the public interest" is relevant to a problem in which both *goals and procedures* are disturbed and controversial. "The public interest" now means "efforts in good faith to reach any kind of agreement and avoid civil war or other forms of destructive conflict." In the recent judicial impasses over the school desegregation problem, I should say that what de Jouvenel and Lippmann say about "the public interest" begins to make sense. Insofar as "the public interest" has any meaning in international relations, the cold war negotiators show some regard for a public interest of this kind. And, in the formerly colonial areas of the world, European settlers and their descendents are being forced back upon a "public order" conception of "the public interest," as the native politicians abolish what were regarded as due process and proper procedures (on the ground that legal process and proper politics were prejudiced in favor of the educated and propertied invaders and their progeny).

THE PUBLIC INTEREST
IN "ORDINARY LANGUAGE"

The broad-minded pragmatism of the foregoing paragraphs may appear to evade the difficulty about generality. We have substituted three definitions of "the public interest" for one completely general definition, and have defined three *kinds* of problems to which the defined conceptions are, respectively, relevant.

Why stop with three different conceptions of "the public interest"? Why only three contexts or types of problems? Why not continue, in the manner of the ordinary language philosophers, to multiply the types of problems and contexts? Why not go on to multiply the models of "the public interest," until the entire enterprise of seeking a general Socratic definition is made to seem ridiculous? Why not resign ourselves to a long series of paradigms or examples, all called "the public interest" because of a family resemblance, but each varying in so many respects, that we are, indeed, on a case-to-case basis in our judgments?

Why not distinguish between meanings of "the public interest" in prescriptions, appraisals, performatives, excuses, commendations, choices, and advices? Here are two cases in point: Citation accompanying honorary degree to a government official: "He has been devoted to serving the public interest." State railroad commission: "The public interest requires that the ABC Railroad Co. continue to operate two passenger trains per day in each direction between *D* and *E*." "Public interest" in the citation permits no deductions, whereas "public interest" in the performative utterance of the railroad commission does.

Another illustration is the shifting meaning of "the public interest" during appraisal of actions and policies. During the latter part of World War II Donald Nelson was the center of a furious controversy in the War Production Board. The issue at that time was conceived primarily in terms of the utilitarian definition of the public interest. As factories and manpower caught up with the demand for munitions, would the public interest be served by permitting reconversion to the production of civilian goods? The calculation of benefits and costs dealt with scarcity, the probability of unemployment and inflation in the post-war period, the breaking of wartime morale, etc. After the war was over, this controversy was studied by a number of social scientists, some of whom—in the course of their investigation—

changed their appraisal of the alternative policies. They shifted
from a utilitarian definition of "the public interest" to a procedural definition. They became convinced that Mr. Nelson had
by a series of actions and inactions allowed his co-ordinating
authority to erode. Whereas, under the utilitarian definition,
they had sympathized with Mr. Nelson, now, under a procedural definition, they condemned him.

If we slide back and forth between different definitions,
depending upon the perception of complex circumstances, should
we not be wary of any generality in "the public interest"? The
pragmatist is saying that some problematic situations become
less problematic when action is guided by one of a group of
ideas that roughly go under the name "the public interest."
Moreover, "the public interest" does not always seem to be the
controlling consideration, even in governmental affairs.[16]

Certainly, there is nothing in logic to prevent a further division of ideas of "the public interest" until we reach the particular judgments in specific action situations. But such a proliferation of scholastic distinctions would overlook the difference
between guiding ideas and the actions that need guidance.

It is true that wise actions, policies, and choices vary endlessly in the relative weights that they give to ideal standards.
In our mixed-up world of conflicting values and loyalties, even
the most sacred customs impose only *prima facie* obligations,
as W. D. Ross used to say. But the fact that judgments in the
particular case are ungeneralizable is not a good reason for
blurring the boundaries of ideal standards. Merely because "due
process of law," "full employment," and "good faith" seem to
be properly sacrificed in different proportions under varying circumstances is not a good reason for blurring "due process," etc.
The fact that an inefficient, uneconomical policy is adjudged to
be in the public interest is not a good reason for refusing to
define the economic requirement of the public interest. The fact
that actions which, under the circumstances, seem to be more

---

16 A summary of part of the studies of the Reconversion Controversy will
be found in my book, *Ethics for Policy Decisions* (1952), Ch. 19. The varying
pre-eminence of "the public interest" as a policy consideration was noted in
Braybrooke's paper.

in the public interest than alternative actions that are more protective of procedural rights does not prove that it is unwise to define the procedural rights in an ideal public interest.

Many of the recent attacks on the generality of normative ideas seem to me to forget the function of general, normative ideas. As C. D. Broad implied, in his criticism of Kant's ethics, a moral standard is a criterion, not a directive.[17] To guide choices under endlessly varying conditions, we need a few criteria, not just one, and not an infinite number of them.

EXISTENTIALIST AMBIGUITY

I shall introduce the existentialist interpretation of "the public interest" by back-tracking to our broad-minded pragmatist's interpretation. You will recall that the pragmatist would try to define the immediate problem and thus he would determine the relevance of a goal conception, a procedural conception, or an order-and-good-faith conception of "the public interest."

An existentialist declares that he cannot unequivocally define his problem. His action situation remains, despite his best efforts, ambiguous. He cannot find a single meaning in what he confronts and in what he is trying to do. There are several prospects, among which choice is arbitrary.

Suppose that you are an American official, employed on a technical assistance mission in an underdeveloped country. What is going on? What are you doing? What role are you playing? Sometimes it looks one way to you; sometimes, another. Here are the alternative "histories":

1. You are participating in the industrialization of humanity, contributing in your small way to a world-wide social change that will reduce poverty and disease.
2. You are working for the national security of the United

---

17 Broad, *Five Types of Ethical Theory* (1930), p. 128. Another way of making this point is to paraphrase a familiar distinction. The following questions are different and demand different answers: (1) What action, in the immediate situation, will be in the public interest? (2) What, in general, do we mean by "the public interest"?

States, countering the aggressive moves of the Communists. You are expected to get results even if you must violate the "conflict-of-interest" rules of your own government in order to secure the co-operation of a foreign government, in which official bribery is the rule rather than the exception.

3. You are conspiring with a baronial group to slow down social change.

4. You are engaged in a struggle for the survival of yourself and your agency, offering justifications for appropriations and protecting your enterprise from issue-hungry Congressmen.

5. You are using up your days, aging, approaching death; the task on which you labor and worry is as transitory as the making of a sand castle on the beach at low tide. There is no assurance that the "cause" which you are serving is giving you any significance; it will not save you from destruction and oblivion.

Suppose further that you detect in the actions of your superior officer what you believe to be gross waste and stupidity. You have suggested to your superior that his actions are contrary to public interest, but he has given you the brush-off. You now ask yourself whether devotion to the public interest requires you to report your damaging information to Washington.[18]

To make your predicament more ambiguous, you do not know with any certainty to what extent other people agree with

---

[18] A number of more or less analogous cases are available for study. Some of the men who squealed and went out of channels became heroes, and some became goats. Anyone venturing into the political arena takes personal chances. Personal fortunes, however, are not our present concern. Our present concern is the nature of "the public interest" and the extent to which it is goal-oriented or procedurally conceived, depending on judgments of the historical processes of which an activity is a part.

In the history of public administration we tend to invoke a goal-oriented notion of the public interest when we read the story of a naval officer like William Sims, going out of channels to secure an innovation that was vital to our national defense, or when we read the story of Harry Slattery, going out of channels to secure a Congressional investigation of Teapot Dome. But we tend to invoke a procedural conception of the public interest, when we read the story of Ewing Mitchell and his complaints to Congressmen about his colleagues and superiors in the Department of Commerce.

any one of these definitions of your situation. Your colleagues in the field, your family, your superiors in Washington, Congress, the electorate, the various elements in the underdeveloped country, the rest of humanity—are they with you, against you, or totally indifferent? You have some evidence, but it points in various directions.

The existentialist cannot reduce the ambiguity of his problem, at least, prior to the deadline for action, and therefore he cannot rationally define "the public interest" or anything else. If somehow one of his decisions involves his ultimate anxieties about life or death, he makes a leap of faith and arbitrarily makes a commitment which assumes that one of the rival orientations is correct. He never escapes from a feeling of anxiety and the sense of responsibility for his choice, for he cannot put the blame on the preponderance of evidence or a commanding God or anything else.

But once he has had a complete, passionate encounter, the existentialist may emerge as an "authentic" person, unalterably committed to one meaning of "the public interest" (or some other norm). There is no science and hardly any logic in his crucial choice. The plural meanings of "the public interest" remain a mystery. But having made an ultimate commitment, the existentialist thereafter proceeds with some rationality (the rationality of choosing efficient means to chosen ends) as if there were no doubt that his goals were the only ones a rational being could choose.

The existentialists point up a peculiar morale problem connected with "the public interest." "The public" does not think very much about "the public interest," and sometimes "the interest possessed by the public" is demonstrably contrary to "the best interests of the public." [19] Hence, Gabriel Marcel can talk about a broken world:

---

19 This contrast is the subject of C. W. Cassinelli's article, "Some Reflections on the Concept of the Public Interest," *Ethics,* 69 (October 1958), 48-61, and a critique by William D. Zarecor, "The Public Interest and Political Theory," *Ethics,* 69 (July 1959), 277-280. Extreme skepticism about an interest possessed by the public (such as Rousseau called "the general will") was, of course, expressed by Arthur F. Bentley in *The Process of Government* (1908),

In the more and more collectivized world that we are now living in, the idea of any real community becomes more and more inconceivable. . . . I am in some danger of confusing myself, my real personality with the State's official record of my activities. . . .[20]

And Hannah Arendt can say:

What makes mass society so difficult to bear is not the number of people involved, or at least not primarily, but the fact that the world between them has lost its power to gather them together, to relate them and to separate them. . . . Goodness, therefore, as a consistent way of life, is not only impossible within the confines of the public realm, it is even destructive of it." [21]

Personally, I am not very sympathetic with much of the existentialist agonizing, especially when a cry-baby attitude is adopted by those whose troubles are the worries of the rich. I must admit, however, that the existentialists have articulated the kind of perplexity that I have encountered among administrators in government, industry, and labor organizations. It is, indeed, disquieting to realize that your best judgment in your most public-spirited moments is repudiated by the very public you thought you were serving.

One way out of the perplexity is to stop thinking in very general terms, to pursue "The Science of 'Muddling Through.' " [22] Committed to your institutional agency and pressured to con-

---

pp. 370-371: "When one condemns (logrolling) 'in principle,' it is only by contrasting it with some assumed pure public spirit which is supposed to guide legislators, or which ought to guide them, and which enables them to pass judgment in Jovian calm on that which is best 'for the whole people.' Since there is nothing which is best literally for the whole people, group arrays being what they are, the test is useless, even if one could actually find legislative judgments which are not reducible to interest-group activities."

20 Gabriel Marcel, *The Mystery of Being*, Vol. I (1960), 34-35.

21 Hannah Arendt, *The Human Condition* (1959), pp. 48-69. Such protests against the impersonality of public life often accompany proposals for "people-to-people" diplomacy, for informality and "group dynamics" techniques, for "problem-solving discussions," for "moral rearmament," for more of the "liberal arts," for "radical" reforms, etc. The existentialists are usually skeptical in their evaluation of these panaceas, but still they cannot accommodate themselves to the impersonality of public life.

22 C. E. Lindblom, "The Science of 'Muddling Through,' " *Public Administration Review*, 19 (Spring 1959), 78-88.

sider many values besides an ideal "public interest," you make decisions by means of successive limited comparisons. But some of us obviously have difficulty accepting such a pluralistic, pragmatic attitude. As one man told me recently, "You just run around putting out fires."

CONCLUSION

We have now reviewed some of the arguments leading to the discounting of assertions concerning "the public interest." Theorists, who want to be scientific, have denigrated "the public interest" as irrelevant, as offering no general guidance. They have found an incurable ambiguity.

I agree with the skeptics that no one can formulate an abstract principle, called "the public interest," which all intelligent men are willing to apply deductively to policy decisions. There seems to be no single definition which will enable us to "prove" that "the public interest" requires:

1. counter-cyclical fiscal measures when unemployment reaches 4 percent;
2. governmental intervention in industry-wide strikes or in collective bargaining that tends to have inflationary consequences;
3. zoning regulations to protect aesthetic interests;
4. the preference of any item in budget requests over any other item;
5. the reform of regulatory agencies because they are influenced in their rule-making by the industries to which the regulatory rules apply.

Even when there is widespread agreement as to the public interest in a given activity, I would go further and say that the public interest in other activities may advise us not to insist upon the satisfaction of the public interest in the immediate instance. "Conflict-of-interest" rules, for example, should not be made as strict as the monastic vows of poverty, chastity, and obedience. A public interest in the staffing of government with

competent men justifies the tolerance of such privacy and such
family financing as competent officials insist upon as a condition
of employment.

But the rival claims of public interests in various activities
do not demonstrate the folly or the impossibility of articulating
those interests. Nor does the improbability of complete agreement on specific public policies disprove the possibility of general criteria or standards, which are properly called "the public
interest." On the basis of the survey which Perry and I made,
I should say that there are three meanings which can reasonably
be attributed to "the public interest" as a set of criteria for
judging proposed governmental actions. Ideally, governmental
action will

1. maximize interest satisfactions (utility),
2. be determined by due process,
3. be motivated by a desire to avoid destructive social conflict
   (good faith).

In judgments of specific policy issues, it is seldom possible
to find an alternative that satisfies all three criteria equally well.
It is seldom possible to eliminate entirely all but one alternative
as claiming to meet the demands of "the public interest." A
pragmatic attempt to define the nature of the problematic situation sometimes reduces our uncertainty as to which of "the
public interest" criteria is most relevant. But in the end the
existentialists are correct: there is a leap of faith, a commitment,
an engagement. As ex-President Coolidge said more prosaically
(after he had affiliated himself with an insurance company):
"You cannot take the risk out of life."

I am conceding more than the existence of disagreements
(hence, the political problem) concerning "the public interest"
in various policy proposals. I am also conceding that intelligent
human beings will not find themselves "of one mind" regarding
"the public interest" in some policy proposals. But this predicament does not justify some of the recent philosophical con-
tentions that a wise man will not try to define what he means
by "the public interest" and that policy discussions are rendered
more confused and futile by sharply defined general standards.